FOUNDATIONS FOR KIDS

NEW TESTAMENT

A 260-DAY BIBLE READING PLAN FOR KIDS

Robby & Kandi Gallaty

LifeWay Press®
Nashville, TN

ISBN 9781535939614
Item 005811045
Dewey Decimal Classification Number: 268.432
Subject Heading: Discipleship—Curricula\God\Bible—Study
Dewey Decimal Classification Number: 248.82
Subject Heading: CHRISTIAN LIFE \ JESUS CHRIST--TEACHINGS

To order additional copies of this resource, write to LifeWay Resources Customer Service; One LifeWay Plaza; Nashville, TN 37234-0113; fax 615.251.5933; phone toll free 800.458.2772; email *orderentry@lifeway.com*, order online at *www.lifeway.com*, or visit the LifeWay Christian Store serving you.

Printed in the United States of America

LifeWay Kids, LifeWay Resources, One LifeWay Plaza, Nashville, TN 37234-0172

ABOUT THE AUTHORS

ROBBY GALLATY is the senior pastor of Long Hollow Baptist Church in Hendersonville, Tennessee. He was radically saved from a life of drug and alcohol addiction. In 2008 he founded Replicate Ministries to educate, equip, and empower people to be disciples who make disciple-makers (replicate.org). He's the author of *The Forgotten Jesus: How Western Christians Should Follow an Eastern Rabbi* (2017), *Rediscovering Discipleship: Making Jesus' Final Words Our First Work* (2015), and *Here and Now: Thriving in the Kingdom of Heaven Today* (2019).

KANDI GALLATY has been investing in the lives of women for over a decade. She's passionate about cultivating a biblical worldview from the truths of Scripture and about teaching women how to steward the life experiences and lessons God has allowed in their lives. Kandi and Robby are the proud, thankful parents of two boys, Rig and Ryder. Kandi is the coauthor of *Foundations: A 260-Day Bible Reading Plan for Busy Believers* (2015) and the author of *Disciple Her: Using the Word, Work, and Wonder of God to Invest in Women* (2019).

MELISSA SWAIN is a wife, mom, teacher, and writer. Melissa has written and edited books, blogs, and journals for various authors and pastors as well as LifeWay Christian Resources. Melissa and her husband, Chris, have lived all over the South serving in various aspects of ministry, but they now call Nashville, Tennessee, home along with their two children and Boston Terrier.

ROBBY GALLATY ON THE HEAR METHOD

When my wife, Kandi, and I, along with the help of our Replicate team, first developed a reading plan called Foundations 260, it was a 260-day reading plan that highlights the foundational passages of Scripture every disciple should know. After failed attempts of reading through the Bible in a year with previous discipleship groups, I wanted a manageable plan that believers who had never read the Bible before could complete. In order to digest more of the Word, the F-260 encourages believers to read less and to keep a H.E.A.R. journal.

After utilizing the F-260 plan for several years, we determined that a plan focusing on the New Testament would be beneficial as well. The New Testament consists of 260 chapters, which allows us to retain the structure of the original F-260 reading plan. While this plan will be great for all disciples, it can be especially effective for new believers or those who are just beginning to read and journal through the Bible.

NOW ... FOUNDATIONS FOR KIDS: NEW TESTAMENT!

We believe that discipleship starts at home. It has always been our dream that as parents go through *Foundations*, they could lead their kids through a similar resource. Just as with *Foundations for Kids*, this resource will equip parents to disciple their children as they work through the same passages of Scripture in *Foundations for Kids: New Testament.*

MEMORIZING SCRIPTURE

While many plans for memorizing Scripture are effective, a simple system has been most effective for me. All you need is a pack of index cards and a committed desire to memorize God's Word. It's easy: write the reference of the verse on one side of the card and the text of the verse on the other. Focus on five verses at a time, and carry your pack of Scripture cards with you.

Throughout the day, whenever you have a few minutes, pull out your pack of Scripture cards and review them. Read the reference first, followed by the verse. Continue to recite the verse until you get a feel for the flow of the passage. When you are comfortable with the text, look only at the reference side of the card in order to test your recall. Adjust this based upon your child's ability to memorize.

THE H.E.A.R. METHOD

Together, families will use this simple method to study and apply God's Word:

HIGHLIGHT Each day has a passage for both younger kids and older kids to read, plus the memory verse for the week. Each day kids will have the opportunity to read and memorize Scripture.

EXPLAIN Each day will have 4 bullets: 3 bullets are shorter and can be read by all kids. The 4th bullet will be longer for older kids and may give additional information from extra verses or be written to an older kids' level.

APPLY Kids will have a learning activity to help them apply the Bible truth.

RESPOND Kids will have the opportunity to respond in prayer.

PARENTS

Parents, help your kids go through the H.E.A.R. method each day. Younger kids may need you to read for them and lead them through the daily devotion. Beginning readers will grow stronger and may only need occasional help. Middle and older kids will be able to read on their own. Regardless of your child's age, spend time discussing the day's reading and how he or she can apply God's truth to everyday life.

TIPS FOR SUCCESS

WHEN: Set a regular time for time together with God.
WHERE: Find a comfortable, quiet place where you and your kids won't be disturbed.
WHY: Communicate with your kids that God wants to have a relationship with them. God speaks through the Bible.
WHAT: Gather your Bible, *Foundations for Kids: New Testament*, and a pencil or markers.
HOW: Explain how important the Bible is. Teach Bible skills as you go. Follow these steps:

1. Pray and ask God to be with your time together and to speak to you. Pray that you will listen and learn.
2. Read the passage from the Bible.
3. Ask your kids what they think the passage means. Read through the Explain section together and talk about the passage and its meaning.
4. Complete the Apply activity together.
5. Review the memory verse for the week. Create a verse card to review and practice learning.
6. Pray together.
7. Hug your kids, tell them how much you love them, and tell them how thankful you are that you could spend this time together with God.

HIGHLIGHT

OLDER SCRIPTURE: Luke 1:26-33
YOUNGER SCRIPTURE: Luke 1:30-33
MEMORY VERSE: Proverbs 1:7

EXPLAIN

- God sent the angel Gabriel to tell a girl named Mary she was going to have a baby.
- Mary's baby would be Jesus—the Savior God had promised to send to save His people.
- God chose Mary and Joseph to be Jesus' parents on earth.
- It had been about 400 years since God spoke to the prophet Malachi. The people had been waiting for the Messiah and the prophet that would prepare the way for Him. God sent Gabriel to announce that Jesus and John were going to be born soon. Jesus would be the Messiah, and John would be the prophet that would prepare the people for Him.

APPLY

God had been quiet for a long time, but He did not forget about His promise. God will always fulfill His promises. Solve the clues below to find out how many years God had been quiet.

RESPOND

PRAY: Heavenly Father, thank You for always fulfilling Your promises.

OLDER SCRIPTURE: Luke 2:4-7, 11-12
YOUNGER SCRIPTURE: Luke 2:4-7, 11-12
MEMORY VERSE: Proverbs 1:7

EXPLAIN

- Mary and Joseph traveled to the city of Bethlehem from their home in Nazareth. While they were there, Jesus was born.
- Angels appeared to shepherds working in the fields and told them the Savior had been born.
- The angels told the shepherds how to find Jesus and His family, and they went to find them.
- Just like God promised, Jesus was born in Bethlehem. God sent the angels to tell the shepherds about Jesus' birth. They ran to find the baby, then they told others about His birth.

APPLY

Shepherds were not liked by many people. God sent the angels to tell the shepherds about Jesus' birth first because He loves everyone and wants us all to know Jesus. Solve the maze to help Joseph and Mary find their way to Bethlehem.

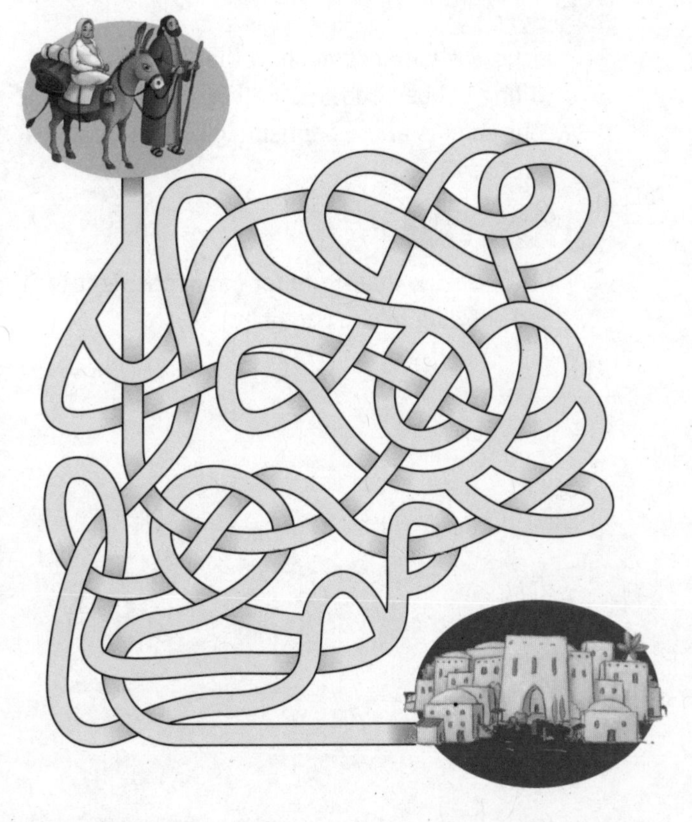

RESPOND

PRAY: Heavenly Father, thank You for sending Jesus for me. Help me remember that the good news about Jesus is for everyone.

HIGHLIGHT

OLDER SCRIPTURE: Luke 3:15-16; 21-22
YOUNGER SCRIPTURE: Luke 3:21-22
MEMORY VERSE: Proverbs 1:7

EXPLAIN

- John the Baptist was teaching in the wilderness. He told the people that he was not the Messiah, but that the Messiah would be coming soon.
- Jesus came to John to be baptized.
- After Jesus was baptized, God spoke. God was very pleased with Jesus.
- John the Baptist was teaching God's Word. People were excited to hear John's teaching and thought he might be the Messiah. John told them he was only pointing them to the true Messiah, Jesus. After John baptized Jesus, God's Spirit came down to Jesus like a dove. God was pleased with His Son.

APPLY

Jesus was baptized to show that He was willing to obey God, His Father. Talk with your parents about baptism.

RESPOND

PRAY: Jesus, thank You for being obedient to God and showing me how to obey.

OLDER SCRIPTURE: Luke 4:1-13
YOUNGER SCRIPTURE: Luke 4:1-4
MEMORY VERSE: Proverbs 1:7

EXPLAIN

- Following His baptism, Jesus went to the wilderness by Himself.
- For 40 days and nights, Jesus didn't eat anything. Satan tried to tempt Jesus with food and power.
- Jesus defeated Satan by using God's Word.
- Jesus spent 40 days and nights in the wilderness by Himself. He was hungry and thirsty. Satan tried to tempt Jesus to turn rocks into food, give up His power to Satan, and have angels come rescue Him. Jesus used God's Word to defeat Satan.

God's Word helps us follow Him and resist temptation. We should read God's Word every day and memorize Scripture to help us follow Him. Fill in the blanks from Proverbs 1:7.

THE ______________________ IS THE

______________________,

______________________ DESPISE WISDOM

______________________.

PRAY: Heavenly Father, help me learn and memorize Your Word.

OLDER SCRIPTURE: Luke 5:4-11
YOUNGER SCRIPTURE: Luke 5:9-11
MEMORY VERSE: Proverbs 1:7

EXPLAIN

- Jesus was teaching near a lake.
- Jesus gave Simon and his friends instructions on how to catch a lot of fish. They were amazed.
- Jesus told Simon, James, and John to come with Him. They left everything and followed Jesus.
- Jesus had been teaching near where Simon, James, and John were fishing. They hadn't caught anything. Jesus gave them instructions, and they obeyed them. They caught so many fish, their nets began to break. Jesus did this to demonstrate His authority through the miraculous catching of fish. Jesus asked them to follow Him, so they left everything and went with Him.

Jesus calls us to be His followers. Write the first letter of each picture in the box above to decode the message.

JESUS TOLD SIMON, JAMES, AND JOHN:

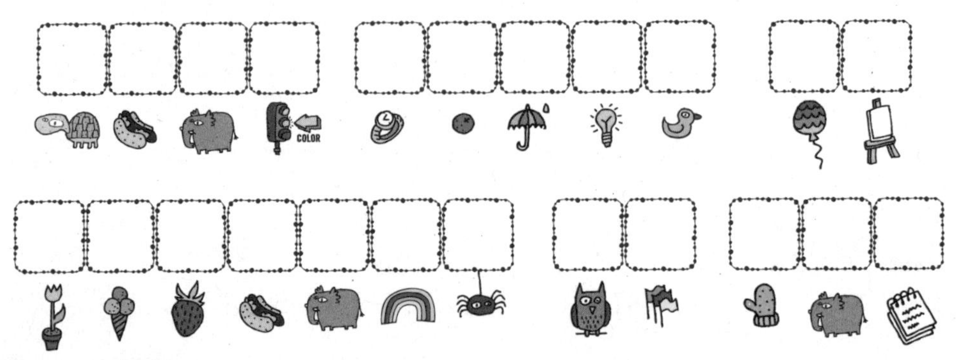

PRAY: God, thank You for calling me to be Your follower.

OLDER SCRIPTURE: Luke 6:27-28, 31
YOUNGER SCRIPTURE: Luke 6:27-28, 31
MEMORY VERSE: Proverbs 2:6

EXPLAIN

- Jesus taught His disciples how they should live.
- Jesus said we should show love, forgiveness, and generosity to others, even when they are unkind to us.
- We are able to love others because of Jesus' love for us.
- Jesus spent time teaching His disciples about how to live as Christians. His way of living is different than how the world says people should live. Jesus called His followers to a higher standard that is only possible because of God's work in us.

Jesus wants us to love, forgive, and show generosity to others even when it is hard. His love for us makes that possible. List ways you can show love, forgiveness, and generosity to others.

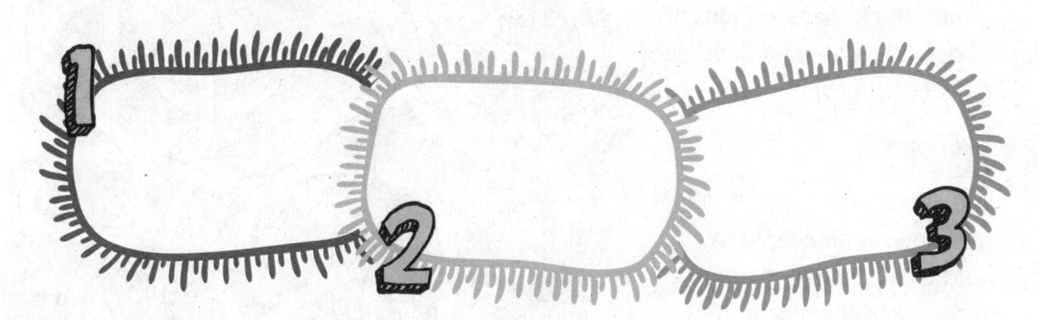

PRAY: Heavenly Father, help me love, forgive, and show generosity to others at all times.

HIGHLIGHT

OLDER SCRIPTURE: Luke 7:12-16
YOUNGER SCRIPTURE: Luke 7:12-16
MEMORY VERSE: Proverbs 2:6

EXPLAIN

- Jesus and His disciples were on their way to a town called Nain, and there were many people traveling with them.
- When they got to the town, Jesus and His disciples saw that a widow's only son had died. She was very sad.
- Jesus had compassion on her, and He raised her son from the dead. People around Him were amazed.
- Jesus traveled from city to city and took time to care for people. He healed the slave of a Roman soldier and the son of a widow. These were people Jews did not think were important, but Jesus showed that He loved all people.

APPLY

Just as Jesus did, we should show love to all people. As you travel from city to city to complete the maze, think about how you can show love to all people.

RESPOND

PRAY: Heavenly Father, help me show love to all people.

HIGHLIGHT

OLDER SCRIPTURE: Luke 8:43-48
YOUNGER SCRIPTURE: Luke 8:47-48
MEMORY VERSE: Proverbs 2:6

EXPLAIN

- Jesus and His disciples were on their way to see a sick girl. Crowds of people surrounded them.
- There was a woman in the crowd who had been sick for 12 years. She had faith that Jesus could heal her, so she squeezed through the crowd to get to Him.
- The woman touched Jesus' clothes and was healed. Jesus told her that she had been healed because of her faith.
- Lots of people were trying to see Jesus and were crowding around to get to Him. Jesus has power over sickness, and He showed mercy and love by healing the sick woman.

APPLY

Jesus has the power to heal. Find the highlighted words from EXPLAIN in the word search.

S D I S C H V H W E L O V W D W
E P Y D Q W E T E A S F H H J E
R O F A I T H U F A I B R E Q R
T W W E R S R I O P L S B M D T
M E R C Y W C R O W D I N G M Y
T R H E A L B I X V Q C N D E G
T T A L Z B W D P E U K E G R F
R O T O U C H E D L Y N R T M D
W W U V R T O U K C E E T Y E S
D Q A E F H E J E S U S R U R A
C R O W B W E R T A Z S C E R C

RESPOND

PRAY: God, thank You for Your power over sickness.

HIGHLIGHT

OLDER SCRIPTURE: Luke 9:46-48
YOUNGER SCRIPTURE: Luke 9:46-48
MEMORY VERSE: Proverbs 2:6

EXPLAIN

- Jesus was with His disciples when they began arguing about which one of them was the greatest.
- Jesus stood a child beside Him and told His disciples that any person who welcomes a child in Jesus' name welcomes Jesus.
- To God, the least of men is considered the greatest to God. Jesus told His disciples to treat other people like they would treat Him.
- Just before these verses, Jesus predicted His death on the cross, but the disciples did not understand His words. They began arguing with one another—they wanted to know which one of them was the greatest disciple. They did not understand what Jesus meant, but Jesus understood their hearts.

APPLY

Jesus taught His disciples—and us—that following Him is about being humble and putting others first. Use the maritime flag code to decode this message from today's reading:

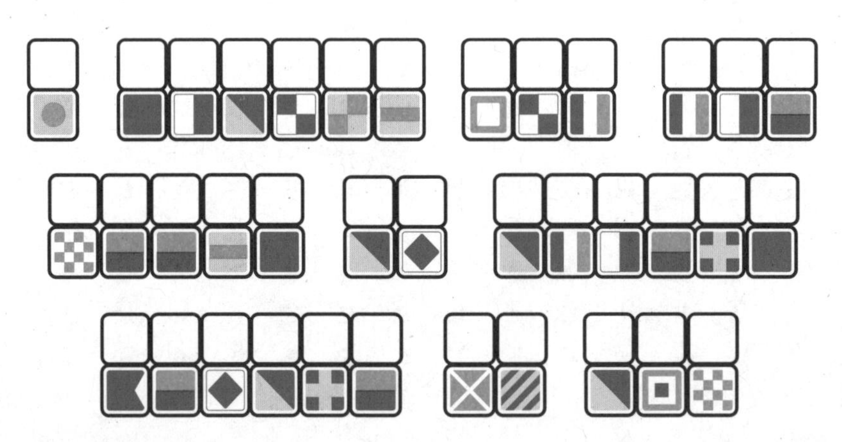

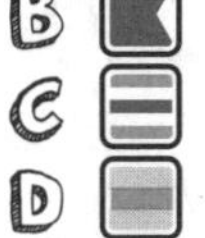

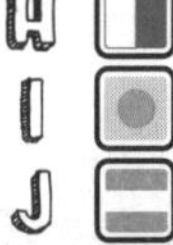

RESPOND

PRAY: Jesus, help me put the needs of others before my own.

OLDER SCRIPTURE: Luke 10:25-28
YOUNGER SCRIPTURE: Luke 10:27
MEMORY VERSE: Proverbs 2:6

EXPLAIN

- An expert in Jewish law was trying to test Jesus and get Him to say something wrong.
- Jesus taught that following Him is following the law, because He is the Messiah God promised.
- Obeying the law means loving Jesus with your whole heart and loving others.
- Some people didn't believe Jesus was the Messiah and were trying to trick Him into saying something wrong. Jesus showed them that He honored the law, and they could find nothing wrong with His teaching.

Obeying God means loving Him and others. Fill in the blanks from Proverbs 2:6.

FOR ______________________________ WISDOM;

______________________________________ COME

________________________ AND

______________________________.

PRAY: Heavenly Father, thank You for sending Jesus to show us how to obey and love.

OLDER SCRIPTURE: Luke 11:1-4
YOUNGER SCRIPTURE: Luke 11:1-4
MEMORY VERSE: Psalm 1:6

EXPLAIN

- The disciples asked Jesus to teach them to pray.
- Jesus prayed, and told the disciples to pray like Him.
- Jesus used prayer to talk to God. Prayer is talking and listening to God.
- Praying is how we talk to God. Jesus talked to God through prayer, and He showed the disciples how to talk to God, too.

APPLY

Jesus taught us to pray so we can talk to God wherever we are. Jesus taught us how to **SIT**. Wait. No He didn't! Solve the puzzle by following the directions to change each word into a new word. This is what Jesus really taught us to do!

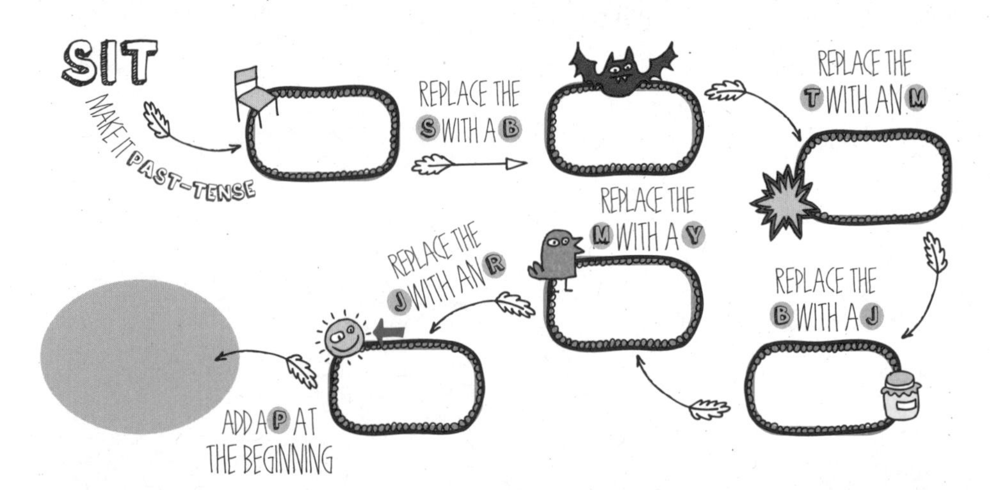

RESPOND

PRAY: Heavenly Father, thank You for sending Jesus to teach us how to live and how to pray.

OLDER SCRIPTURE: Luke 12:31-34
YOUNGER SCRIPTURE: Luke 12:31-34
MEMORY VERSE: Psalm 1:6

EXPLAIN

- Jesus taught His disciples how to live without worrying. Jesus said God takes care of all things, but He will take even better care of you, so you should trust God and not be anxious.
- Jesus taught that the things on earth do not last forever, but the things God gives in heaven will last forever.
- Jesus taught His disciples not to become distracted by earthly worries and possessions. God provides for every need, just as He provides for all of His creation. Jesus taught that His followers should focus on heavenly treasure that will last forever.

Put a check mark beside possessions you and your family own. Then cross out the ones that will not last forever. Jesus instructs us to focus our hearts on heavenly treasures, not things we have on earth.

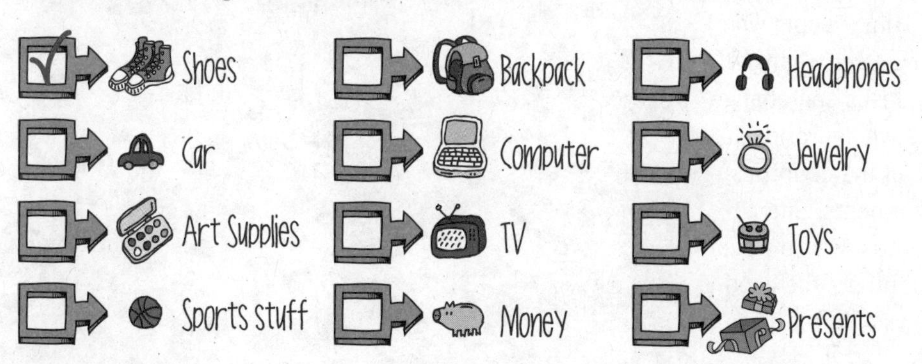

PRAY: God, thank You for giving me good things in heaven that will last forever.

WEEK 3 DAY 3

HIGHLIGHT

OLDER SCRIPTURE: Luke 13:20-21
YOUNGER SCRIPTURE: Luke 13:20-21
MEMORY VERSE: Psalm 1:6

EXPLAIN

- Jesus was teaching through parables—stories that have meaning.
- Jesus used a parable about yeast spreading through dough. Just a little yeast spreads through all the dough and makes the whole batch rise.
- The good news of Jesus spreads and changes the lives of everyone who follows Him.
- Jesus often used familiar people, places, and things in His parables. Sometimes these familiar things would help people more easily understand what He was teaching about. Jesus taught that the good news about God spreads to reach a lot of people.

APPLY

The good news of Jesus changes each person who trusts in Him. People who have been changed by Jesus can change the whole world. Color in all the countries, continents, and islands, where we can tell others the good news of Jesus.

RESPOND

PRAY: God, thank You for sending Jesus. Help me share the good news about Him.

OLDER SCRIPTURE: Luke 14:12-14
YOUNGER SCRIPTURE: Luke 14:12-14
MEMORY VERSE: Psalm 1:6

- One Sabbath, while Jesus was eating, He saw the dinner guests taking the best seats for themselves. In response, He taught the guests about humility, or putting others' desires ahead of your own.
- Jesus encouraged selfless behavior among His followers. He said to include poor and hurting people—those who cannot repay someone with gifts or party invitations.
- Jesus taught that His followers will be blessed by caring for people who cannot do nice things in return.
- Jesus was eating with the Pharisees. The Pharisees were watching Jesus carefully. They wanted to trick Him. Instead, Jesus taught the Pharisees, who were prideful and very concerned with themselves, how to be humble. Jesus is the best example of humility. Everything He said and did was perfect and for God's glory and the good of His followers.

God values and honors a humble attitude. Jesus humbled Himself when He came to earth to pay the price for our sin. Which dinner guest has a humble attitude? Follow the paths to find out.

PRAY: Heavenly Father, help me put the needs of others ahead of my own needs.

HIGHLIGHT

OLDER SCRIPTURE: Luke 15:3-7
YOUNGER SCRIPTURE: Luke 15:3-7
MEMORY VERSE: Psalm 1:6

EXPLAIN

- Jesus told stories called *parables* to help people understand what He was teaching.
- Jesus told a parable about a shepherd who lost a sheep. The shepherd went looking for the sheep and celebrated when he found it.
- Jesus said all of heaven celebrates when just one person is rescued from sin.
- The Pharisees and scribes were speaking against Jesus for hanging out with sinners. Jesus told them a parable—a shepherd with 100 sheep lost one, and he left the 99 safe sheep alone to find the lost one. Jesus came to save those who were lost, just like the shepherd searched for his lost sheep. The Pharisees should have rejoiced over a sinner who had found life in Christ!

APPLY

All people matter to God, and He is overjoyed when just one person is rescued from sin. We should celebrate too! Discuss: What do you think it looks like when God celebrates?

RESPOND

PRAY: Heavenly Father, thank You for celebrating every person who loves You. Help me celebrate, too.

HIGHLIGHT

OLDER SCRIPTURE: Luke 16:10-12
YOUNGER SCRIPTURE: Luke 16:10
MEMORY VERSE: Psalm 3:3

EXPLAIN

- Jesus was teaching His disciples with a parable—a story with meaning.
- Jesus' story was about a man who was not responsible with his boss's things.
- Jesus wanted the people to understand that being wise and faithful stewards is important.
- When Jesus told a parable, He often used familiar people, places, and things. He told about a man who was not a good steward of his boss's property and had to fix his mistakes. Being faithful, even with just a little, is important to God.

APPLY

When we are faithful and take care of what God gives us, we honor God. Fill in the blanks to complete this week's memory verse.

BUT ____

____

MY GLORY ____

____.

RESPOND

PRAY: Heavenly Father, help me honor You with my faithfulness.

OLDER SCRIPTURE: Luke 17:11-19
YOUNGER SCRIPTURE: Luke 17:15-16
MEMORY VERSE: Psalm 3:3

EXPLAIN

- Jesus was traveling to Jerusalem and came to a village with 10 men who were sick with a skin disease.
- When the sick men saw Jesus, they asked Him to heal them, and He did.
- The 10 men were excited to be healed, but only one of them returned to Jesus to thank Him.
- During this time, people who had serious diseases had to stay far away from everyone else. Jesus saw these sick men, and when they asked Him for healing, He healed them. Being healed meant they would be able to go back to their families and worship God together. Only one man returned to thank Jesus and praise God.

APPLY

When Jesus changes our life, we should show thankfulness to Him in worship. Discuss: How can we show God that we are thankful?

RESPOND

PRAY: God, thank You for changing the lives of people who ask You.

OLDER SCRIPTURE: Luke 18:35-43
YOUNGER SCRIPTURE: Luke 18:40-43
MEMORY VERSE: Psalm 3:3

- Jesus was walking with His disciples when a blind man called out to Him.
- Jesus asked the man what he wanted. The man asked Jesus to heal his blindness.
- Jesus healed the blind man because of his faith in Jesus. The man immediately followed Jesus and praised God. So did everyone else!
- Not long before Jesus gave sight to the blind man, He told His disciples about His death. They had not fully understood Jesus—the meaning was hidden to them. The blind man believed that Jesus is the Messiah and has power over all things, including sickness and death. Jesus healed the blind man, and many people worshiped God.

Decode the message below to learn one thing that is true about Jesus.

PRAY: Jesus, thank You for having power over sickness and death. Help me to trust that You are all-powerful and in control of all things.

HIGHLIGHT

OLDER SCRIPTURE: Luke 19:39-40
YOUNGER SCRIPTURE: Luke 19:39-40
MEMORY VERSE: Psalm 3:3

EXPLAIN

- Jesus was about to enter Jerusalem. He sent the disciples to get a donkey for Him to ride on.
- As Jesus and the disciples were going along the road, people were spreading their robes on the road and praising God.
- The Pharisees wanted Jesus to rebuke people for praising Him. Jesus told them that if people do not worship God, the stones would cry out in their place.
- Jesus was on His way to Jerusalem before Passover. As He passed by, people were praising God because of all the miracles they had seen Jesus do. The Pharisees wanted Jesus to tell them to stop, but Jesus would not. He let the Pharisees know that if the people didn't praise God, His creation would.

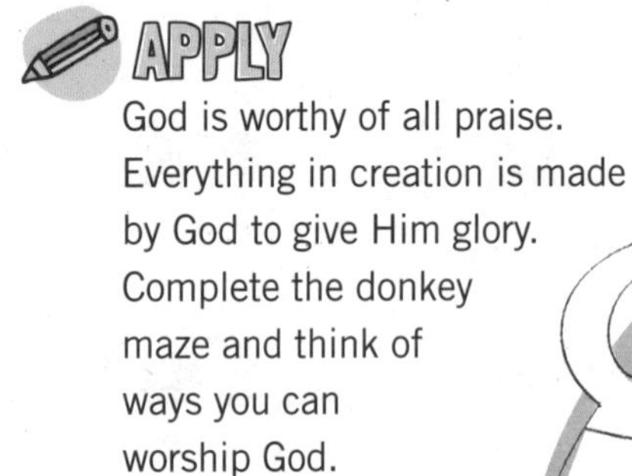

APPLY

God is worthy of all praise. Everything in creation is made by God to give Him glory. Complete the donkey maze and think of ways you can worship God.

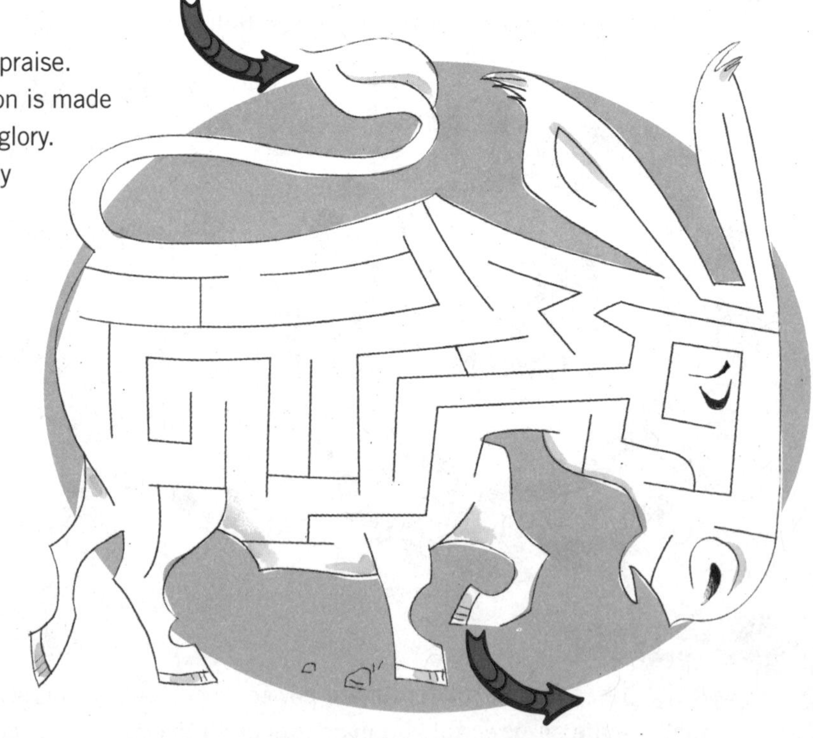

RESPOND

PRAY: Heavenly Father, thank You for being holy and worthy of praise.

OLDER SCRIPTURE: Luke 20:20-26
YOUNGER SCRIPTURE: Luke 20:26
MEMORY VERSE: Psalm 3:3

EXPLAIN

- Religious leaders were trying to trick Jesus into saying something against God's law. No one can trick Jesus because He is God.
- Jesus taught that people are made in God's image and should give themselves to worshiping and obeying Him.
- Jesus showed the religious leaders that He will never break God's law because He is the Messiah.
- The religious leaders did not like Jesus and kept trying to trick Him into saying something against God's law. Jesus did not fall for their tricks. Jesus is holy and will never break God's law. He fulfills the law because He is God's promised Messiah.

Jesus is the Messiah, the promised Son of God. Who is the Messiah? Fill in the boxes with a square in a dark color and the boxes with a circle in a light color.

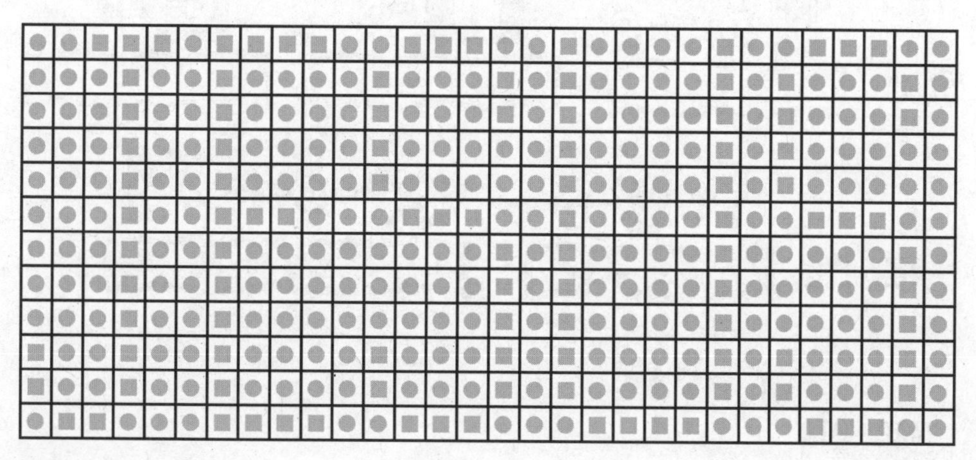

PRAY: God, thank You for sending Jesus to be the Messiah.

HIGHLIGHT

OLDER SCRIPTURE: Luke 21:1-3
YOUNGER SCRIPTURE: Luke 21:1-3
MEMORY VERSE: Proverbs 3:11

EXPLAIN

- Jesus was at the temple where people were giving their offerings and worshiping God.
- Some people gave a lot, but one widow gave two tiny coins.
- Jesus said that the widow had given more than anyone else because she was poor and gave all she had.
- Jesus had just spoken to His disciples about people who took advantage of widows. He saw a widow who gave all she had to God's temple. Even though the amount of money was small, Jesus said she had given more than anyone else there. She gave because she obeyed God and trusted in Him.

APPLY

Faith and obedience to God are important to Him. Solve the rebus puzzle below.

RESPOND

PRAY: Heavenly Father, help me have faith and obey You.

OLDER SCRIPTURE: Luke 22:14-16
YOUNGER SCRIPTURE: Luke 22:14-16
MEMORY VERSE: Proverbs 3:11

EXPLAIN

- Jesus was observing the Passover meal with His disciples.
- The Jews celebrated Passover to remind them of when God saved them from death in Egypt.
- Jesus told His disciples He would be killed, but they did not understand.
- Since the very first Passover during captivity in Egypt, the Jewish people had continued to celebrate Passover to remind them of how God saved them from death. Jesus told the disciples He would die to save people from their sin, but they did not understand.

APPLY

Jesus became our Passover lamb to save us from our sin. Write Proverbs 3:11 in the circle to help you memorize this week's verse.

RESPOND

PRAY: Jesus, thank You for becoming our Passover lamb to save us from sin.

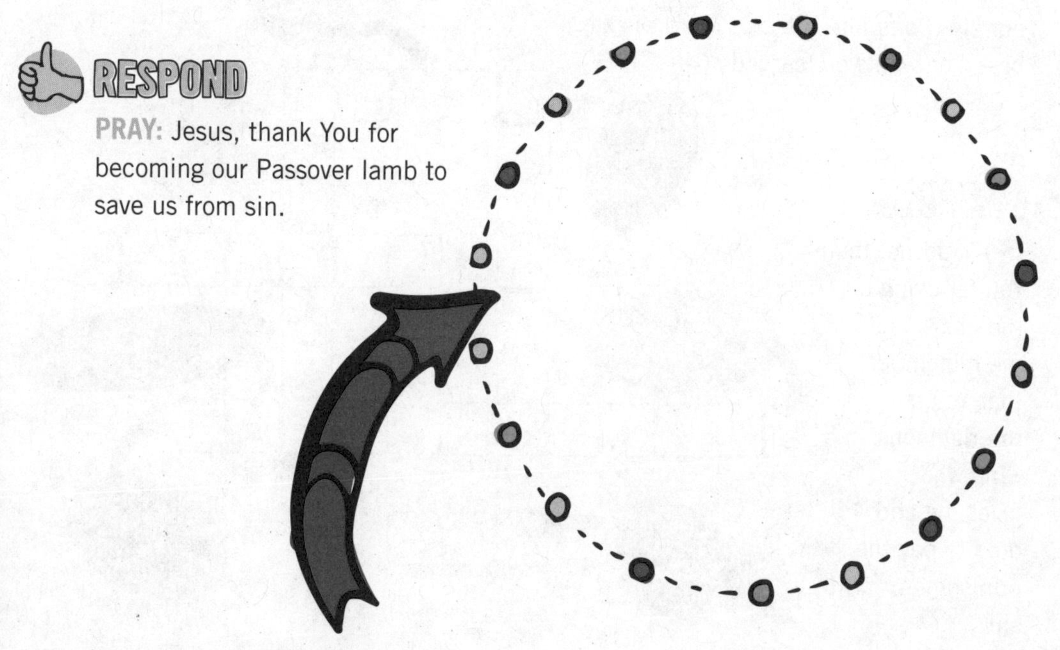

WEEK 5 DAY 3

HIGHLIGHT

OLDER SCRIPTURE: Luke 23:44-46
YOUNGER SCRIPTURE: Luke 23:44-46
MEMORY VERSE: Proverbs 3:11

EXPLAIN

- Jesus was crucified on a cross between two criminals.
- The sky grew dark and the sun's light failed. Jesus gave His Spirit to God and died.
- A soldier who saw Jesus die realized Jesus was innocent because He was the Son of God. The soldier glorified God.
- A sign saying "This is the King of the Jews" had been written above Jesus on the cross. The soldiers had written this sign to mock Jesus, but one of the soldiers watched Jesus carefully and realized that He really was the righteous King, the Messiah. Jesus sacrificed Himself for all who believe in Him.

APPLY

Jesus died on the cross to take the punishment for our sin. Complete the crossword puzzle based on what you learned today.

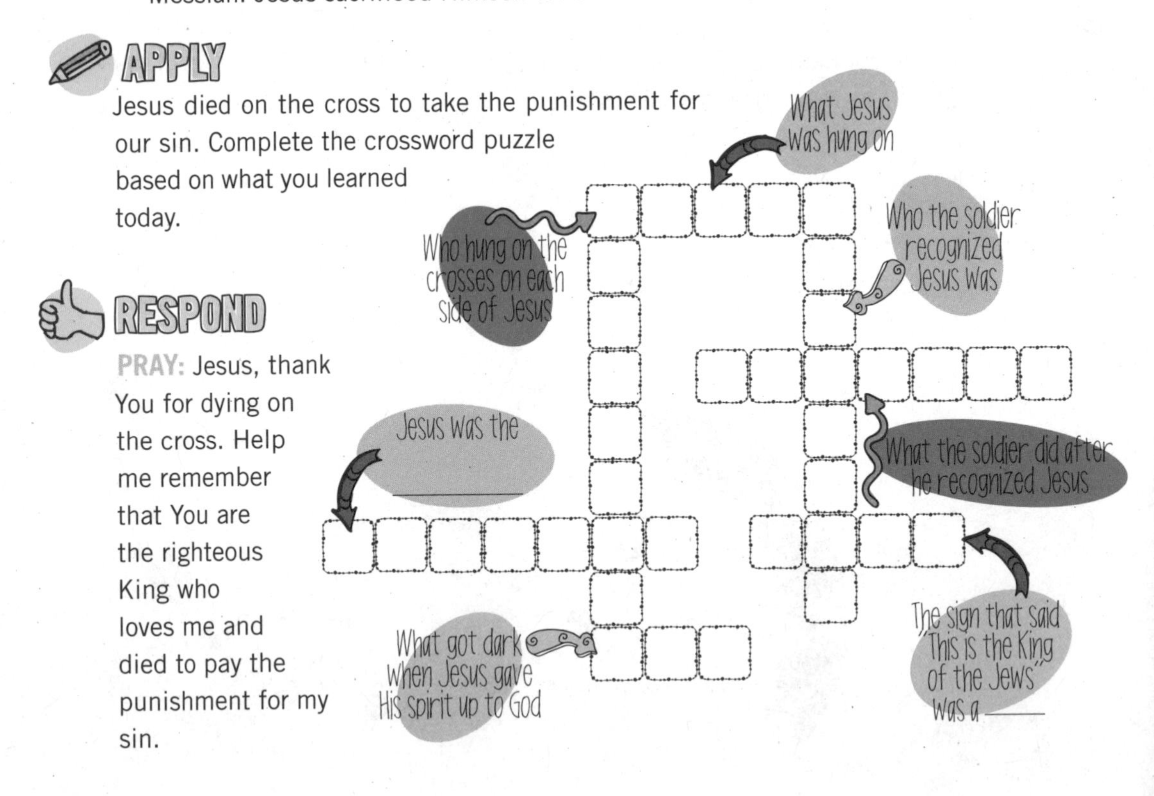

RESPOND

PRAY: Jesus, thank You for dying on the cross. Help me remember that You are the righteous King who loves me and died to pay the punishment for my sin.

OLDER SCRIPTURE: Luke 24:1-8
YOUNGER SCRIPTURE: Luke 24:1-3
MEMORY VERSE: Proverbs 3:11

EXPLAIN

- Jesus died on the cross and was buried in a tomb. On the third day, some women went to the tomb.
- When the women got to the tomb, the stone was rolled away, and Jesus wasn't there!
- The women saw two men in dazzling clothes who reminded them that Jesus had told them He would rise on the third day.
- Friends of Jesus went to take care of His body in the tomb. But when they got there, His body was gone! Two men appeared in dazzling clothes, and the women were afraid. But the men reminded them that Jesus had told them He would rise on the third day.

APPLY

Jesus rose from the dead just like He said He would. Discuss: How do you think the women felt when Jesus was gone, and the two men appeared?

RESPOND

PRAY: Jesus, thank You for rising from the dead. Help me tell others the good news of Your resurrection.

OLDER SCRIPTURE: Acts 1:6-11
YOUNGER SCRIPTURE: Acts 1:8
MEMORY VERSE: Proverbs 3:11

EXPLAIN

- Jesus was preparing to go to heaven. He gave final instructions to the disciples.
- The disciples wanted to know if Jesus would restore Israel soon. Jesus said some things are only for God to know, but they should tell everyone about Him.
- Jesus went up into heaven on a cloud.
- Before Jesus went back to heaven, He gave His disciples instructions to tell others about Him. He did not want them to worry about waiting around for Him to return—He wanted them to focus on telling others the good news about Him. Jesus will come back one day, but only God knows the day and time.

APPLY

We do not know when Jesus will return, but we should tell everyone about Him until He comes back. Where should we tell people about Jesus? Everywhere. Even to the ends of the earth. Complete the globe maze and think about who you can tell about Jesus.

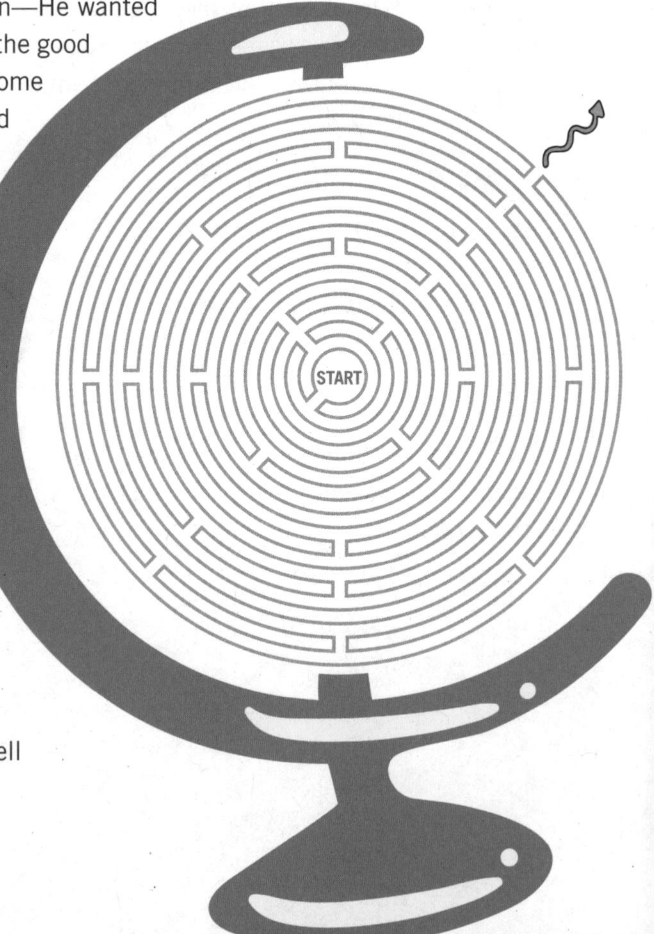

RESPOND

PRAY: Jesus, give me courage to tell others about You.

HIGHLIGHT

OLDER SCRIPTURE: Acts 2:32-39
YOUNGER SCRIPTURE: Acts 2:36
MEMORY VERSE: Psalm 9:9

EXPLAIN

- At Pentecost, Peter preached to people about Jesus.
- Peter told the people that Jesus is the Messiah they had been waiting for.
- Peter told them to repent of their sin and be baptized in the name of Jesus so they could receive the Holy Spirit.
- At Pentecost, the Holy Spirit came and gave understanding to the people that Jesus was the Messiah. Peter made it clear that God's salvation and promises are for everyone, not just Jews. Many people repented and believed in Jesus and received the Holy Spirit.

APPLY

God gives the Holy Spirit to anyone who repents and believes. Cross out every other circle and write the remaining letters in the empty circles to solve the puzzle.

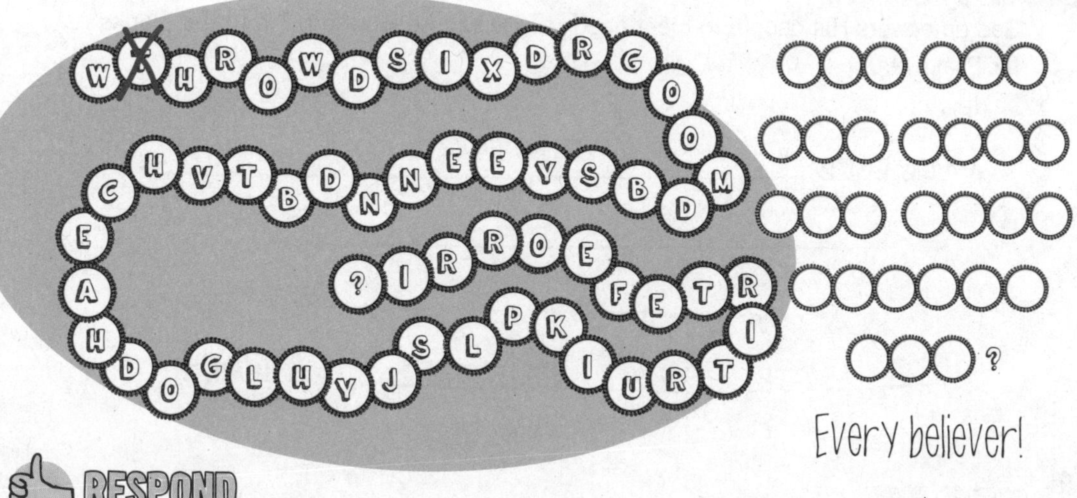

RESPOND

PRAY: Heavenly Father, thank You that Your promises are for everyone.

OLDER SCRIPTURE: Acts 3:2-8
YOUNGER SCRIPTURE: Acts 3:6-8
MEMORY VERSE: Psalm 9:9

EXPLAIN

- Peter and John were entering the temple when a man who could not walk asked for their help.
- The man had never been able to walk. At the temple gate, he begged for money and other things he needed. Peter and John gave the man a different kind of help than he expected.
- Peter and John healed the man in the name of Jesus! The man jumped up, walked, and praised God. The man went to the temple to worship God, walking and leaping. Other people began to praise God, too.
- Peter and John had been preaching and doing miracles in Jesus' name. The lame man wanted help but did not expect the kind of help Peter and John gave him. He was excited to be healed and praised God.

APPLY

God empowers His people to meet needs so He will be glorified. Fill in the blanks for Psalm 9:9.

THE LORD ______________________________

______________________________.

A ______________________________

______________________________ TROUBLE.

PRAY: Heavenly Father, help me meet the needs of others so You will be glorified.

HIGHLIGHT

OLDER SCRIPTURE: Acts 4:19-20
YOUNGER SCRIPTURE: Acts 4:19-20
MEMORY VERSE: Psalm 9:9

EXPLAIN

- Peter and John continued preaching the good news of Jesus, but the religious leaders did not like it. Many people believed in Jesus because of Peter and John's preaching.
- The religious leaders arrested Peter and John. Peter and John had done nothing wrong, so they were released.
- Many people were believing in Jesus because of Peter and John's preaching and miracles. Religious leaders tried to stop Peter and John from preaching and even had them put in jail. Persecution did not keep Peter and John from preaching the good news about Jesus.

APPLY

God wants us to tell people about Him, even if we are persecuted. Complete the puzzle on the right. In each row, you will create a new word by changing one letter in the current word. The letter to change is highlighted with a yellow arrow and an orange circle. The picture clue will help you figure out each new word.

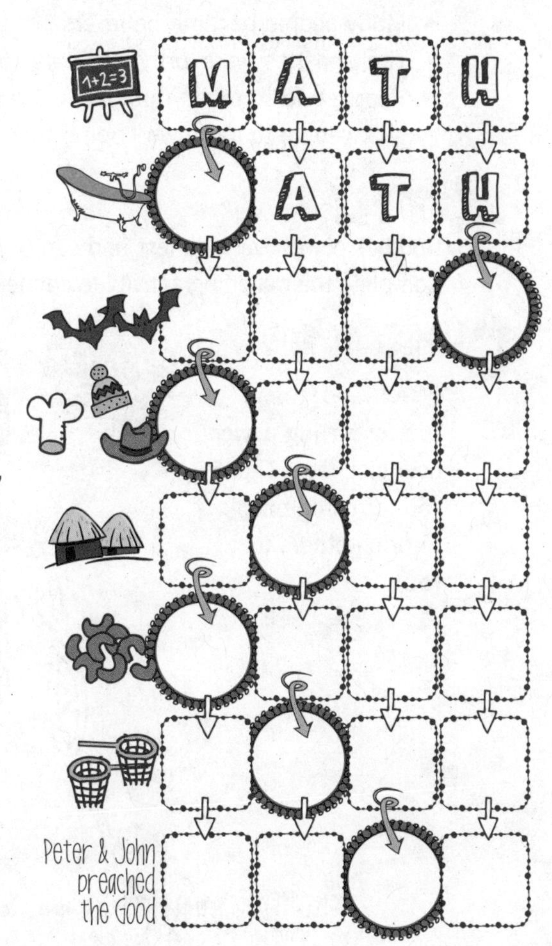

RESPOND

PRAY: God, help me tell people about You.

OLDER SCRIPTURE: Acts 5:12-16
YOUNGER SCRIPTURE: Acts 5:12-16
MEMORY VERSE: Psalm 9:9

- The apostles (Jesus' chosen disciples) were healing people through God's power in Jesus' name.
- Some would bring sick people from other towns to see the apostles.
- Many people became believers because of God's work through the apostles.
- The apostles were bringing glory to God, and sick people were being healed. People had so much faith in God to work through the apostles, they would bring sick people to the town hoping to be healed as apostles walked by.

God has power over sickness and can work through people to bring Himself glory. Complete the matching activity to connect the true sentences from today's reading.

PRAY: God, thank You for having power over sickness. Thank You for using people to bring others to You.

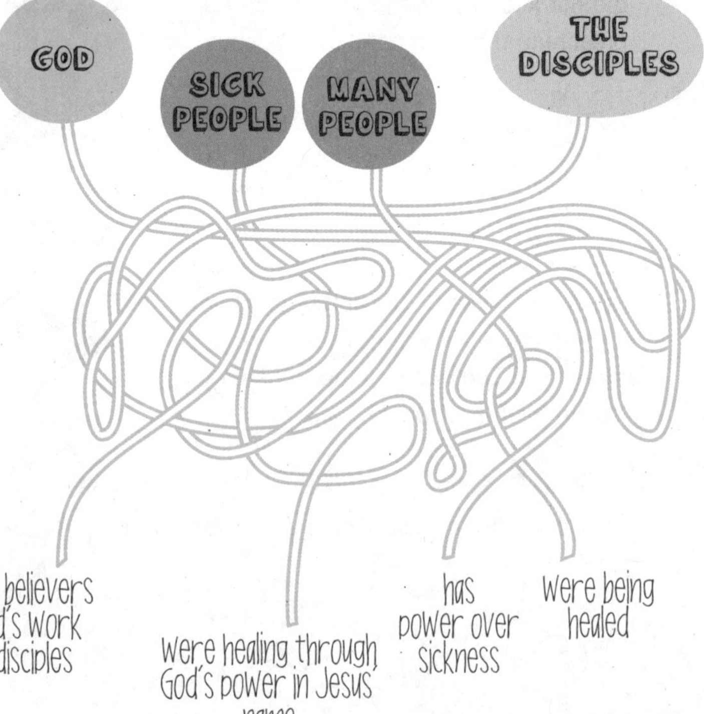

HIGHLIGHT

OLDER SCRIPTURE: Acts 6:1-6
YOUNGER SCRIPTURE: Acts 6:1-6
MEMORY VERSE: Psalm 9:9

EXPLAIN

- More and more people became believers in Jesus.
- The disciples couldn't do the work of taking care of everyone and preach, too.
- Seven men were chosen who were wise and full of the Spirit to serve by making sure the believers were cared for.
- The number of believers had grown so much, there were too many for the disciples to take care of by themselves. It was important to choose wise believers to help. God calls the church to love and care for one another.

APPLY

We can all use our abilities to serve God. Discuss: What abilities do you have that you can use to serve God?

RESPOND

PRAY: Heavenly Father, help me use my abilities to serve You.

OLDER SCRIPTURE: Acts 7:54-60
YOUNGER SCRIPTURE: Acts 7:54-60
MEMORY VERSE: Proverbs 4:23

EXPLAIN

- Stephen performed signs and wonders in the name of Jesus. This made the Jewish leaders angry, and they arrested Stephen.
- The Jewish leaders took Stephen before the Jewish court where he preached about Jesus.
- The Jewish leaders were angry with Stephen and killed him.
- Stephen was killed for his faith in Jesus, but many people heard the good news because of his faithfulness and boldness to tell others about Jesus. What people intended for harm, God used for good.

We can be faithful and bold to tell others about Jesus in truth and love.

Jesus told us we would be persecuted for ________ ____ ________.

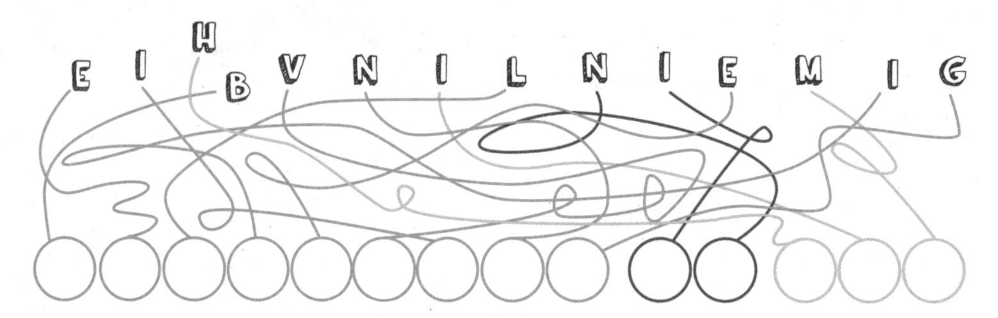

PRAY: Heavenly Father, help me be strong and brave when I am persecuted for trusting in You.

OLDER SCRIPTURE: Acts 8:34-38
YOUNGER SCRIPTURE: Acts 8:34-38
MEMORY VERSE: Proverbs 4:23

EXPLAIN

- An angel of the Lord told Philip to go down the road from Jerusalem to Gaza.
- On the way, Philip met a man who served the queen of Ethiopia. He was reading the Book of Isaiah.
- Philip explained the good news of Jesus to the man, and he believed in Jesus.
- Philip obeyed God's instructions to go down the road to Gaza. He met a man who was reading the Book of Isaiah but didn't understand it. Philip explained that this Scripture was talking about Jesus. The man understood, and he decided to follow Jesus. He wanted to obey Jesus' command and be baptized right away.

APPLY

We should always be ready to tell people about Jesus and follow Him in obedience, no matter where we are. Discuss: What does it mean to obey God?

RESPOND

PRAY: God, please help me always be ready to tell people about You and obey You.

HIGHLIGHT

OLDER SCRIPTURE: Acts 9:1-9
YOUNGER SCRIPTURE: Acts 9:3-6
MEMORY VERSE: Proverbs 4:23

EXPLAIN

- Saul persecuted Christians. He hurt them and arrested them for teaching about Jesus.
- As Saul was traveling to Damascus to arrest Christians, Jesus appeared to him in a bright light and explained what he was doing was wrong.
- Saul became a believer in Jesus and started preaching about Jesus.
- Saul wanted to hurt and kill the disciples of God. God changed Saul's heart and chose him to tell people about Jesus. Saul (later called Paul) traveled all over telling others about Jesus.

APPLY

Jesus changed Saul's heart when Saul repented of his sin and believed in Jesus. Jesus wants everyone to trust in Him for salvation. Write Proverbs 4:23 in the circle to memorize this week.

RESPOND

PRAY: Jesus, thank You for having the power to change my heart.

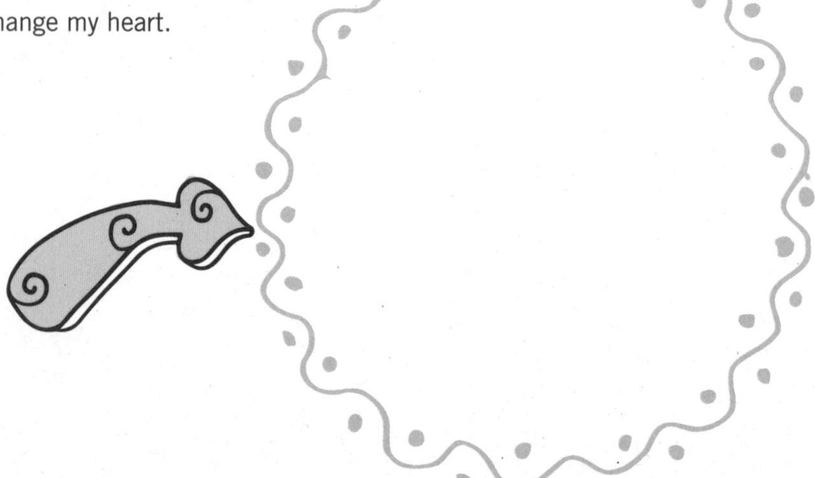

HIGHLIGHT

OLDER SCRIPTURE: Acts 10:34-36
YOUNGER SCRIPTURE: Acts 10:34-36
MEMORY VERSE: Proverbs 4:23

EXPLAIN

- Peter was speaking to the Gentiles (non-Jewish people) about Jesus.
- Peter understood that God doesn't have favorites—He loves everyone and wants them all to believe.
- God sent Jesus for everyone to trust and believe in Him.
- Peter wanted to make it clear that the good news of Jesus is for everyone—Jews and Gentiles. Because God loves everyone equally, He wants everyone to know and trust in Him.

APPLY

Who is the good news of Jesus for? Find the answer by placing the first letter of each picture in the circle below it.

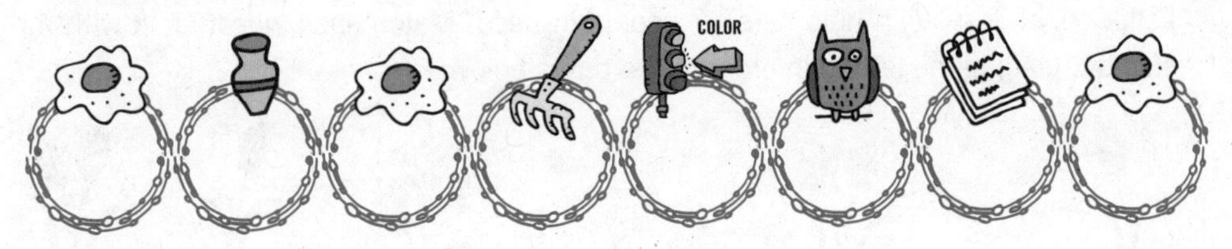

RESPOND

PRAY: Heavenly Father, thank You for loving me!

HIGHLIGHT

OLDER SCRIPTURE: Acts 11:27-30
YOUNGER SCRIPTURE: Acts 11:27-30
MEMORY VERSE: Proverbs 4:23

EXPLAIN

- The Holy Spirit told one of the men at Antioch that there would be a famine (shortage of food) in Rome.
- The disciples decided they would send help to believers who lived where the famine was.
- Barnabas and Saul took the gifts to the believers in Judea from the church at Antioch.
- A famine in the land meant that food would be hard to get. When the believers at Antioch learned this, they wanted to help the believers in Judea. They decided to send gifts to help to the people through Barnabas and Saul.

APPLY

Followers of Jesus can help care for people in need. Match each wheat stalk with its shadow, placing the letters in order in the boxes below.

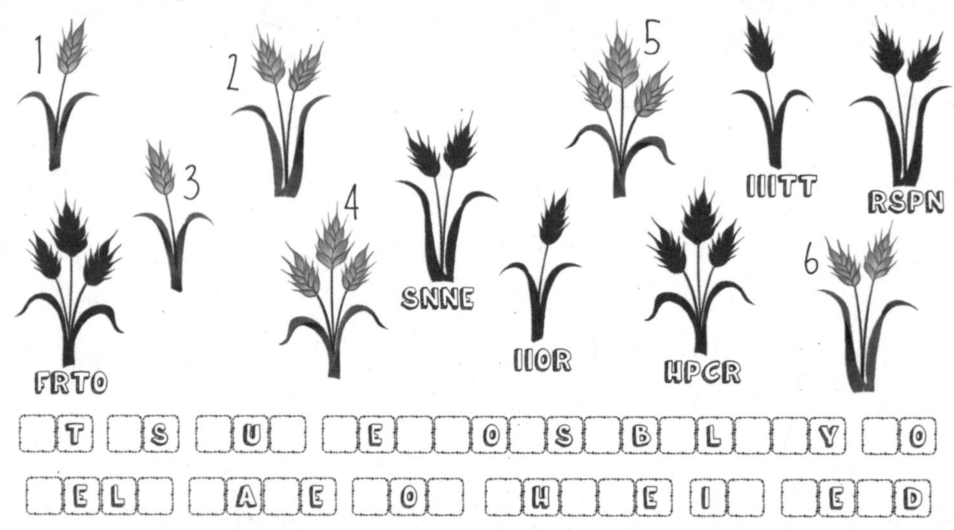

RESPOND

PRAY: Heavenly Father, show me how I can help care for people in need.

HIGHLIGHT

OLDER SCRIPTURE: Acts 12:6-11
YOUNGER SCRIPTURE: Acts 12:6-11
MEMORY VERSE: Psalm 16:11

EXPLAIN

- King Herod put Peter in jail and planned to kill him because he was preaching about salvation in Jesus.
- God sent an angel to rescue Peter from prison.
- Peter's friends had gathered together to pray for him. When Peter came to the door where they were praying, they were shocked.
- God rescued Peter because his work for God wasn't finished yet.

APPLY

Can anyone stop God's plan to share the good news of Jesus? Find out who can stop the good news of Jesus by following the path below.

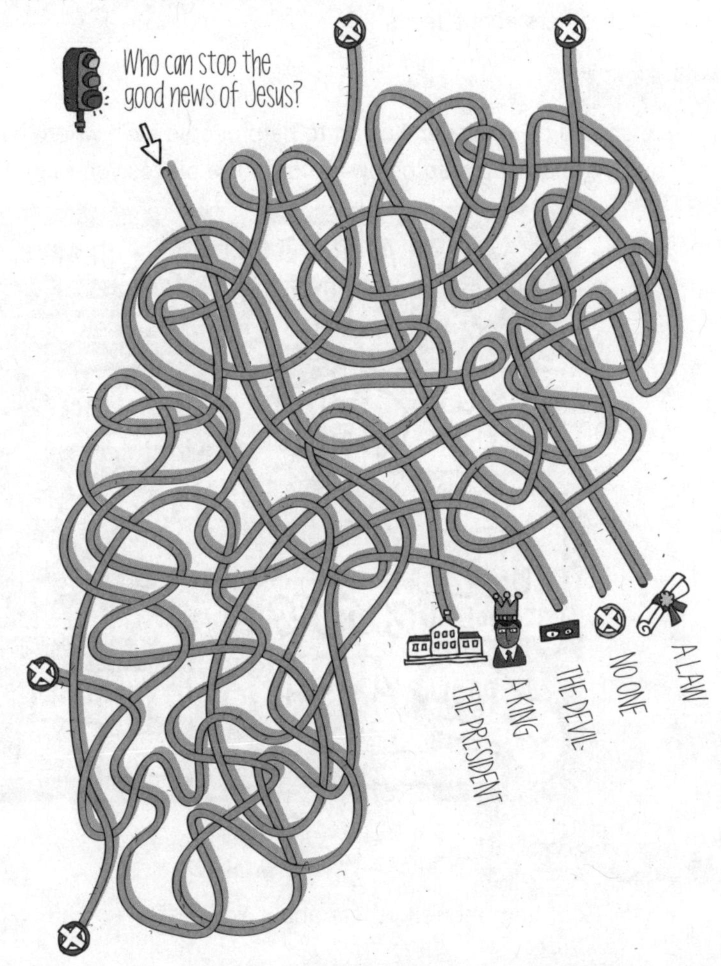

RESPOND

PRAY: Jesus, thank You that You and Your good news can't be stopped by anyone.

OLDER SCRIPTURE: Acts 13:1-3
YOUNGER SCRIPTURE: Acts 13:1-3
MEMORY VERSE: Psalm 16:11

- The church in Antioch wanted everyone to hear the good news about Jesus.
- The church sent men out to tell others about Jesus.
- Barnabas and Saul (also called Paul) were sent to tell others about Jesus.
- Jesus commanded His followers to make disciples when He gave the Great Commission. The disciples taught others how to obey the Great Commission and tell others about Jesus.

We should do whatever we can to help people everywhere hear about Jesus. Look at the neighborhood map below. Color in the places you might tell people about Jesus.

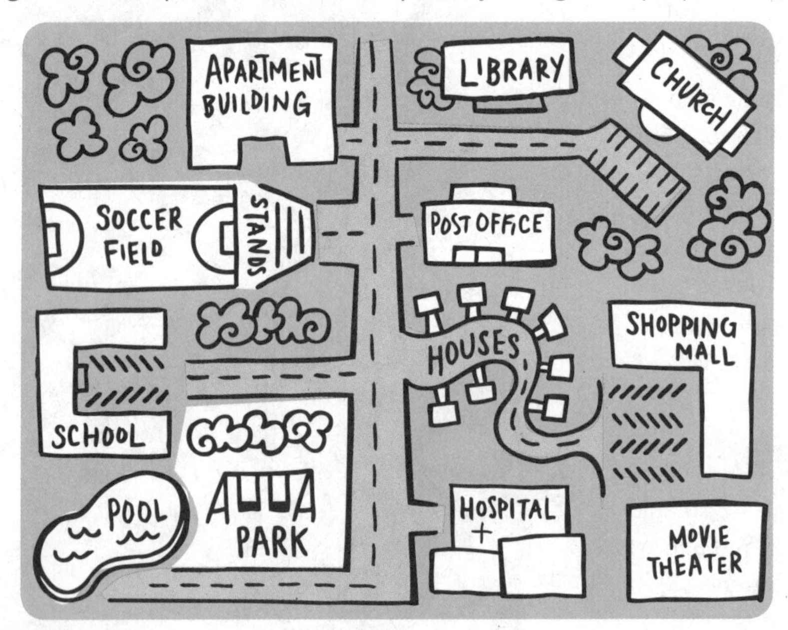

PRAY: God, help me tell others about You.

OLDER SCRIPTURE: Acts 14:21-22
YOUNGER SCRIPTURE: Acts 14:21-22
MEMORY VERSE: Psalm 16:11

EXPLAIN

- Paul endured suffering and persecution for preaching about Jesus, but he continued to tell more people about Jesus.
- The apostles continued going from town to town, telling people about Jesus as they went.
- They also encouraged believers to stay strong, even though there would be struggles in their lives.
- The apostles were made to leave towns and people even tried to kill them, but that did not stop them from telling people about Jesus everywhere they went. They also encouraged believers to be strong in their faith through difficult times.

APPLY

We should encourage each other to love Jesus, even when things are hard. Discuss: How can you encourage others to love Jesus when things are hard?

RESPOND

PRAY: Jesus, help me to love You and encourage others to love You when things are hard.

OLDER SCRIPTURE: James 1:2-3
YOUNGER SCRIPTURE: James 1:2-3
MEMORY VERSE: Psalm 16:11

EXPLAIN

- James, Jesus' younger brother, wrote to the believers in Jerusalem about how to live.
- He told the believers to be joyful and continue to live in faith even in hard circumstances.
- James told the church that Christians will go through difficult times, but God gives wisdom and strength as believers go through them.
- James gave lots of instructions about how to live as a follower of Jesus. James knew that believers would face hard times, and should be joyful and steadfast because it would help increase their faith.

APPLY

When we follow Him, God gives us wisdom and strength so we can keep going when things are hard. Write about 3 occasions when you faced a hard time. Was it difficult to be joyful during those times?

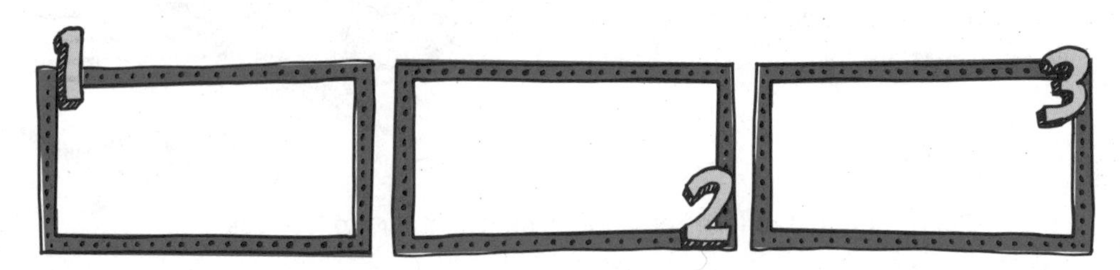

RESPOND

PRAY: Heavenly Father, thank You for giving me strength to follow You, even when things are hard.

OLDER SCRIPTURE: James 2:14-17
YOUNGER SCRIPTURE: James 2:14-17
MEMORY VERSE: Psalm 16:11

EXPLAIN

- James wrote to believers about how to live.
- He taught that Christians must not only believe in Jesus but follow His commands as well.
- James said belief and trust in Jesus should lead to acts of obedience. Christians can follow God's commands with the help of the Holy Spirit.
- James wrote a lot about faith. He wanted disciples of Jesus to understand that faith is just the beginning of following God. When believers have true faith, obedience will always follow.

Trust in Jesus always leads to actions of joyful obedience. We must follow God's plan and trust in Him as He helps us obey Him. Fill in the blanks of Psalm 16:11.

YOU ______________________________

PATH OF LIFE ______________________________

____

______________________________.

PRAY: Jesus, help me to have faith in You and show it by my actions.

HIGHLIGHT

OLDER KIDS: James 3:13-18
YOUNGER KIDS: James 3:13
MEMORY VERSE: Psalm 18:2

EXPLAIN

- James taught Christians how to live for God in their actions, attitudes, and words.
- James said God's wisdom is different than the wisdom of people.
- God's wisdom is pure, full of mercy, and unchanging.
- There are two kinds of wisdom—wisdom that comes from God and wisdom that comes from people. God's wisdom is pure, but people's wisdom is not. Followers of Jesus learn the difference by reading the Bible and obeying Jesus.

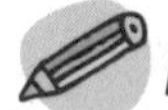

APPLY

God's wisdom is always best! Through your actions, attitudes, and words, you can reflect God's wisdom to others.
Discuss: What is one way you can reflect God's wisdom?

RESPOND

PRAY: Heavenly Father, help me reflect Your wisdom to others through my actions, attitudes, and words.

OLDER KIDS: James 4:7-10
YOUNGER KIDS: James 4:7-8
MEMORY VERSE: Psalm 18:2

EXPLAIN

- James taught Christians how to live as disciples of Jesus.
- He wrote that if Christians seek God and draw near to Him, He will be near to them.
- God is honored when His children humble themselves before Him and repent of sin.
- James wrote about how to follow God. Following God is more than following rules—it's also being pure in our hearts and minds and drawing close to God. God wants His followers to trust in Him, repent of sin, and draw close to Him.

APPLY

God is honored when we are humble before Him, and He draws near to us. Write Psalm 18:2 in the box to help you memorize it this week.

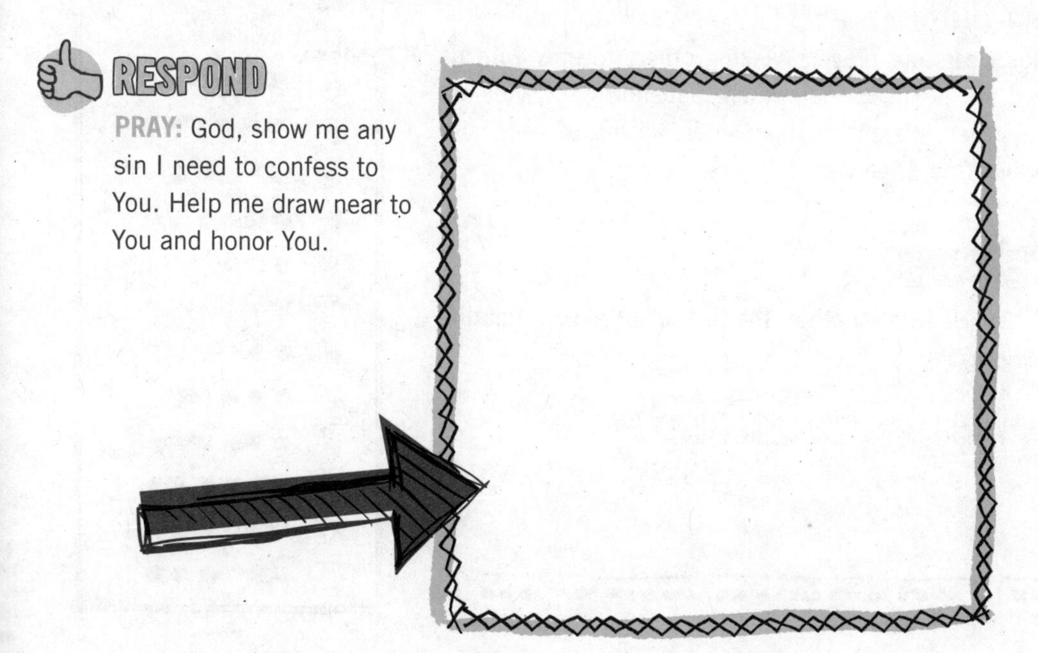

PRAY: God, show me any sin I need to confess to You. Help me draw near to You and honor You.

HIGHLIGHT

OLDER KIDS: James 5:13-14
YOUNGER KIDS: James 5:13-14
MEMORY VERSE: Psalm 18:2

EXPLAIN

- James ended his letter to believers by talking about how to treat one another.
- The Book of James encourages believers to pray to God when they are sad *and* happy.
- James reminds Christians to ask others to pray with them and for them.
- Prayer is talking to God. James wanted believers to understand that they can talk to God about everything going on in their lives. He also wanted them to ask others to pray for them and with them when they were sick or in need.

APPLY

God hears our prayers. Asking others to pray with us and for us shows that we are depending on God, not ourselves. We should pray when we are in need and praise God when we are happy.

RESPOND

PRAY: Heavenly Father, thank You for always hearing my prayers.

When does God hear our prayers?

___	___	___	___	___	___
•—	•—••	•——	•—	—•——	•••

MORSE CODE

A	•—
B	—•••
C	—•—•
D	—••
E	•
F	••—•
G	——•
H	••••
I	••
J	•———
K	—•—
L	•—••
M	——
N	—•
O	———
P	•——•
Q	——•
R	•—•
S	•••
T	—
U	••—
V	•••—
W	•——
X	—••—
Y	—•——
Z	——••

HIGHLIGHT

OLDER KIDS: Acts 15:9-11
YOUNGER KIDS: Acts 15:11
MEMORY VERSE: Psalm 18:2

EXPLAIN

- Some Christians in Antioch were teaching that people had to do special things in order to become a Christian.
- Paul and Barnabas told them that God sees everyone, Jews and Gentiles, in the same way.
- Paul and Barnabas explained that everyone is saved from sin by trusting in Jesus, whether they are a Jew or Gentile.
- Some people were teaching that Gentiles (non-Jews) had to do special things in order to become Christians. Paul and Barnabas taught that everyone is saved through Jesus' sacrifice, not things we do. God saves everyone in the same way. No one's actions saves them—only faith in Jesus saves.

APPLY

Jesus is the only way to salvation, and faith in Him is all we need to be saved from our sins. Find highlighted words above in the puzzle below.

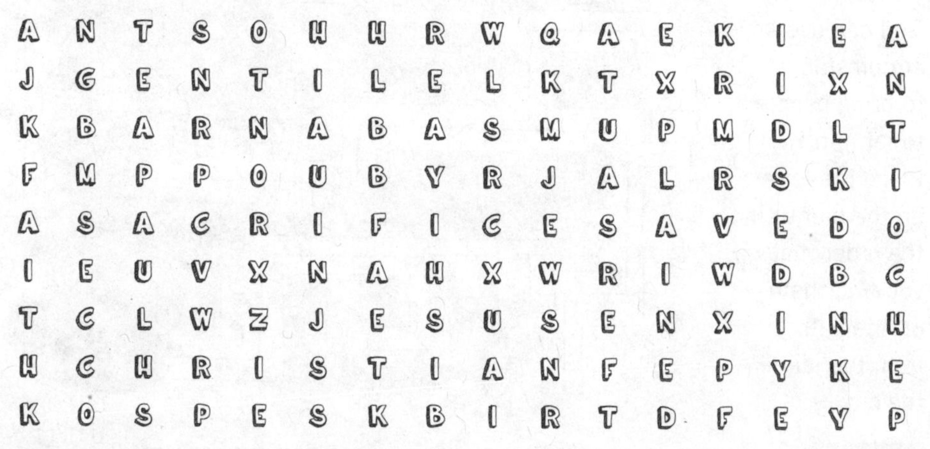

RESPOND

PRAY: God, thank You for sending Jesus to save us from our sin.

HIGHLIGHT

OLDER KIDS: Acts 16:25-34
YOUNGER KIDS: Acts 16:29-31
MEMORY VERSE: Psalm 18:2

EXPLAIN

- Paul and Silas were arrested and put in jail, but they still praised and worshiped God.
- There was an earthquake. All the prisoners could have escaped, but no one did.
- Because of Paul and Silas's faithfulness to God, the man in charge of the jail and his whole family believed in Jesus.
- If the prisoners had escaped, the jailer would have been in big trouble. Instead, the prisoners stayed where they were. The jailer asked Paul and Silas what he could do to be saved. They told him to believe in Jesus. The jailer and his family began following Jesus. Later, when they were set free, Paul and Silas continued preaching about Jesus.

APPLY

God wants us to trust and praise Him, even in difficult times. God can use any circumstance to bring people to faith in Him. Place the letters on the blanks in the order that you find them on the path from the jail to the city.

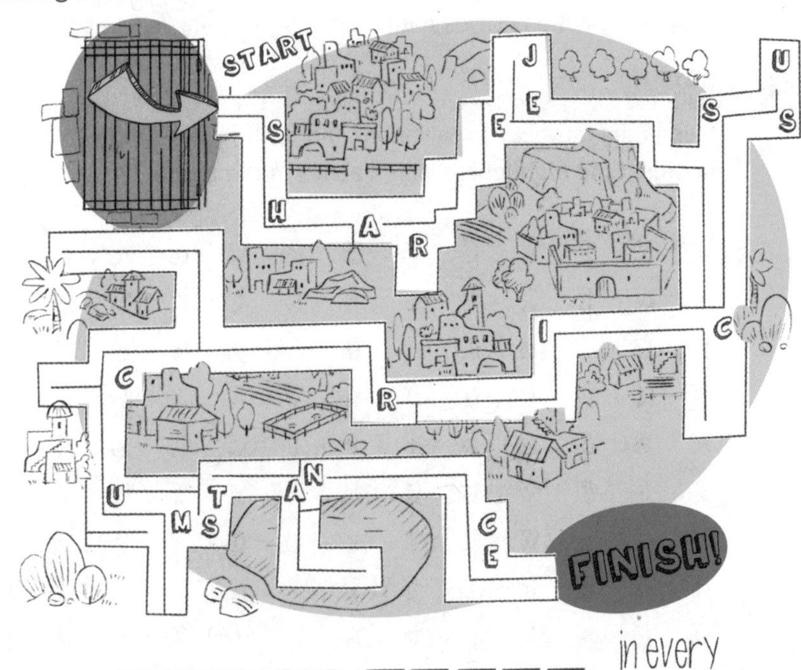

RESPOND

PRAY: Heavenly Father, _ _ _ _ _ _ _ _ _ _ in every _ _ _ _ _ _ _ _ _ _ _ _ _. help me trust in You no matter my circumstances.

HIGHLIGHT

OLDER KIDS: Galatians 1:11-12
YOUNGER KIDS: Galatians 1:11-12
MEMORY VERSE: Psalm 19:14

EXPLAIN

- Paul couldn't always stay with believers for a long time, so he wrote letters to encourage them. The Book of Galatians is his letter to the church in Galatia.
- Paul warned the church in Galatia not to believe people who were teaching things about Jesus that were not true.
- Paul told the believers he was preaching the good news that was revealed to him directly from Jesus.
- Paul wanted the believers in Galatia to understand that sometimes people taught things that were not true about God. He told them that what he was teaching was not from people, but from Jesus, and could be trusted.

APPLY

The only true gospel is the one Jesus taught. Decode the phrase from today's devotion by placing the first letter of each picture in the box above it.

RESPOND

PRAY: Jesus, thank You for teaching us the truth.

OLDER KIDS: Galatians 2:19-21
YOUNGER KIDS: Galatians 2:19-21
MEMORY VERSE: Psalm 19:14

EXPLAIN

- Paul wrote to the church in Galatia to encourage them in their faith.
- He wanted believers to understand that, even though the Old Testament law is important, it did not save people from sin.
- Because Jesus fulfilled the law by sacrificing Himself for us, all people are saved by faith in Jesus.
- Jewish people were used to living by the law given in the Old Testament. They sometimes had a hard time understanding that Jesus was all they needed for salvation. Paul explained that only faith in Jesus saves someone from sin.

Only Jesus can save us from our sins. Color the squares to find out what we need to be saved.

COLOR BOXES WITH TRIANGLES BLUE
COLOR BOXES WITH CIRCLES RED

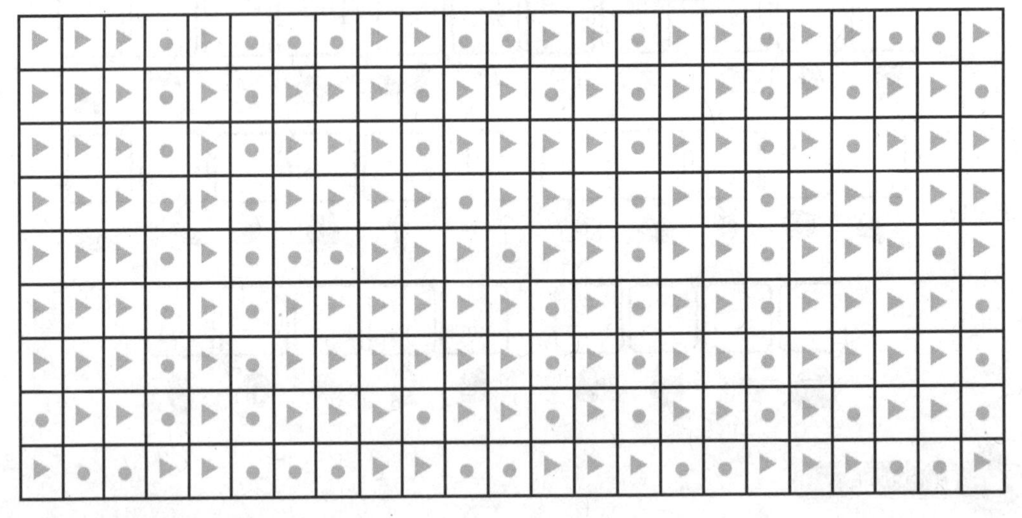

PRAY: Heavenly Father, thank You for sending Jesus to save us from our sins.

OLDER KIDS: Galatians 3:27-29
YOUNGER KIDS: Galatians 3:27-29
MEMORY VERSE: Psalm 19:14

EXPLAIN

- Paul's letter to the church in Galatia taught about being part of God's family.
- Paul wanted Christians to understand that all believers are valuable and important in Jesus. There are no favorites.
- He taught everyone that Christians are all one family—God's family.
- In his letter, Paul taught the church in Galatia about a lot of things, but he wanted to make sure they understood that God's family is one family, and everyone is saved in the same way—through faith in Jesus.

Christians are all part of the same family—God's family. Paul wanted people to know that everyone in God's family is important. Complete today's crossword puzzle using the clues.

RESPOND

PRAY: God, thank You for making all believers one big family.

HIGHLIGHT

OLDER KIDS: Galatians 4:6-7
YOUNGER KIDS: Galatians 4:6-7
MEMORY VERSE: Psalm 19:14

EXPLAIN

- Paul continued his letter to the church in Galatia by talking about God's family.
- Paul said that all people are saved from our sin in the same way—through repenting of sin and trusting in Jesus' sacrifice.
- When we are saved from our sins, we are adopted into God's family.
- Sometimes Jews and Gentiles had trouble thinking about being in the same family. Paul reminded them again that once we are saved from our sins, we are all part of God's family—the same family.

APPLY

When we receive God's salvation through Jesus, we are adopted into His family. Write Psalm 19:14 in the box and work to memorize it this week.

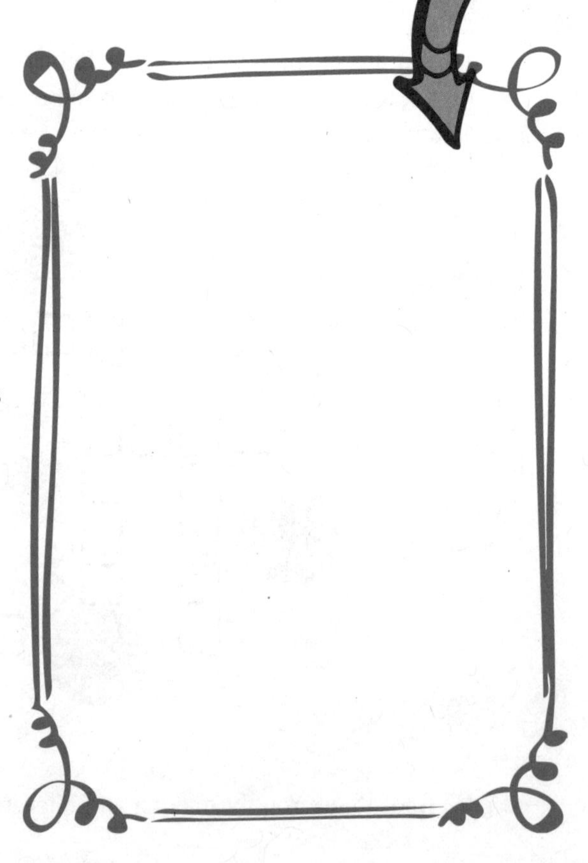

RESPOND

PRAY: God, thank You for allowing us to be adopted into Your family when we trust in Jesus.

OLDER KIDS: Galatians 5:13-14
YOUNGER KIDS: Galatians 5:13-14
MEMORY VERSE: Psalm 19:14

EXPLAIN

- Paul wrote a letter to the believers in Galatia to encourage them in their faith.
- Paul wanted them to understand that Christians are to serve each other in love.
- Followers of Jesus have a responsibility to serve and care for one another.
- Paul wrote to the church in Galatia to remind them that they are to love each other as much as they love themselves. God calls Christians to serve others in love.

APPLY

It is our responsibility to love and care for others. Solve the maze to deliver Paul's letter to the Galatians.

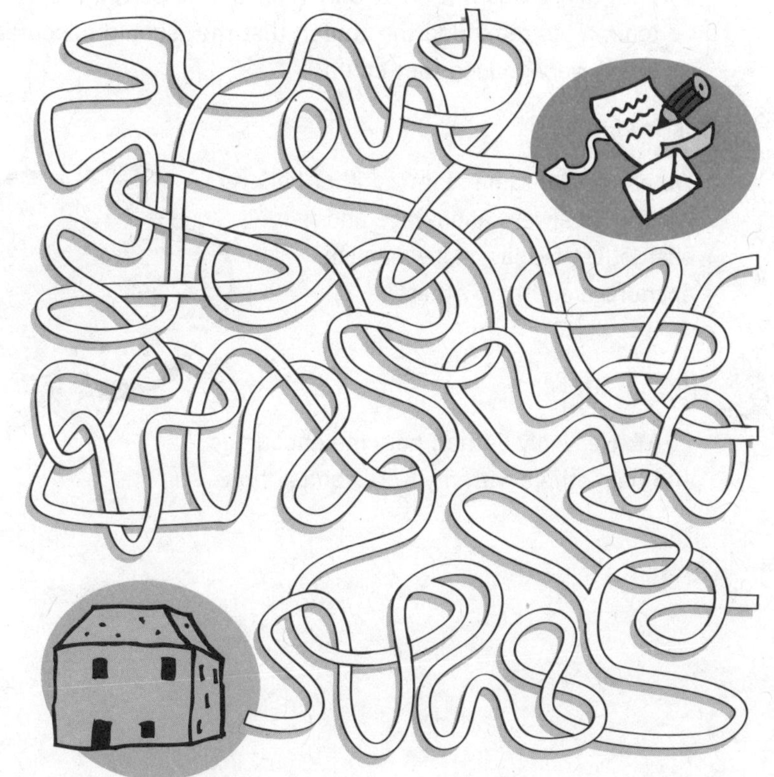

RESPOND

PRAY: Heavenly Father, help me to love and care for others today.

HIGHLIGHT

OLDER KIDS: Galatians 6:10
YOUNGER KIDS: Galatians 6:10
MEMORY VERSE: Psalm 23:1

EXPLAIN

- Paul's letter to the church at Galatia encouraged them to care for one another.
- Paul said Christians should take every opportunity to help others and do things that are good for each other.
- Paul encouraged the people to look for opportunities to care for and serve others, especially followers of Jesus.
- Loving and taking care of each other is an important part of being a Christian. Paul talked about it a lot. Christians are all part of the same family, the same team. Paul reminded the church that they should encourage and help each other every chance they could.

APPLY

We are on the same team as other believers. We should always encourage and help each other. Discuss: How can you encourage and help others?

RESPOND

PRAY: Heavenly Father, help me encourage and help others with my words and actions.

OLDER KIDS: Acts 17:22-24
YOUNGER KIDS: Acts 17:24
MEMORY VERSE: Psalm 23:1

EXPLAIN

- Paul was preaching and teaching in Athens.
- He noticed that the people of Athens worshiped, but they worshiped false gods.
- Paul wanted to make sure that the people of Athens knew about the one true God, and explained it in a way they could understand.
- Paul noticed that the people of Athens were worshiping lots of things, but not the God who made heaven and earth—and them. Paul saw an altar "To an Unknown God" and used it to teach the people about the One True God—a God that could be known personally, the God who made everything. Some people thought Paul was crazy, but others wanted to hear more.

APPLY

We can explain the good news of Jesus in the way people understand it best, but it is always the same message. Complete the decoder to find a word that means good news.

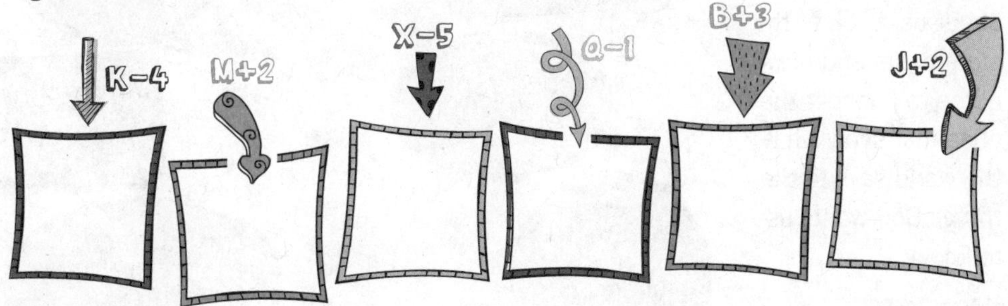

PRAY: Heavenly Father, thank You that Your good news never changes.

HIGHLIGHT

OLDER KIDS: Acts 18:9-11
YOUNGER KIDS: Acts 18:9-11
MEMORY VERSE: Psalm 23:1

EXPLAIN

- Paul traveled from place to place teaching about Jesus.
- Some people didn't like that Paul was preaching about Jesus. They tried to make things hard for him.
- God told Paul not to be afraid to keep teaching. God would be with Paul and take care of him.
- When people tried to make things hard for Paul or make fun of him, he could have become discouraged, but Paul listened to God more than he listened to people. God used Paul to spread the good news about Jesus.

APPLY

God's instructions are more important than what other people say or think about us. Look at the statements and draw a line to connect the ones that show what the world says to the things God wants us to know.

RESPOND

PRAY: Heavenly Father, help me always remember what You think about me is more important than what anyone else thinks.

OLDER KIDS: 1 Thessalonians 1:2-6
YOUNGER KIDS: 1 Thessalonians 1:2-4
MEMORY VERSE: Psalm 23:1

EXPLAIN

- Paul wrote to the believers in Thessalonica to encourage them in their faith.
- Paul was thankful because they had been faithful to serve God, even when they were persecuted, or punished for speaking about their faith.
- They were an example to the people around them of how Christians should live out their faith in difficult circumstances.
- When followers of Jesus obey and follow God in faith, they show others how to respond during difficult times. Paul was thankful for the believers in Thessalonica because they had looked at his example, then set an example of faithfulness for others.

You can show others God's love by the way you act and treat others. Fill in the blank spaces to complete this week's memory verse.

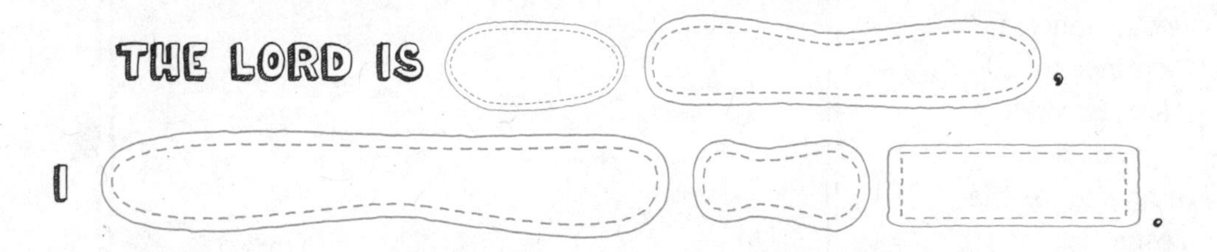

PRAY: God, help me show Your love to others by the way I act.

HIGHLIGHT

OLDER KIDS: 1 Thessalonians 2:13
YOUNGER KIDS: 1 Thessalonians 2:13
MEMORY VERSE: Psalm 23:1

EXPLAIN

- Paul wrote to the Christians in Thessalonica to strengthen their faith.
- Paul and Timothy wanted the believers in Thessalonica to know how much they loved them and praised God for them.
- Paul and Timothy were encouraged that the believers had welcomed the good news about Jesus and believed it was the Word of God.
- Paul and Timothy knew that the believers in Thessalonica were sometimes persecuted, but they were still following Jesus. They praised God for the believers receiving the good news about Jesus and continuing to follow Jesus even when things were hard.

APPLY

When we encourage each other in our faith in Jesus, it helps us continue to follow Him. Decorate a sign to encourage others to trust in Jesus.

RESPOND

PRAY: Heavenly Father, help me encourage others to trust in You.

OLDER KIDS: 1 Thessalonians 3:12-13
YOUNGER KIDS: 1 Thessalonians 3:12-13
MEMORY VERSE: Proverbs 10:27

EXPLAIN

- Paul prayed for the Thessalonian believers in his letter.
- He wanted the believers to love everyone, just as he and Timothy loved them.
- Paul prayed that God would make their hearts blameless, and they would continue to obey and follow God.
- Paul wanted the believers in Thessalonica to continue to love others, and obey God. He prayed that they would continue to do those things as they continued to love God.

APPLY

Our love for others and love and obedience to God are some of the most important ways we can show our faith in Him. List 3 ways you can show love to others.

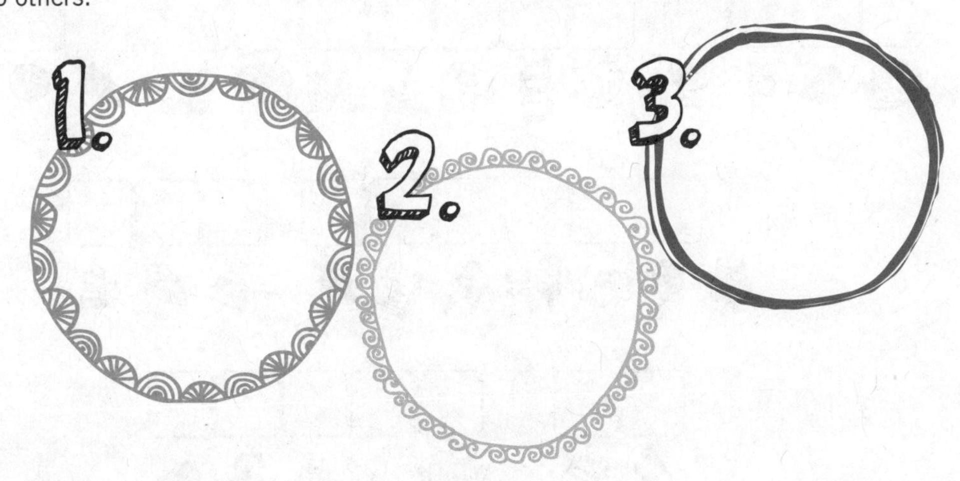

PRAY: God, help me love others, love You, and obey You.

OLDER KIDS: 1 Thessalonians 4:1-2, 7-8
YOUNGER KIDS: 1 Thessalonians 4:1-2
MEMORY VERSE: Proverbs 10:27

EXPLAIN

- Paul wrote to the believers in Thessalonica to continue growing in their faith.
- Paul encouraged them to continue honoring God through their obedience and to keep following His commands even more than they had before.
- Paul reminded them that, as disciples of Jesus, they had been called to live in holiness.
- Paul wanted the believers in Thessalonica to understand that it wasn't Paul telling the people to obey God's commands—it was God telling them to obey.

We should honor God and follow His commands out of gratitude for what Jesus has done for us, how He has changed us, and to point others to Jesus. Use the first letter of each picture to decode the question and find the answer.

PRAY: Heavenly Father, help me follow Your commands and glorify You.

HIGHLIGHT

OLDER KIDS: 1 Thessalonians 5:18
YOUNGER KIDS: 1 Thessalonians 5:18
MEMORY VERSE: Proverbs 10:27

EXPLAIN

- Paul ended his letter to the believers in Thessalonica by urging them to practice thankfulness.
- He gave final instructions in his letter, encouraging the believers to follow God and take care of each other.
- Paul said it is God's will for believers to give thanks in every circumstance.
- Paul loved the believers in Thessalonica and wanted to encourage them to continue following and trusting God. In his letter, Paul encouraged them to practice thankfulness in all circumstances, to love and encourage one another, and to follow God's will.

APPLY

Because we have Jesus, we can practice thankfulness in all circumstances. Write Proverbs 10:27 below and work to memorize it this week.

RESPOND

PRAY: God, help me always be thankful, no matter my circumstances.

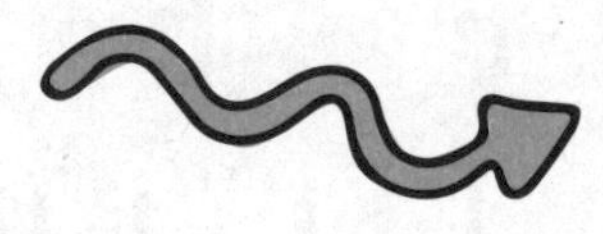

OLDER KIDS: 2 Thessalonians 1:5
YOUNGER KIDS: 2 Thessalonians 1:5
MEMORY VERSE: Proverbs 10:27

EXPLAIN

- Paul wrote a second letter to the believers in Thessalonica to encourage them during hard times.
- The church was being persecuted for following God.
- Paul urged believers to remain strong in following God so He would be glorified.
- The believers in Thessalonica were suffering persecution, and Paul wanted to encourage them. He reminded them that God knew about their suffering and would one day make everything right.

APPLY

We should stay faithful through tough times so God will be glorified through us. Follow the instructions below to answer the question at the bottom of the page.

PRAY: Heavenly Father, help me stay faithful to You so You will be glorified.

Cross out every **THIRD** letter.
Cross out every **YELLOW** letter.
Cross out every **RED** letter.

I T T G A P O E R L X J C F V
U T S C V E B W P O K H G V
G T A U H Y G B V B N J U W
I T U B C Y A F E T S I S N C

When should we be faithful? ______________________

HIGHLIGHT

OLDER KIDS: 2 Thessalonians 2:1-4
YOUNGER KIDS: 2 Thessalonians 2:1-4
MEMORY VERSE: Proverbs 10:27

EXPLAIN

- The believers in Thessalonica were concerned about when Jesus would come back.
- Paul reminded them that no one knows when Jesus will return, but He will return. Someone might say they know when Jesus will come back, but they don't. Only God knows!
- The Thessalonian believers were spending too much time worrying about when Jesus was coming back and not focusing on living for God in faith. Paul encouraged them to live each day trusting in His plan so they would be ready when Jesus does return.

APPLY

We do not know when Jesus will return, but we know He will. We must be faithful to tell others the good news about Him until He comes back. Find and circle six things you can use to tell someone that Jesus will come back.

RESPOND

PRAY: Heavenly Father, help me be faithful to tell others the good news until Jesus comes back.

HIGHLIGHT

OLDER KIDS: 2 Thessalonians 3:3-5, 13
YOUNGER KIDS: 2 Thessalonians 3:13
MEMORY VERSE: Proverbs 11:25

EXPLAIN

- Paul taught the believers in Thessalonica that God is faithful and strong.
- He reminded them that God would guard and strengthen them.
- Paul encouraged them to continue following Jesus. He also warned them not to become tired of doing good, but to persevere or continue.
- Sometimes people start something and it gets old or boring so they start to lose interest. Paul wanted to make sure followers of Jesus don't become lazy when following Jesus. Believers should depend on Jesus for strength to keep following Him.

APPLY

We can be encouraged that God gives us everything we need to keep following and trusting Him. We should always encourage others who follow Jesus. Discuss: How can you encourage others to follow Jesus?

RESPOND

PRAY: Jesus, help me follow You and encourage others who follow You, too.

HIGHLIGHT

OLDER KIDS: Acts 19:1-5
YOUNGER KIDS: Acts 19:1-5
MEMORY VERSE: Proverbs 11:25

EXPLAIN

- Paul traveled to a town called Ephesus to teach people about Jesus.
- Paul loved talking to people about Jesus. He tried to help them understand that Jesus is the Messiah.
- Many people heard the gospel and were saved.
- Paul taught many people about the good news of Jesus. He helped others understand who Jesus was, the Messiah who died for sin so people can have a relationship with God.

APPLY

God teaches us we have a responsibility to tell others about Jesus. Write the word next to each picture, changing a letter or two from each word to work out the puzzle.

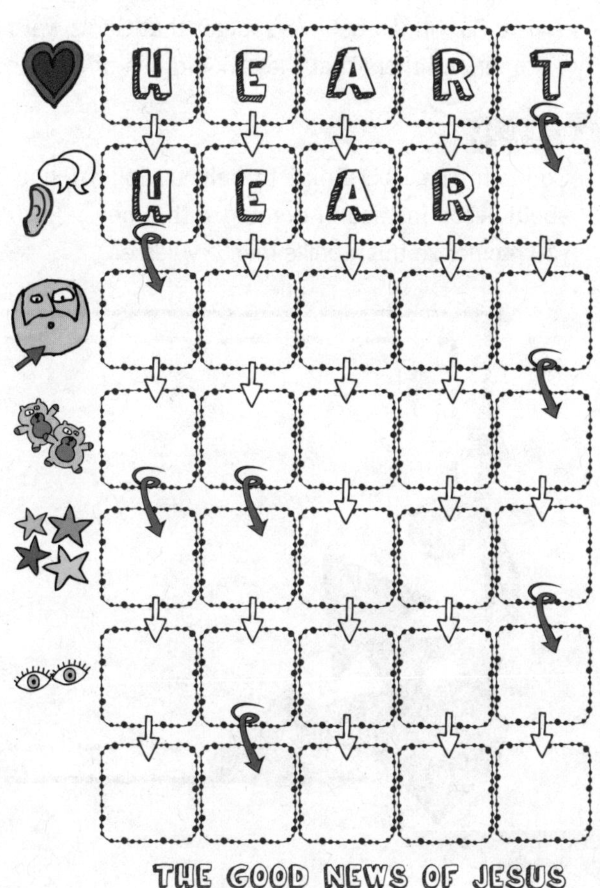

RESPOND

PRAY: Heavenly Father, help me follow and honor You no matter what. Please give me opportunities to share the good news of Jesus with others.

OLDER KIDS: 1 Corinthians 1:26-31
YOUNGER KIDS: 1 Corinthians 1:30-31
MEMORY VERSE: Proverbs 11:25

- Paul wrote a letter to the believers in Corinth to remind them of who they are as followers of Jesus.
- A group of people argued among themselves, but Paul wanted them to focus on Jesus, His message, and the Holy Spirit instead.
- Paul reminded them that God's ways are higher than their ways, and His wisdom is better than anything the world can offer.
- The Corinthian believers forgot that God's ways are always best. God used Paul to remind them that they should live differently because they follow Jesus.

God sent the Holy Spirit to help us follow Him. We should trust God and share about Jesus instead of arguing with other believers. Write Proverbs 11:25 to help you memorize this week's memory verse.

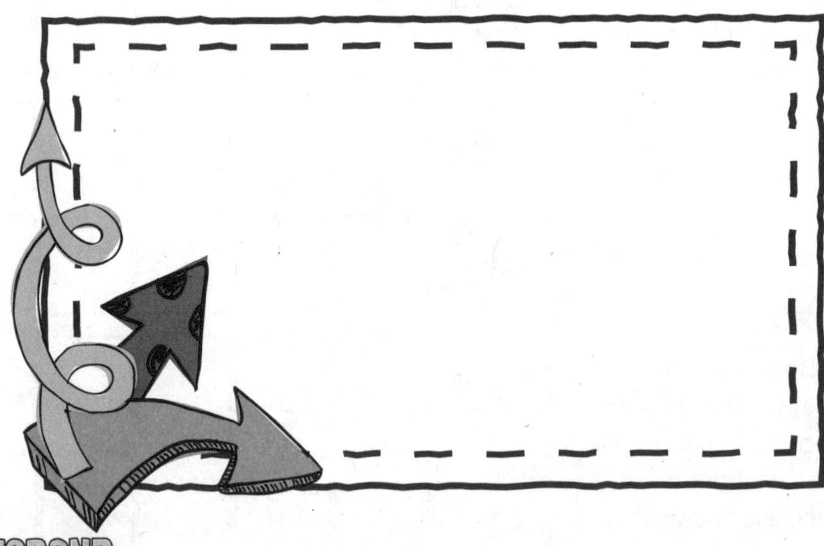

PRAY: God, help me to remember that Your ways are always best.

OLDER KIDS: 1 Corinthians 2:10-13
YOUNGER KIDS: 1 Corinthians 2:10
MEMORY VERSE: Proverbs 11:25

EXPLAIN

- Paul wrote a letter to the believers in Corinth to remind them that their faith in Jesus should change how they live.
- Paul taught the believers about wisdom from God that they receive through the Holy Spirit.
- The Holy Spirit helps Christians understand God and His truths.
- God gives the Holy Spirit to believers when they trust in Jesus for salvation. The Holy Spirit helps Christians understand God's wisdom and how to tell the difference between God's wisdom and the world's wisdom. Without the Holy Spirit, we cannot understand those things.

The Holy Spirit helps us understand God and His truths. Match the following statements to read four truths about the Holy Spirit.

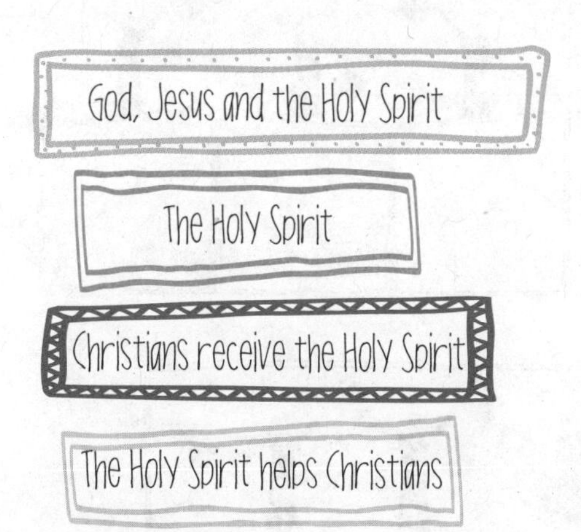

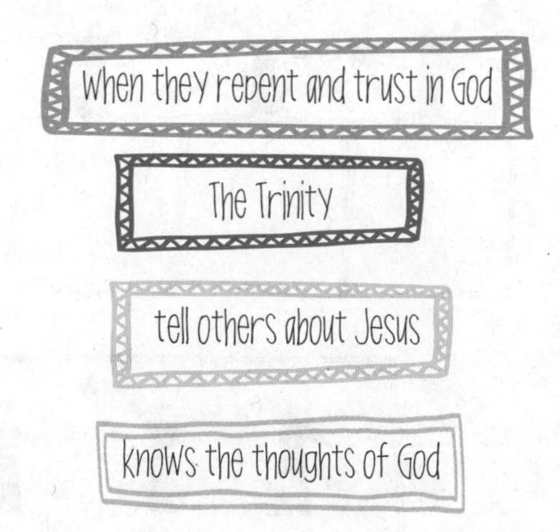

PRAY: Heavenly Father, thank You for sending the Holy Spirit to help us understand Your Word.

HIGHLIGHT

OLDER KIDS: 1 Corinthians 3:16
YOUNGER KIDS: 1 Corinthians 3:16
MEMORY VERSE: Proverbs 11:25

EXPLAIN

- Paul continued challenging the believers in Corinth to grow in their faith.
- Paul reminded them that they are God's servants, each with their own purpose.
- Paul warned them that their bodies were a place for the Holy Spirit, and that made their bodies holy.
- Mature believers are called to work together and treat one another with respect. A believer's body is special because the Holy Spirit lives inside, and all followers of Jesus should treat themselves and others with respect and love.

APPLY

When we are followers of Jesus, the Holy Spirit lives in us. Use the flag code to solve the puzzle and learn how we should treat ourselves and others.

RESPOND

PRAY: Heavenly Father, thank You for sending the Holy Spirit for us. Help me to treat myself and others with respect.

OLDER KIDS: 1 Corinthians 4:1-5
YOUNGER KIDS: 1 Corinthians 4:1-2
MEMORY VERSE: Proverbs 12:2

EXPLAIN

- Paul taught the church in Corinth about their responsibility as Christians.
- Paul explained that they were managers over what God has given them.
- Paul explained that their focus should be on making sure they were faithful to God. They should not worry about what others thought of them.
- Paul taught the Corinthian church that they were called to be good stewards, or managers, of God's truth, that is, the gospel. Their job was not to judge others but to be faithful and obedient to God.

APPLY

God cares about our faithfulness and our attitude. List 3 ways you can be faithful to the gospel.

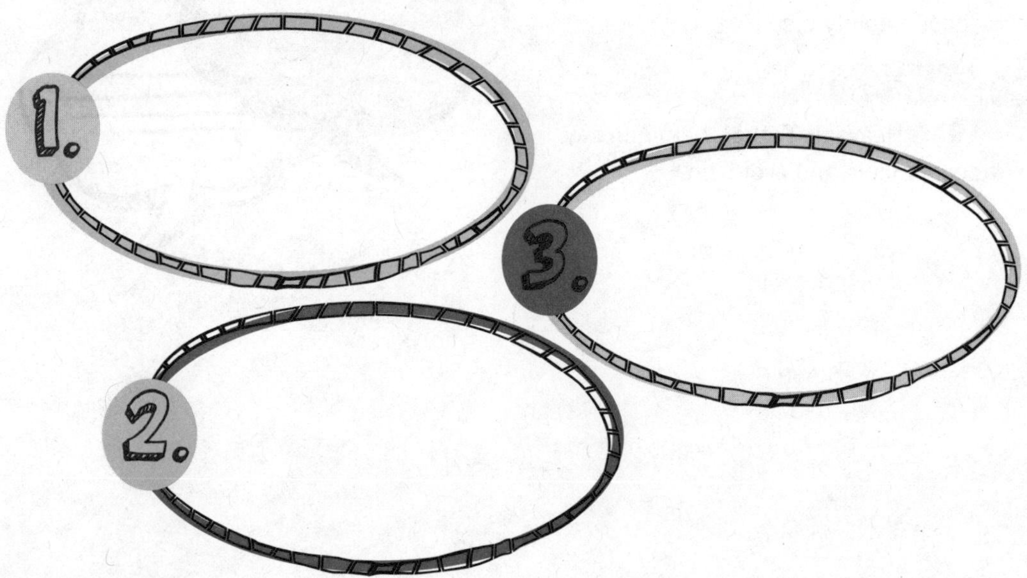

PRAY: God, help me be faithful to You.

OLDER KIDS: 1 Corinthians 5:6
YOUNGER KIDS: 1 Corinthians 5:6
MEMORY VERSE: Proverbs 12:2

- Paul told the believers at Corinth how God wanted them to live.
- Paul explained that sin can spread like yeast spreads through dough.
- Christians are called to help each other overcome temptation in one another's lives. This is called *accountability*.
- The church in Corinth was dealing with sin in the church, but Paul said they did not respond in the proper way. They should have been sad about the sin, but they were not. Christians are called to help each other overcome sin.

We should hold one another accountable to avoid sin. Discuss: What does accountability mean?

PRAY: Heavenly Father, help me stay accountable and avoid sin.

HIGHLIGHT

OLDER KIDS: 1 Corinthians 6:19-20
YOUNGER KIDS: 1 Corinthians 6:19-20
MEMORY VERSE: Proverbs 12:2

EXPLAIN

- Paul's letter to the Corinthians taught them how to live as followers of Jesus.
- Paul wanted believers to understand they should glorify God with their bodies.
- Christians must choose to care for their bodies differently because they are a special dwelling place for the Holy Spirit.
- Followers of Jesus live differently by choosing to care for their bodies in their attitudes, actions, thoughts, and words. When Christians take care of the bodies God gave them, they glorify Him.

APPLY

We can glorify God by taking care of our bodies. Write *T* next to the true statements and *F* next to the false statements.

- God wants me to honor Him with my actions, attitudes, thoughts and words.
- It does not matter if I make healthy choices or not.
- My body belongs to me. I can do what I want to do.
- I should respect my body because I have the Holy Spirit in me.
- When I take care of the body God gave me, I glorify Him.

RESPOND

PRAY: Heavenly Father, help me to take care of the body You gave me.

OLDER KIDS: 1 Corinthians 7:23-24
YOUNGER KIDS: 1 Corinthians 7:23-24
MEMORY VERSE: Proverbs 12:2

- In his letter, Paul answered questions for the believers in Corinth.
- Paul wanted them to understand that Christians should be content to serve God wherever they are.
- God wants His children to serve Him anytime, anywhere. We don't have to wait until we are somewhere special to serve Him.
- Everyone has different circumstances in life, but God calls each of His disciples to serve Him right where they are.

Living for God is more important than what we are going through in our lives. When can we serve God? Solve the puzzle to find out!

RESPOND

PRAY: Heavenly Father, help me to live for You right where I am.

OLDER KIDS: 1 Corinthians 8:13
YOUNGER KIDS: 1 Corinthians 8:13
MEMORY VERSE: Proverbs 12:2

EXPLAIN

- Paul taught the believers at Corinth and answered their questions about the cultures and traditions of their time.
- Some unbelievers offered food to false gods, and the believers were arguing about whether or not they should eat that food.
- Paul explained that if something they choose to do causes harm to someone else or causes them to sin, they should not do it.
- There was a debate among the believers about whether they were allowed to eat foods that had been offered to false gods. Paul told them it's not about the food, but about how their actions affect the people around them.

Our actions should not cause others to sin. How others see Jesus through our lives is more important than what we want to do. We should always live in such a way that helps others see Jesus. Work to memorize Proverbs 12:2 by writing it in the box.

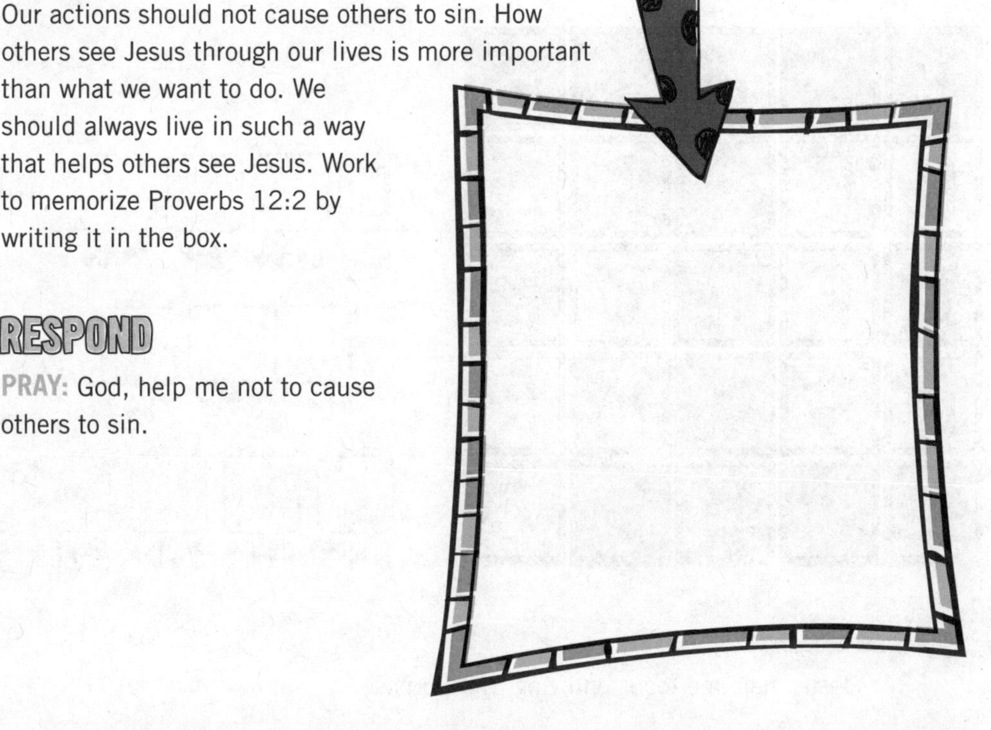

RESPOND

PRAY: God, help me not to cause others to sin.

HIGHLIGHT

OLDER KIDS: 1 Corinthians 9:24-27
YOUNGER KIDS: 1 Corinthians 9:24-27
MEMORY VERSE: Psalm 25:5

EXPLAIN

- Paul told the believers in Corinth that the Christian life is like a race.
- When you run a race, you run with purpose, focusing on the finish line.
- In a regular race, only one person wins the prize, but this race is for everyone who believes in Jesus. The Christian's prize is living forever with God.
- When Paul taught about a race, he was not talking about racing against other people. He was talking about reaching for a goal—the prize—at the end. Paul meant that Christians should live with a purpose—following Jesus.

APPLY

The prize for Christians who run the race is life with God. Following God should always be our purpose for running the race.

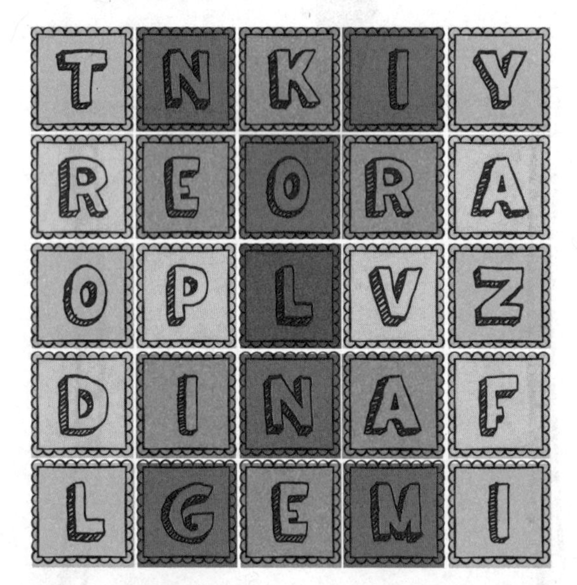

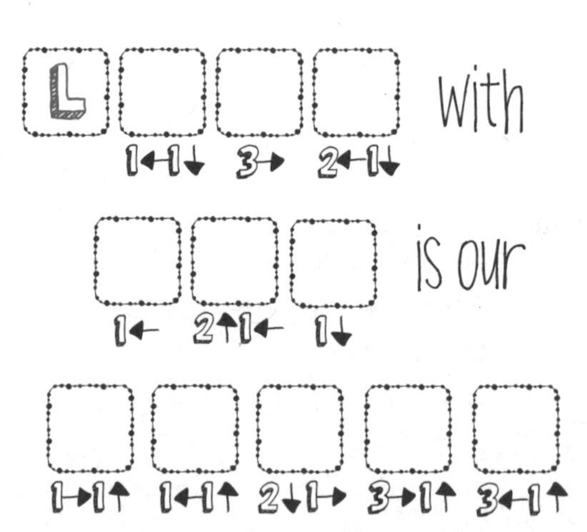

RESPOND

PRAY: Jesus, help me focus on living with purpose.

HIGHLIGHT

OLDER KIDS: 1 Corinthians 10:31
YOUNGER KIDS: 1 Corinthians 10:31
MEMORY VERSE: Psalm 25:5

EXPLAIN

- Paul taught the Christians in Corinth how to grow in their faith.
- Paul explained that there are a lot of things that are not sinful, but that doesn't mean they are good or helpful to practice.
- Whatever Christians do, it should be for the glory of God.
- Paul taught the Corinthian Christians to understand that while something may not be sinful, it may not be the best thing for us and others. If something causes someone else to sin, it does not glorify God. Christians must choose to glorify God over doing what they want.

APPLY

Everything we do should be for God's glory. Use the table on the right to decode the message below.

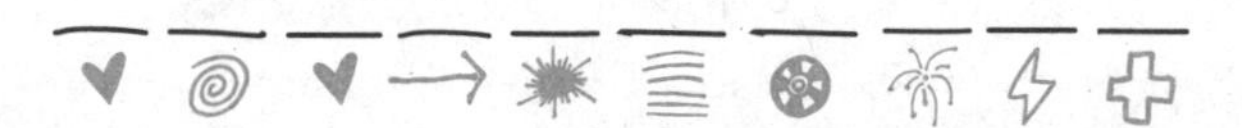

A	B	C	D	E	F	G	H	I	J	K	L	M	N	O	P	Q	R	S	T	U	V	W	X	Y	Z

RESPOND

PRAY: Heavenly Father, help me always glorify You.

OLDER KIDS: 1 Corinthians 11:3
YOUNGER KIDS: 1 Corinthians 11:3
MEMORY VERSE: Psalm 25:5

- Paul taught the church that believers are under God's authority.
- Paul explained that Christ is the head of the church, and God is the head of Christ.
- God set up authority for us as believers, and when we remain under God's authority, we glorify Him.
- Paul helped the Corinthian church understand that God's plan includes authority. God set up authority for Christians to submit to God and glorify Him.

God is our ultimate authority. We are called to submit to and obey Him. Discuss: What does authority mean?

PRAY: Heavenly Father, thank You for being my ultimate authority.

HIGHLIGHT

OLDER KIDS: 1 Corinthians 12:12-20
YOUNGER KIDS: 1 Corinthians 12:12
MEMORY VERSE: Psalm 25:5

EXPLAIN

- Paul told the believers in Corinth that Christians are all part of one body, or family, of Christ.
- Paul explained that as believers, we are all different with different jobs, but we are supposed to work together like a body.
- Paul said it is good that people are all different with different strengths so that they can help each other.
- Just like our feet, hands, and eyes are all different parts of our body, they all have their own special jobs. If one of them is missing or not working properly, it makes a difference to the entire body. Paul explained that each believer is an important part of the body of Christ.

APPLY

God made us all different so we can be helpful in the body of Christ. Fill in the spaces to complete this week's memory verse.

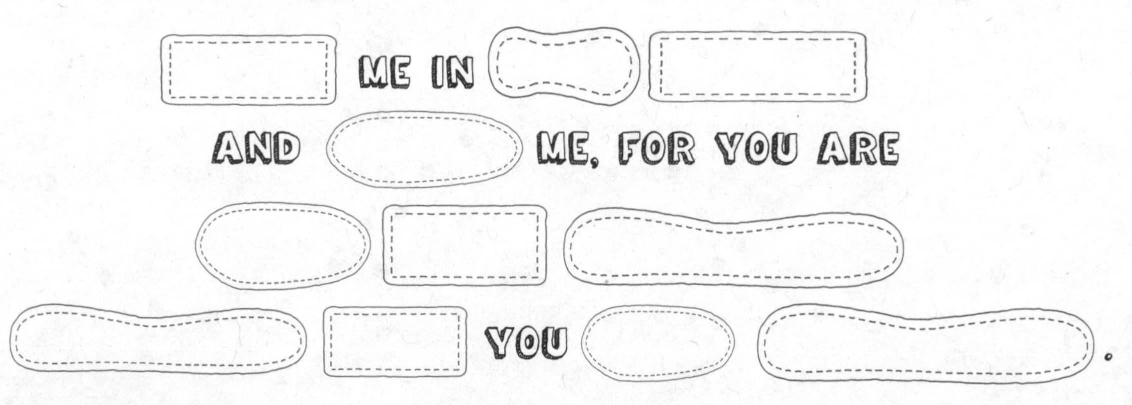

RESPOND

PRAY: God, thank You for making us all different. Help me help me do my part as part of Your family.

OLDER KIDS: 1 Corinthians 13:4-7
YOUNGER KIDS: 1 Corinthians 13:4-5
MEMORY VERSE: Psalm 25:5

EXPLAIN

- Paul wanted the believers in Corinth to understand how to love others.
- Paul made it clear that you can do many great things, but if you don't love others through patience, kindness, humility, and forgiveness, those great things mean nothing.
- All Christians and their abilities are important, but loving each other is the most important.
- Paul taught that Christians can have all kinds of special talents and abilities, but if we don't know how to love, we have nothing. He also taught what love is and how love behaves.

APPLY

Loving others is important and helps Christians be part of the body of Christ. List 3 ways you can show love to others.

PRAY: Heavenly Father, thank You for loving me. Help me to love others in a way that honors You.

OLDER KIDS: 1 Corinthians 14:40
YOUNGER KIDS: 1 Corinthians 14:40
MEMORY VERSE: Proverbs 13:13

EXPLAIN

- Paul wrote to the believers at Corinth about church meetings.
- Paul made it clear that orderly worship is important.
- Worship gatherings are for glorifying God, not people. If people are disruptive during worship or distract others with their actions, they are not glorifying God.
- God is a God of order. Orderly worship helps Christians worship and glorify God together.

It is hard for us to glorify God if we are distracting others or paying attention to something besides worshiping God. When we gather to worship God, our goal should be to focus on Him, not worry about other things going on around us. Place a check mark beside the things you've done at churches you've visited.

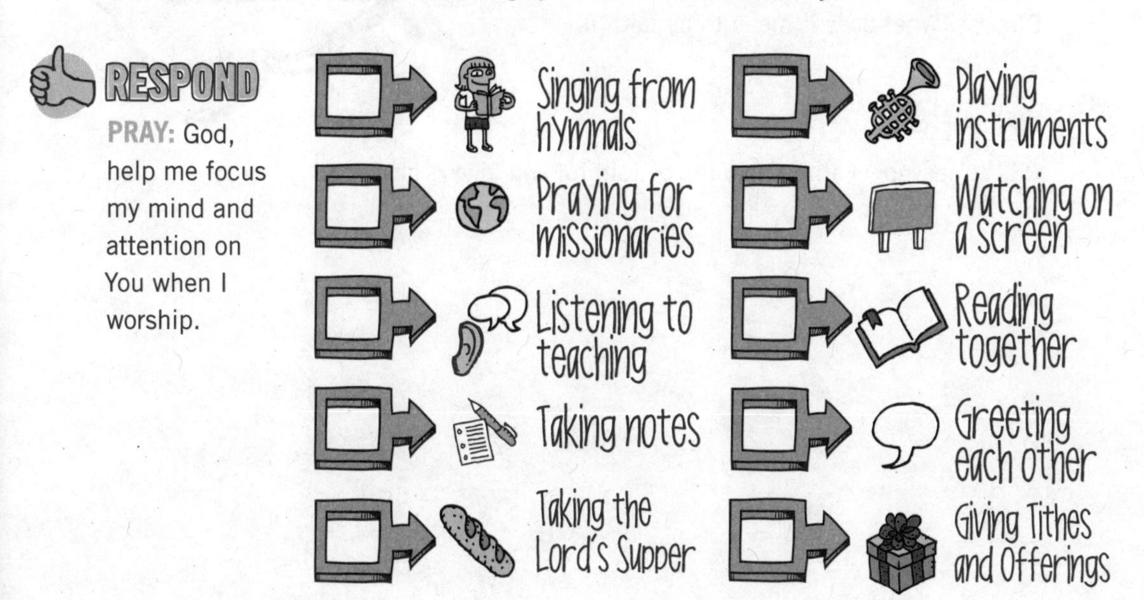

HIGHLIGHT

OLDER KIDS: 1 Corinthians 15:58
YOUNGER KIDS: 1 Corinthians 15:58
MEMORY VERSE: Proverbs 13:13

EXPLAIN

- Paul finished his first letter to the believers in Corinth by reminding them that God would make all things new one day.
- Paul's final encouragement was to remind believers to be faithful and give their best to God.
- Paul wanted the believers to understand that the work they do for God is meaningful and has an eternal importance.
- Paul reminds us to be faithful in our work and strong in our faith. Everything we do for God makes a difference.

APPLY

God wants us to be faithful and always do our best to continue growing in our faith. Discuss: What does it mean to be faithful?

RESPOND

PRAY: Heavenly Father, help me be faithful and always give You my best.

HIGHLIGHT

OLDER KIDS: 1 Corinthians 16:13-14
YOUNGER KIDS: 1 Corinthians 16:13-14
MEMORY VERSE: Proverbs 13:13

EXPLAIN

- Paul gave the believers in Corinth some final instructions on how to live.
- Paul encouraged them to be alert and strong as they lived out their faith.
- He reminded them that every action they did should be done in love.
- Paul wanted to remind the believers again that they must be courageous and strong but also do everything with love. If we do things with love, we will treat others well, which glorifies God.

APPLY

Everything we do should be done with love. Find and circle six hearts that don't match the others.

RESPOND

PRAY: God, help me do everything in love.

OLDER KIDS: 2 Corinthians 1:20-22
YOUNGER KIDS: 2 Corinthians 1:20
MEMORY VERSE: Proverbs 13:13

EXPLAIN

- Paul wrote another letter to the church in Corinth to strengthen their faith.
- Paul reminded the Christians that God's promises are always "yes" in Christ. Believers can always trust God to keep His promises.
- Paul reminded the believers in Corinth that God's promises are true, and He will always fulfill them.
- Paul wanted Christians to see that God has kept His promises all throughout Scripture. God doesn't change—He is the same forever.

APPLY

God always keeps His promises, and we can trust He will fulfill them. Write out this week's memory verse to help you memorize it this week.

RESPOND

PRAY: Heavenly Father, thank You for always keeping Your promises. Help me to trust You.

OLDER KIDS: 2 Corinthians 2:9-10
YOUNGER KIDS: 2 Corinthians 2:10
MEMORY VERSE: Proverbs 13:13

EXPLAIN

- Paul wrote a second letter to the church in Corinth to challenge them to grow in their faith.
- Someone in the church had sinned, and then repented (confessed their sin to God and asked for forgiveness).
- Paul said that the church should forgive and show grace and mercy to the person who had repented.
- Just as the people in Corinth had been forgiven for the things they had done wrong, Paul said they should forgive their friend in the church who had sinned and then repented. Paul wanted to make sure there were no hard feelings between them because Satan could use that to cause trouble in the church.

If someone repents and asks us to forgive them, we should. Because we have been forgiven so much, we are called to forgive others. Follow the paths to write each letter in the correct circle.

God Wants us to

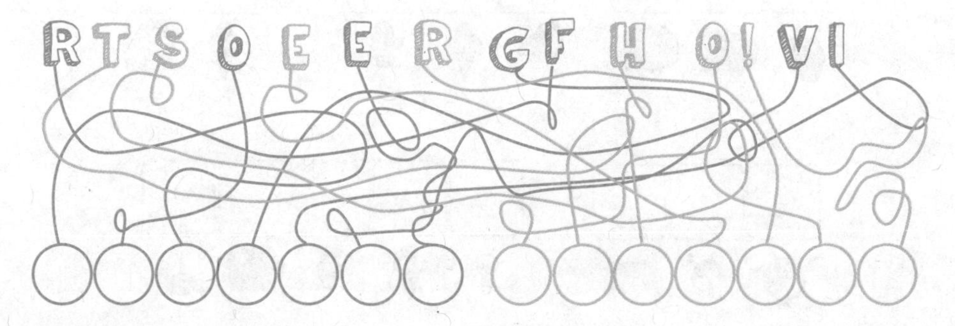

PRAY: God, help me forgive others. Thank You for forgiving me.

HIGHLIGHT

OLDER KIDS: 2 Corinthians 3:4-6
YOUNGER KIDS: 2 Corinthians 3:4-6
MEMORY VERSE: Psalm 27:10

EXPLAIN

- Paul reminded the church in Corinth that every believer's confidence comes from God.
- Paul told the believers in Corinth that their changed lives were proof of his ministry.
- When Christians share the good news of Jesus and disciple others, everyone can see their changed lives—it is no secret.
- Paul felt he did not need to prove himself as a minister of Jesus' good news. His proof was the changed lives of the people in the churches he had ministered to. Disciples make more disciples.

APPLY

Christians can live in confidence knowing that God works in us and through us for His glory and our good. Write the first letter of each picture in the box above to solve the code.

RESPOND

PRAY: Heavenly Father, help me share Jesus with others.

OLDER KIDS: 2 Corinthians 4:7-10
YOUNGER KIDS: 2 Corinthians 4:7-10
MEMORY VERSE: Psalm 27:10

EXPLAIN

- In this letter to the believers in Corinth, Paul wrote that believers have the treasure of the gospel to share with others.
- Paul said our treasure is in clay jars, and if we are broken or have hard times, Jesus shines through us to brings glory to God.
- Paul wanted believers to understand that even though we have Jesus, life will not always be easy.
- Paul used clay jars as an example because that was something everyone understood. Clay jars get broken, and whatever is inside of them shows through the cracks. Paul used this example to teach that when people are broken, Jesus shines through their weaknesses. That way, God gets the glory in their lives.

APPLY

We can give glory to God and show His work in our lives even during tough times. Color in the clay jars that are broken to reveal what shines through in our weakness.

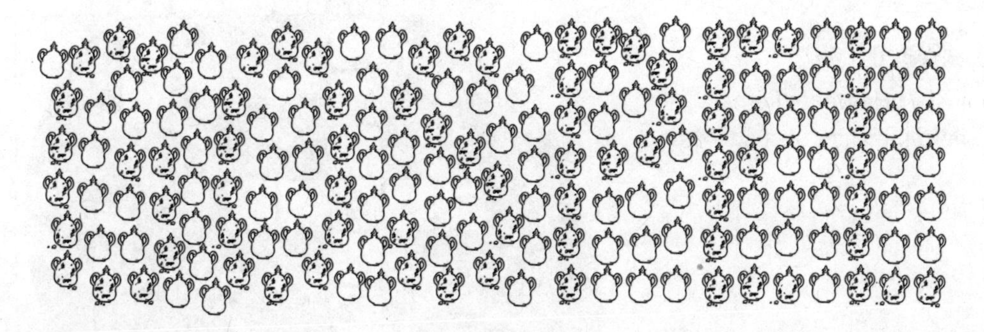

RESPOND

PRAY: Heavenly Father, thank You for using my weaknesses to show others Your strength.

OLDER KIDS: 2 Corinthians 5:17-20
YOUNGER KIDS: 2 Corinthians 5:17
MEMORY VERSE: Psalm 27:10

EXPLAIN

- Paul told the believers at Corinth that anyone who trusts Jesus for salvation is a new creation.
- Because of Jesus' forgiveness, Christians should share that good news with other people.
- Followers of Jesus are called to be ambassadors, or representatives, for Jesus.
- Jesus' sacrifice and forgiveness is for everyone who believes and trusts in Him. Christians should be grateful and worship Jesus for His sacrifice for us. Understand that is the job of every believer to represent Jesus and tell others about His forgiveness.

APPLY

We can show Jesus to others by the way we live. Use the clue letters to fill in the crossword using the highlighted words above.

RESPOND

PRAY: Heavenly Father, help me show Jesus to others.

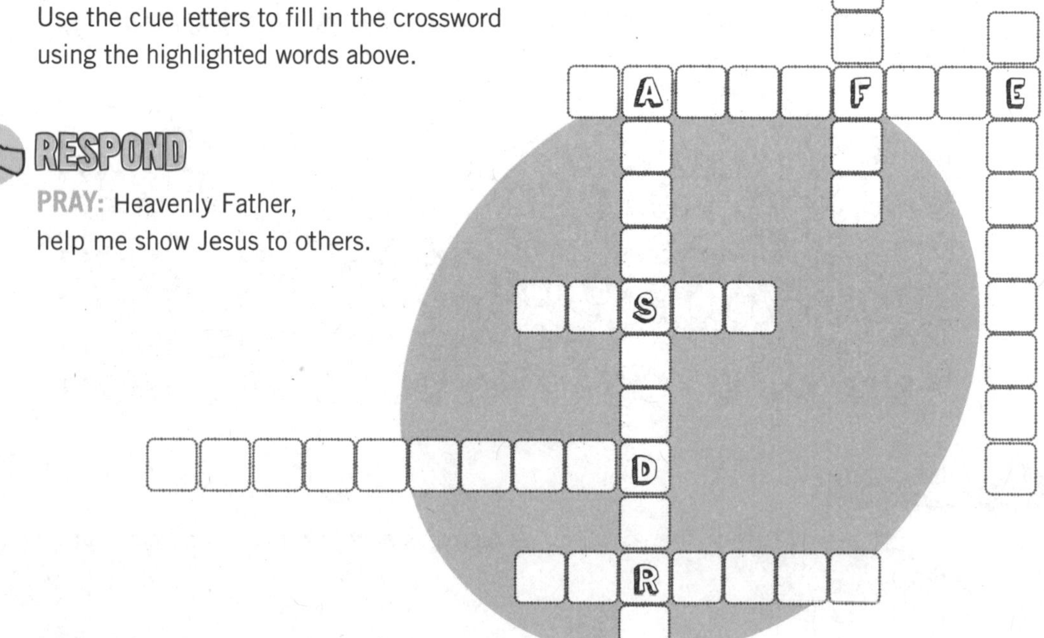

HIGHLIGHT

OLDER KIDS: 2 Corinthians 6:1-2
YOUNGER KIDS: 2 Corinthians 6:1-2
MEMORY VERSE: Psalm 27:10

EXPLAIN

- Paul wrote to the church in Corinth to teach them about obedience.
- Paul told the believers that when they hear God's Word, they should act on it right away.
- Paul quoted the Old Testament, Isaiah 49:8, to help believers understand that the Old Testament prophecy was being fulfilled. Now is the day of salvation.
- Paul wanted the believers to understand how important God's Word is, and that when they hear it, they should not wait to respond.

APPLY

We should always respond to God's message right away. Discuss: How do we respond to God's Word?

RESPOND

PRAY: Heavenly Father, help me always respond to Your Word right away.

OLDER KIDS: 2 Corinthians 7:10
YOUNGER KIDS: 2 Corinthians 7:10
MEMORY VERSE: Psalm 27:10

EXPLAIN

- Paul wrote to the Corinthian church to explain grief about sin.
- Paul told them that godly grief leads Christians to turn away from sin, and that is good.
- Worldly grief is not healthy because it does not lead Christians to repent and turn away from sin.
- Sadness is not always a bad thing. If Christians are not sad about sin, we will not turn away from it and seek to obey God. When sadness over sin leads to repentance and obedience to God, it is a good thing.

APPLY

Godly sadness leads us to turn away from our sin. God forgives us when we ask Him. Write Psalm 27:10 in the box to help you memorize it this week.

RESPOND

PRAY: Heavenly Father, thank You for forgiving me when I ask.

OLDER KIDS: 2 Corinthians 8:1-7
YOUNGER KIDS: 2 Corinthians 8:7
MEMORY VERSE: Proverbs 14:12

EXPLAIN

- Paul shared with the believers in Corinth about the churches in Macedonia.
- Even though the churches in Macedonia were poor, they raised money for poor Christians in Jerusalem.
- Paul reminded the church that Jesus taught to give generously and sacrificially.
- Paul shared about the Macedonian church's generosity with the Christians in Corinth to encourage them to continue giving generously because of their love for God and others.

APPLY

We do not have to be rich in order to give and help others. When we recognize how much Jesus has given for us and to us, we will want to give generously and help others. Discuss: What does it mean to be generous?

RESPOND

PRAY: Heavenly Father, help me be generous and give help to others.

OLDER KIDS: 2 Corinthians 9:6-8
YOUNGER KIDS: 2 Corinthians 9:7
MEMORY VERSE: Proverbs 14:12

EXPLAIN

- Paul challenged the believers in Corinth to give freely and cheerfully—not because someone forced them.
- God loves it when believers give generously with a happy heart.
- Cheerful giving is an example of how to obey God with joy, not out of duty.
- Our attitude is important when we give. When we give with an attitude of joy, our giving is a blessing to us and to others. When we give generously, we don't have to worry about meeting our own needs because God will provide.

We bring glory to God when we give with a heart of joy and selflessness. Our giving is a thankful response because God has given to us. Fill in the boxes with the clues provided to complete the sentence below.

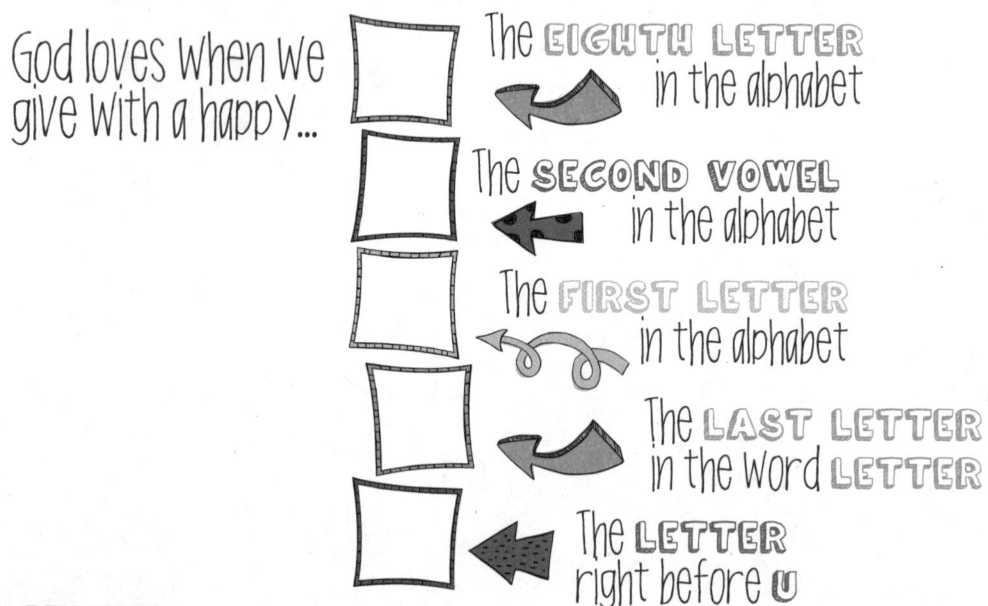

PRAY: Heavenly Father, help me give with an attitude that honors You.

HIGHLIGHT

OLDER KIDS: 2 Corinthians 10:7
YOUNGER KIDS: 2 Corinthians 10:7
MEMORY VERSE: Proverbs 14:12

EXPLAIN

- Paul wrote his second letter to the church in Corinth to remind them that His authority to share about Jesus comes from God.
- Some people criticized Paul, saying that he wasn't a good speaker and wasn't a powerful minister of the gospel.
- Paul reminded them that anyone who belongs to Jesus can be confident in Him.
- Paul needed to address some things people had said about him. He wanted to make sure that the Christians in Corinth knew that their confidence is in Christ, not in what others say or think.

APPLY

We can be confident in Jesus no matter what others think or say about us. Find the highlighted words from today's devotion.

J C K L O I U Y T F G H R B J G
M R O S P O W E R F U L P N S B
V I C N X D F G H J N C A E P T
R T N W F Q A Z C C V B U G E S
W I E I T I V G O S P E L M A N
B C V C S Z D A R S D E W R K U
I I U H G T D E I S W E R T E M
M Z N X B V E T N G V B H J R L
S E D F G H J R T T B V C S E U
L D I U Y T Y T H E D S M C C C
Y U I O C H R I S T I A N S P O

RESPOND

PRAY: Jesus, help me remember my confidence is in You, not what others think.

HIGHLIGHT

OLDER KIDS: 2 Corinthians 11:30
YOUNGER KIDS: 2 Corinthians 11:30
MEMORY VERSE: Proverbs 14:12

EXPLAIN

- In Paul's second letter to the church in Corinth, he addressed some things people had been saying about him.
- Paul wanted the believers to understand that he cared for them. He had dealt with a lot of hard things and been in a lot of trouble because of he preached the good news of Jesus.
- Paul told them that in his own power, he was weak, and in his weakness, God's power would show through.
- Paul felt he had to remind the church in Corinth of all that he had been through because of preaching the gospel. He wanted them to understand that his hardships didn't make him special, but in fact, made him weak. Paul was grateful for his weaknesses because he knew God showed His strength through human weakness.

APPLY

When we admit our weakness, God is able to work through us in a way that others can see His power. We see God's power when we understand our own weakness. Change one letter at a time to discover the answer.

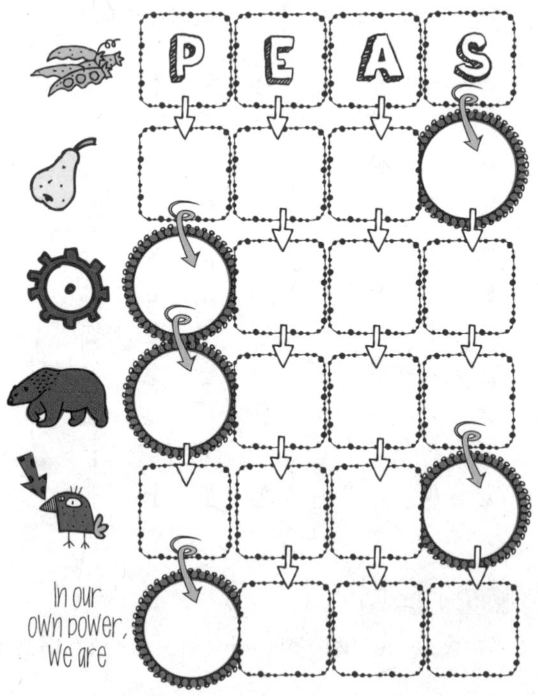

RESPOND

PRAY: Heavenly Father, help me see Your power through my weakness.

OLDER KIDS: 2 Corinthians 12:9-10
YOUNGER KIDS: 2 Corinthians 12:9-10
MEMORY VERSE: Proverbs 14:12

- Paul told the Corinthians about some trials he had in his life.
- Paul asked God to take his trials away, but instead, God gave Paul the grace to be able to handle the hard things he was going through.
- Paul told the Corinthian believers that when he has to depend on God, he's strong, because God is strong. He learned that God is enough, even in difficult times.
- God doesn't always take our troubles away. When He doesn't take them away, God will give us His grace and strength to depend on Him and handle it with His help.

God cares about our struggles. He will give us His grace and strength to be able to depend on Him to handle what we are going through. Write the words next to each picture, then use the letters in the red boxes to unscramble the answer.

PRAY: Heavenly Father, thank You for loving me. Remind me that Your grace and strength are enough, no matter what.

What did God give Paul to be able to get through his trouble?

HIGHLIGHT

OLDER KIDS: 2 Corinthians 13:5-6
YOUNGER KIDS: 2 Corinthians 13:5-6
MEMORY VERSE: Proverbs 14:26

EXPLAIN

- Paul finished his letter to the church in Corinth with some final instructions about their faith.
- Paul's goal in writing to the Corinthians was to encourage them to grow in their spiritual relationship with Christ.
- Paul told them they should look at their own lives to see if they were Christians, and if they were, to make sure they were growing in their faith.
- Paul challenged the believers in Corinth to look at themselves and to examine themselves and the strength of their faith. Were they Christians? And if so, were they living like it? True followers of God are changed by God to live for Him.

APPLY

We need other believers to challenge us to grow in our faith and encourage us as we grow. We should look at our own life to see if we are SNOWING in our walk with Christ. Wait, that can't be right. Follow the directions to find the right word!

RESPOND

PRAY: Heavenly Father, help me to grow in my walk with Christ.

OLDER KIDS: Mark 1:16-20
YOUNGER KIDS: Mark 1:16-18
MEMORY VERSE: Proverbs 14:26

EXPLAIN

- Mark wrote about Jesus and His ministry.
- Jesus was walking along the sea of Galilee when He called to some fishermen to follow Him and be His disciples.
- The men dropped what they were doing right away and followed Jesus.
- Jesus had already been baptized by John and tempted by Satan. Jesus was ready to begin His public ministry, and asked men to follow Him. These men did not fully understand that Jesus was the Messiah, but they responded right away.

APPLY

We should always respond to Jesus right away. Discuss: What does it mean to respond to Jesus?

RESPOND

PRAY: Jesus, help me respond to You right away when You speak to me.

OLDER KIDS: Mark 2:2-5
YOUNGER KIDS: Mark 2:2-5
MEMORY VERSE: Proverbs 14:26

EXPLAIN

- Jesus was teaching in a house. So many people were gathered that there was no more room inside.
- Some men took their paralyzed friend to see Jesus, but they couldn't get near Him because there were so many people.
- The men dug a hole in the roof and lowered their friend to Jesus. Jesus saw their faith. He forgave their friend's sins and healed him (Mark 2:11). The man's life was changed!
- The paralyzed man's friends cared enough about him to do whatever it took to get him to Jesus. It doesn't always mean digging a hole in a roof, but sometimes it takes a lot of effort to introduce someone to Jesus.

Helping your friends meet Jesus will change their lives because Jesus has power over sin. List 3 ways you can help others know Jesus.

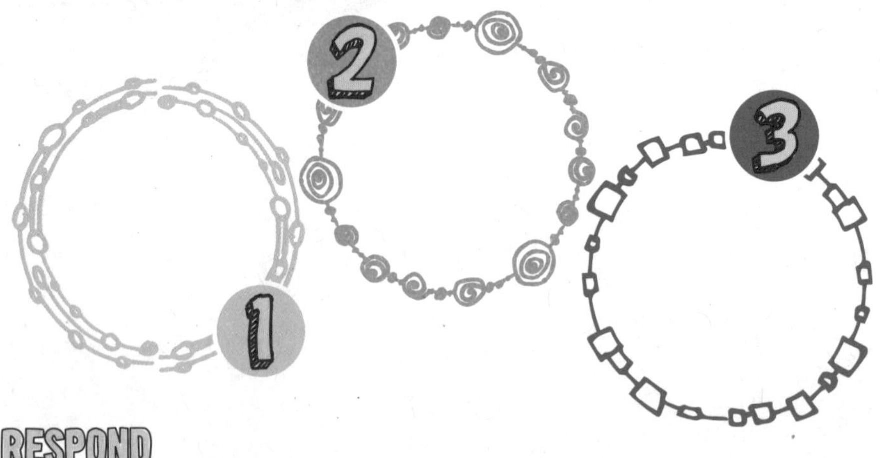

PRAY: Heavenly Father, help me introduce my friends to You.

OLDER KIDS: Mark 3:1-6
YOUNGER KIDS: Mark 3:1-2, 5
MEMORY VERSE: Proverbs 14:26

EXPLAIN

- Jesus was in the synagogue on the Sabbath day.
- A man with a withered hand came to Jesus. The Pharisees watched closely to see if Jesus would heal the man on the Sabbath day.
- Jesus healed the man! The Pharisees were upset with Him because they thought Jesus had broken God's law by healing on the Sabbath, but Jesus had not broken any laws.
- It was against the law to work on the Sabbath. The Pharisees were trying to catch Jesus breaking God's law, but Jesus knew what they were doing. He knew that healing the man would not break God's law, but Jesus would show love and compassion to the man. God's law is meant to help people, not hurt them.

Loving and caring for others is obedience to God's law. Fill in the blanks to reveal the memory verse, Proverbs 14:26.

______________________________ THE LORD

______________________________ CHILDREN

______________________________ REFUGE.

PRAY: Heavenly Father, help me to love and care for others.

HIGHLIGHT

OLDER KIDS: Mark 4:36-41
YOUNGER KIDS: Mark 4:37-39
MEMORY VERSE: Proverbs 14:26

EXPLAIN

- Jesus and the disciples were crossing the sea on a boat. Jesus took a nap on the boat.
- A bad storm began, and they were in danger. The disciples were afraid; they woke Jesus because they thought they would all die.
- Jesus spoke to the wind and waves, and He told them to calm down. The wind stopped, and the water became calm. The disciples were amazed—even the winds and waves obeyed Him!
- Jesus' disciples knew He was someone special, but they did not quite understand that He was the Son of God. After He calmed the storm with His words, the disciples were amazed, and they began to understand a little more who Jesus really was.

APPLY

Jesus has power over creation because He is the Son of God. Put a check mark next to the things Jesus has power over.

RESPOND

PRAY: Heavenly Father, thank You for being in control of creation.

HIGHLIGHT

OLDER KIDS: Mark 5:38-42
YOUNGER KIDS: Mark 5:40-42
MEMORY VERSE: Psalm 33:4

EXPLAIN

- Jairus, a synagogue leader, asked Jesus to come to his house to heal his sick daughter.
- On the way to his house, some of Jairus's friends ran to tell him that his daughter had died, and not to bother Jesus anymore.
- Jesus continued to Jarius's house with Peter, James, and John. When He arrived, Jesus told them she was not dead, but asleep. He told her to get up and walk, and she did. Jesus raised her from the dead and healed her completely. Jesus showed love and compassion to Jairus and his family.
- Jarius and his friends knew Jesus could heal sickness, but they did not understand that He had power over death too. Jesus told Jarius to believe and not be afraid. Jesus went to Jairus's house and raised his daughter from the dead, because Jairus believed in Jesus' power.

APPLY

Jesus has power over sickness and death because He is the Messiah. Use the maritime flags to decode the message:

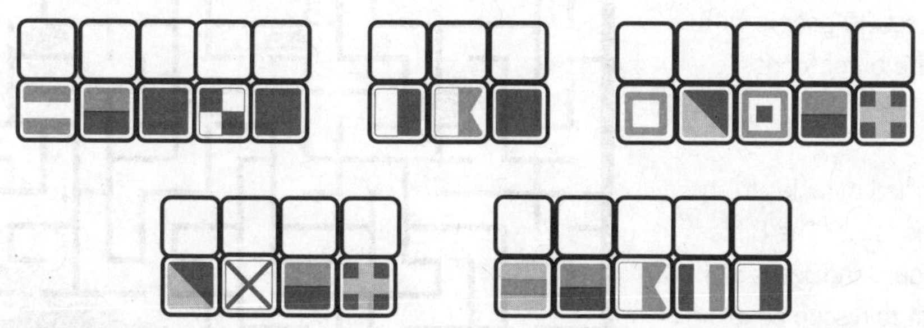

RESPOND

PRAY: Heavenly Father, thank You for giving Jesus power over sickness and death.

HIGHLIGHT

OLDER KIDS: Mark 6:39-44
YOUNGER KIDS: Mark 6:39-44
MEMORY VERSE: Psalm 33:4

EXPLAIN

- Jesus and His disciples were trying to rest, but people saw them and followed them. Jesus had compassion on the people and began to teach them.
- There were many people, and they had no food. Jesus sent the disciples to gather whatever food they could find.
- The disciples found five loaves of bread and two fish. Jesus blessed the food and told the disciples to give some to everyone. That little bit of food fed everyone with 12 baskets of food left over!
- When Jesus saw the people coming to Him, He did not want to leave them. He taught them, and then He showed them He is God by the miracle He performed. Jesus fed over 5,000 people with just a little bit of food!

APPLY

Jesus performed miracles to show everyone who He is. The Bible helps us understand Jesus is the Messiah sent to rescue people from sin. Complete the maze.

RESPOND

PRAY: God, help me understand more about Jesus as I read my Bible.

OLDER KIDS: Mark 7:6-8
YOUNGER KIDS: Mark 7:6-8
MEMORY VERSE: Psalm 33:4

EXPLAIN

- Scribes and Pharisees were asking Jesus about why His disciples didn't follow all of their traditions.
- Jesus said the Scribes and Pharisees only cared about the rules, traditions, and what people saw them do instead of loving God with all their hearts.
- Jesus told them that they made their own rules more important than God's law.
- Jesus never broke God's law, but He did not follow all the traditions and rules the Scribes and Pharisees followed. Jesus told them that loving God with all their hearts was more important than the traditions and rules they followed.

APPLY

God wants us to honor Him with our whole heart. When we do that, we will also honor Him with our actions, too. Draw a line to match each sentence below to recreate the story you read today.

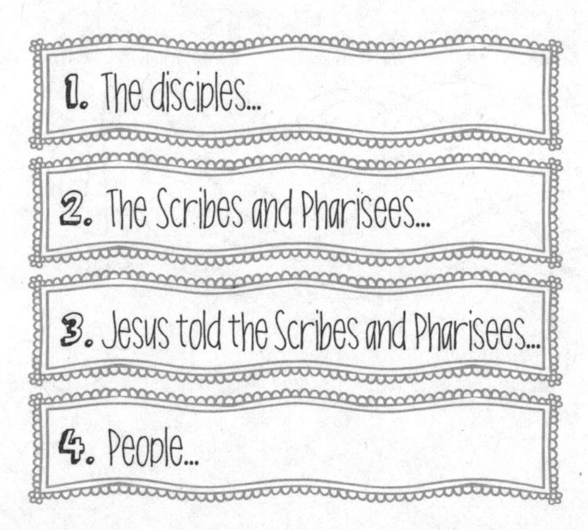

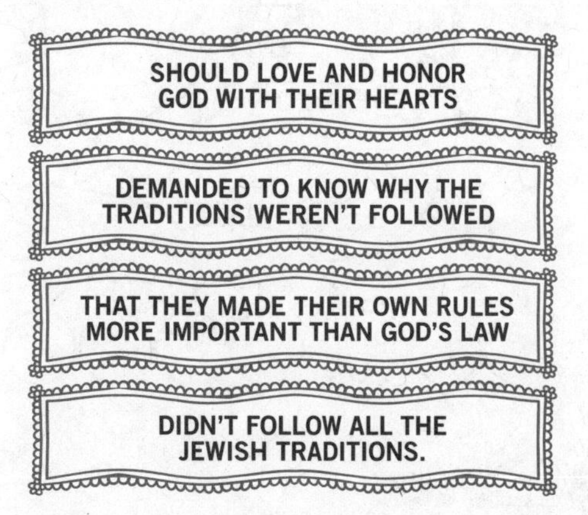

PRAY: Heavenly Father, help me honor You with my heart and my actions.

HIGHLIGHT

OLDER KIDS: Mark 8:27-30
YOUNGER KIDS: Mark 8:27-30
MEMORY VERSE: Psalm 33:4

EXPLAIN

- Jesus spent time with His disciples as He taught people and performed miracles.
- Jesus asked the disciples to tell Him who people thought He was. Then, He asked who *they* thought He was.
- Peter answered, "You are the Messiah!" The disciples were starting to understand who Jesus really was.
- Jesus knew that people weren't really sure who He was. Many did not understand that He was the Messiah sent by God to fulfill the prophecy of the Old Testament. The disciples spent a lot of time with Jesus, and even they did not see that He was the Messiah right away.

APPLY

Jesus is _______ _______ ____________, sent by God to save us. Find the missing words by following the paths below.

RESPOND

PRAY: Heavenly Father, thank You for sending Jesus to save us, just as You promised.

OLDER KIDS: Mark 9:23-24
YOUNGER KIDS: Mark 9:23-24
MEMORY VERSE: Psalm 33:4

EXPLAIN

- A father brought his son who could not speak to see Jesus.
- The father believed Jesus could heal his son.
- Jesus healed the boy because of the father's faith.
- A man brought his son to Jesus for healing. Jesus told the man that everything is possible for the one who has faith in Him. Jesus healed the boy so God would be glorified and more people would have faith in Him.

Following Jesus means we must trust Him. Fill in the blanks of the memory verse, Psalm 33:4.

FOR ____________________ OF THE LORD

____________________,

____________________.

PRAY: Heavenly Father, help me to trust You.

HIGHLIGHT

OLDER KIDS: Mark 10:13-16
YOUNGER KIDS: Mark 10:13-16
MEMORY VERSE: Proverbs 15:1

EXPLAIN

- Jesus was attracting large crowds of people who wanted to see Him.
- Some people brought young children to Jesus so He could bless them.
- Jesus' disciples thought children were a distraction. They thought Jesus was too busy to deal with kids. Jesus corrected the disciples. He invited the children close to Him!
- Jesus blessed the children and told the disciples that the kingdom of heaven belongs to them too. Jesus welcomes children and offers His gift of eternal life to them, just like adults.

D	S	Y	R	G
Q	G	H	A	T
C	O	☺	U	N
E	P	U	L	R
Z	I	M	X	N

☺... ←2 ☐
☺... ↑1 ☐
☺... ↓2 ←1 ☐
☺... ↓1 →1 ☐
☺... ↑2 ←2 ☐
☺... →1 ↑2 ☐
☺... ↓1 ←2 ☐
☺... ↓2 →2 ☐

APPLY

Faith in Jesus is not just for adults. Who else can have faith in Jesus? To find the answer, begin with the smiling face in the center and write the letter for each set of directions. Begin in the center space each time.

RESPOND

PRAY: Jesus, thank You for loving me. Help me have faith in You.

OLDER KIDS: Mark 11:4-10
YOUNGER KIDS: Mark 11:4-10
MEMORY VERSE: Proverbs 15:1

EXPLAIN

- Jesus and the disciples were going into Jerusalem. He sent them to find a certain donkey so he could ride on it.
- Jesus rode the donkey into Jerusalem to keep the promise about the Messiah in Zechariah 9:9. People praised Jesus as King as He entered Jerusalem.
- Jesus showed that He was humble and accessible to all people by riding a common donkey.
- Jesus entered Jerusalem on a donkey to fulfill the prophecy spoken about Him many years before by the prophet Zechariah. Jesus came as a humble king. His actions told the people that He is the righteous Messiah that has come. The people chose to praise Him on their own, which shows how much they believed in Him.

APPLY

Jesus is our humble King. Discuss: What does it mean to be humble?

RESPOND

PRAY: Jesus, thank You for being our humble King.

OLDER KIDS: Mark 12:13-17
YOUNGER KIDS: Mark 12:13-14
MEMORY VERSE: Proverbs 15:1

- Some religious leaders were trying to trick Jesus into saying something wrong.
- Jesus knew what they were trying to do, and He would not be tricked.
- Jesus answered them in a way that followed man's laws and honored God.
- Some of the religious leaders who didn't like Jesus were trying to get Him in trouble. They wanted to find a way to prove He wasn't the Messiah. But Jesus showed His authority by always knowing what they were doing, and amazed them by always answering in a way that honored God.

Starting with the first box (H), place all the letters along the path into the blue boxes in order. Then do the same with each color.

PRAY: Heavenly Father, help me always honor You.

OLDER KIDS: Mark 13:32-37
YOUNGER KIDS: Mark 13:32-33
MEMORY VERSE: Proverbs 15:1

EXPLAIN

- Jesus was talking about His return to earth.
- He told the disciples that only God knows when He will return.
- Jesus taught His disciples to be alert for His return and be faithful while He is away.
- To explain how they should wait for His return, Jesus used an example of a master leaving his house and his servants waiting for him to return. Just as servants would be working and waiting for their master to return home, Christians should be working and waiting for Jesus to return.

We do not know when Jesus will return, but we should remain faithful and live for Him until He comes back. Fill in the blanks to complete the memory verse Proverbs 15:1:

A ______________ ANSWER TURNS AWAY

______________, BUT A HARSH WORD

______________.

PRAY: Heavenly Father, help me remain faithful until Jesus returns.

HIGHLIGHT

OLDER KIDS: Mark 14:17-20
YOUNGER KIDS: Mark 14:17-20
MEMORY VERSE: Proverbs 15:1

EXPLAIN

- Jesus knew He would be betrayed by one of the disciples, and He told them so.
- The disciples could not imagine themselves betraying Jesus because they loved Him.
- Even though Jesus could have stopped His betrayal, He allowed it to happen. He knew it was part of God's plan for saving people from their sin.
- Jesus endured a lot of suffering. Even before He was physically harmed, Jesus was betrayed by a close friend. He knew it would happen in advance and could have stopped it, but He allowed it to happen because of His obedience to the Father and His love for people.

APPLY

Jesus loves us so much, He allowed Himself to suffer so we can be saved from our sins. Write the name of each item in the column below it to reveal the missing word from today's reading.

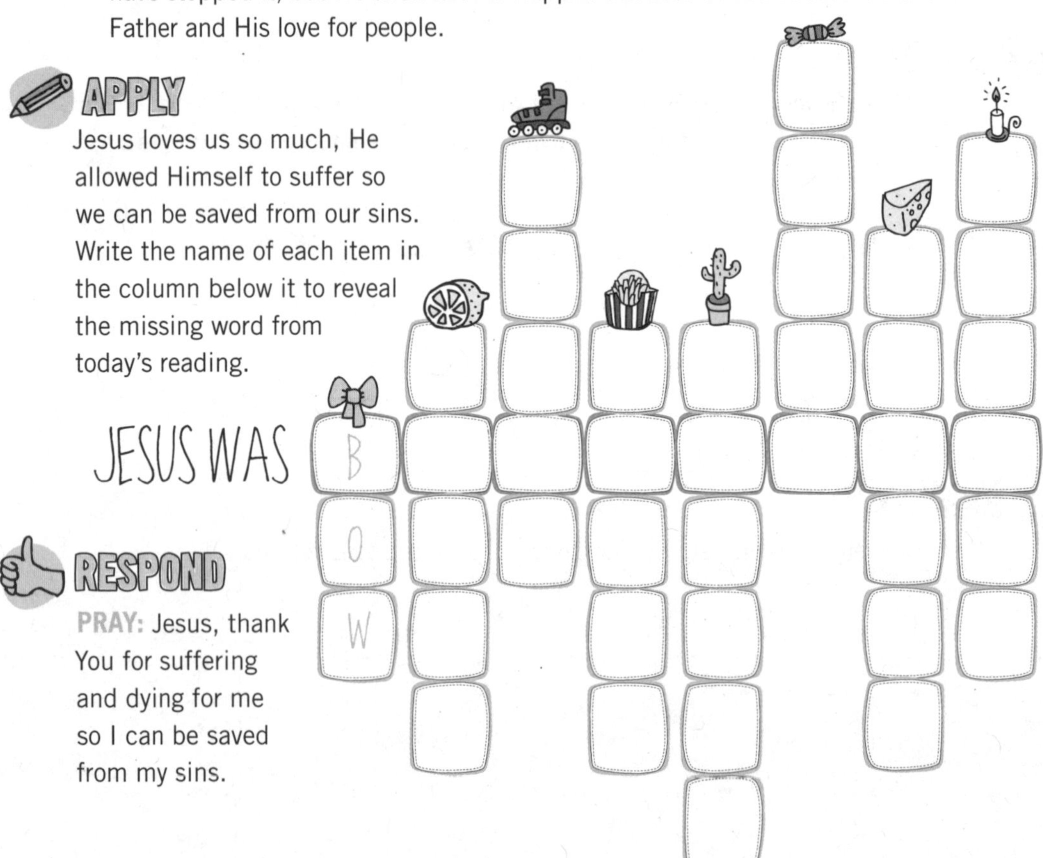

RESPOND

PRAY: Jesus, thank You for suffering and dying for me so I can be saved from my sins.

HIGHLIGHT

OLDER KIDS: Mark 15:37-39
YOUNGER KIDS: Mark 15:37-39
MEMORY VERSE: Psalm 37:4

EXPLAIN

- Jesus was crucified on the cross as punishment for sin, even though He had never sinned.
- Not everyone realized Jesus was the Messiah, but the soldier understood it when he saw Jesus die.
- Jesus died for everyone.
- When Jesus died, the curtain in the temple was ripped. This is important because the curtain had separated the people from the place where God dwelt in the temple. Jesus paid the price for sin, which separates people from God. The curtain was ripped because it was no longer needed. Because of Jesus' payment of sin, everyone can have access to God when they believe and trust in Him.

APPLY

Decode the message to reveal the main point from today's reading:

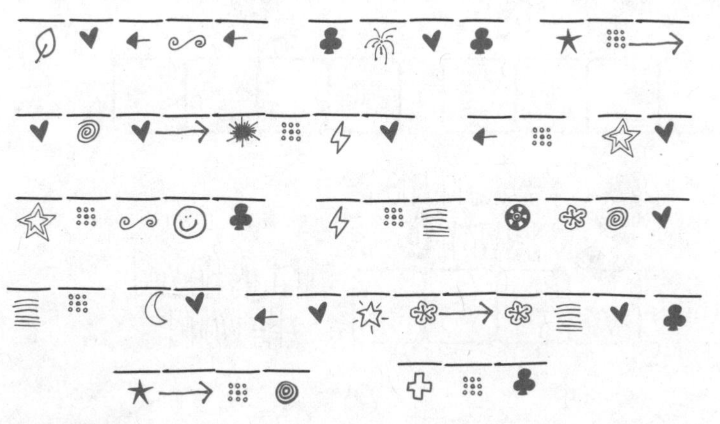

A
B
C
D
E
F
G
H
I
J
K
L
M
N
O
P
Q
R
S
T
U
V
W
X
Y
Z

RESPOND

PRAY: Heavenly Father, thank You for sending Jesus to pay the price for my sin.

OLDER KIDS: Mark 16:1-8
YOUNGER KIDS: Mark 16:4-7
MEMORY VERSE: Psalm 37:4

EXPLAIN

- Three days after Jesus died, some women who were friends of Jesus went to the tomb to anoint His body with spices.
- When they got to the tomb where Jesus was buried, the stone was rolled away from the opening.
- A man dressed in all white told them not to be afraid—Jesus had risen and was alive! This man was an angel (Matthew 28:2-3).
- Jesus had told His followers that He would rise after three days, but they did not understand. The women were amazed and afraid at what they were told. They ran back to tell their friends that Jesus' body was gone and He was alive (Matthew 28:8).

Jesus conquered death and sin so we can be forgiven of our sin. Solve the puzzle to reveal the secret message.

PRAY: Jesus, thank You for defeating sin and death. I worship You, my risen Savior.

HIGHLIGHT

OLDER KIDS: Romans 1:16-17
YOUNGER KIDS: Romans 1:16-17
MEMORY VERSE: Psalm 37:4

EXPLAIN

- Paul wrote a letter to the Christians in Rome to help them see Jesus was the Savior they had been waiting for.
- Paul was not ashamed to teach about God or His Word.
- He wanted the Roman Christians to understand that Jesus' salvation is for everyone, not just a certain group of people.
- Paul had once hated Christians, but since Jesus changed him, he told Christians that he was not ashamed of the gospel of Christ. Paul's life was changed by his faith in Jesus, and he wanted others to have the same opportunity.

APPLY

We should not be ashamed of the good news of Jesus. It's for everyone! Fill in the blanks to complete the memory verse, Psalm 37:4.

______________________ IN THE LORD, AND HE

____.

RESPOND

PRAY: Heavenly Father, thank You that Your forgiveness is for everyone.

OLDER KIDS: Romans 2:11
YOUNGER KIDS: Romans 2:11
MEMORY VERSE: Psalm 37:4

- Paul's letter to the Christians in Rome reminded them that God is holy and gracious.
- He explained that every person is born a sinner, so every person needs God's forgiveness.
- God loves and forgives everyone who asks Him. He does not show favorites.
- Some Christians thought they were better than others, and this caused a problem. Paul wanted them to understand that all people matter to God.

When we trust in God for salvation, our hearts will change and we will understand that we need His forgiveness. Decode the message below by replacing each letter with the letter that comes BEFORE it in the alphabet.

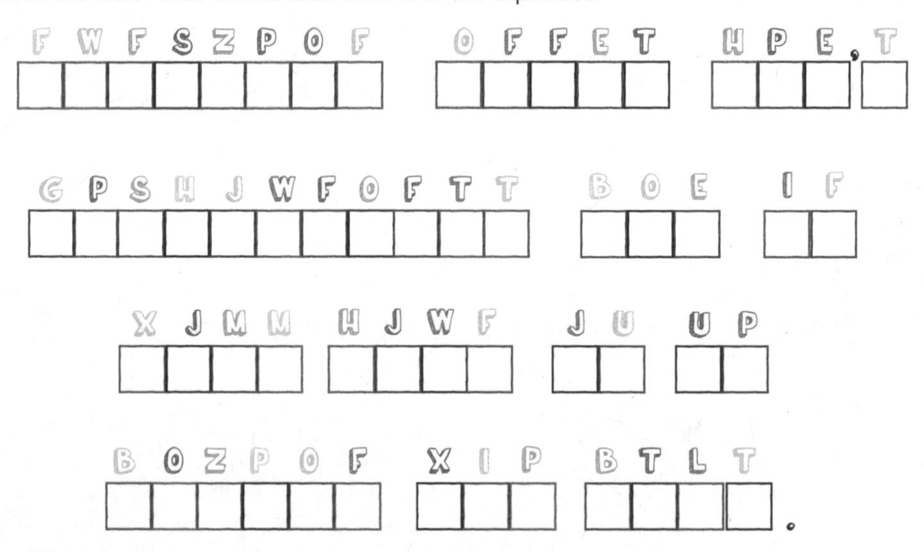

PRAY: Heavenly Father, thank You for loving me and forgiving me when I ask.

OLDER KIDS: Romans 3:21-24
YOUNGER KIDS: Romans 3:23
MEMORY VERSE: Psalm 37:4

EXPLAIN

- Paul explained that Jewish people needed God's grace just as much as Gentiles (people who were not Jews).
- Paul told the Roman Christians that grace through faith in Jesus is the only way to salvation.
- Paul wanted the people to understand that salvation did not come from following the law, or the rules from the Old Testament. This is why they needed a Rescuer—Jesus.
- Paul explained that the Jews were not better than the Gentiles. Everyone has sinned and needs grace and faith in Jesus to be saved.

APPLY

Who has sinned and needs faith in Jesus for salvation? Everyone! Complete the activity by matching the correct statements together.

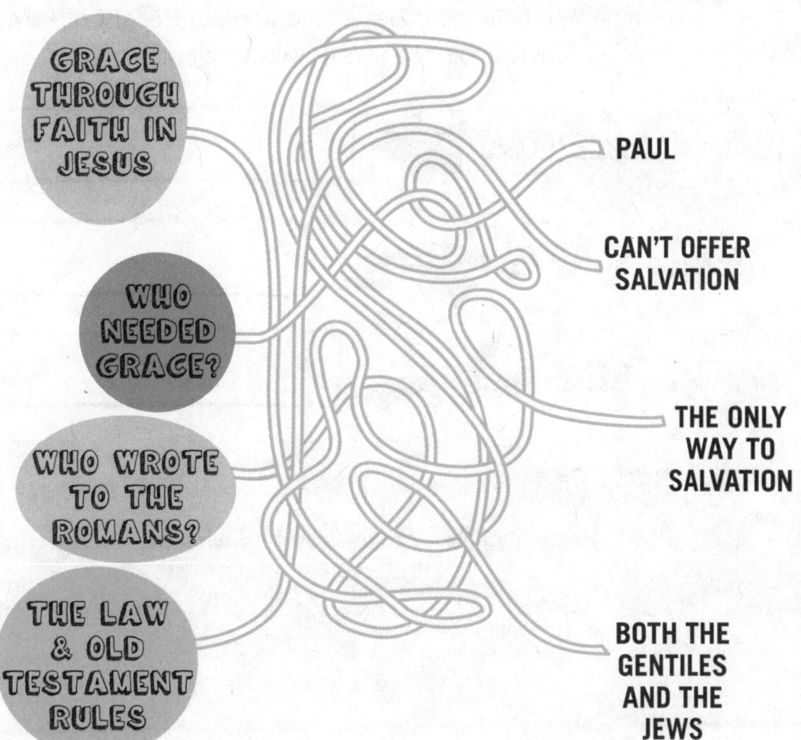

RESPOND

PRAY: Heavenly Father, thank You for offering grace and salvation for everyone through Jesus.

OLDER KIDS: Romans 4:23-25
YOUNGER KIDS: Romans 4:23-25
MEMORY VERSE: Psalm 37:23

- Paul wrote to the Christians in Rome to help them understand faith and salvation.
- Paul reminded them that Abraham had faith in God.
- Just like Abraham had faith in God, Christians in New Testament times could have faith in God, too. All people are saved by faith, not by the things they do.
- Abraham was the father of the Jewish nation and important to Jewish history. Paul used Abraham as an example because he knew it would help the Jewish Christians understand more about faith in God.

Anyone who believes in Jesus and accepts His gift of salvation will be forgiven of his sins. Unscramble the sets of words below.

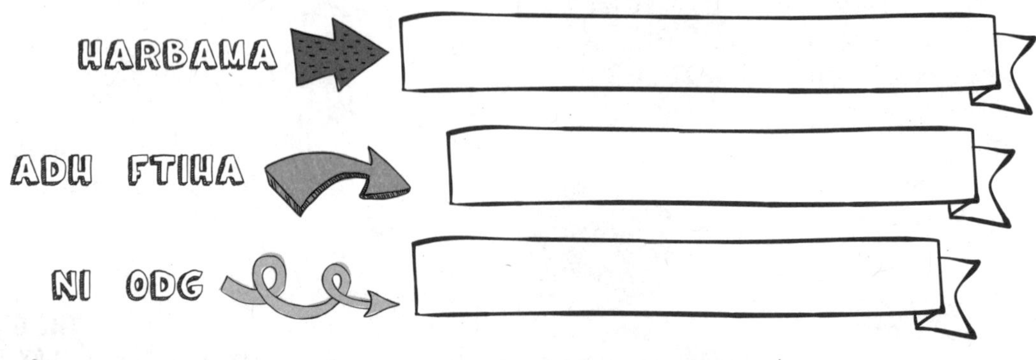

PRAY: Heavenly Father, thank You for loving me and offering salvation to me.

OLDER KIDS: Romans 5:6-8
YOUNGER KIDS: Romans 5:6-8
MEMORY VERSE: Psalm 37:23

EXPLAIN

- Paul reminded the Roman Christians that Jesus died for sin, knowing that people could not have a right relationship with God on their own.
- God loved people so much that He sent Jesus to die for us while we were still sinners.
- God sent Jesus to take the punishment for sin, and He gives grace to everyone who trusts in Him for salvation.
- God gave grace when He didn't have to. He knew how sinful people are, but He sent Jesus to die for us anyway. God's salvation is for us—forever.

APPLY

God showed us grace when He sent Jesus to take the punishment for sin when He didn't have to. He continues giving us grace every day. As you solve the code below, think about the ways God gives you grace every day.

RESPOND

PRAY: Heavenly Father, thank You for giving grace and salvation through Jesus to everyone who trusts in You.

OLDER KIDS: Romans 6:12-13
YOUNGER KIDS: Romans 6:12-13
MEMORY VERSE: Psalm 37:23

EXPLAIN

- Paul taught Christians about how they should live as followers of Jesus.
- Paul told them Christians should not continue to live like they did before they knew Jesus, letting sin rule their lives.
- They should let God use their lives for His glory.
- When a person becomes a Christian, she is no longer a slave to sin or a weapon for unrighteousness. Believers in Jesus are freed by God's salvation and become God's weapons for His glory.

Trusting God for salvation and giving our lives to Him is freedom to live for Him. Look at the weapons below. Can you find the identical ones? Draw a line between each matching pair.

PRAY: Heavenly Father, help me live my life for Your glory.

HIGHLIGHT

OLDER KIDS: Romans 7:15
YOUNGER KIDS: Romans 7:15
MEMORY VERSE: Psalm 37:23

EXPLAIN

- Paul talked about the law and how it helps people understand right from wrong and points others to Jesus.
- Paul told the Christians in Rome that he was not perfect—far from it!
- No one is perfect or has ever been perfect, except Jesus. Everyone struggles with sin, even those following Jesus.
- Jesus gives His followers power to resist sin and follow Him.

APPLY

No matter how much we hate sin, we will continue to struggle with it. But Jesus gives us the power to choose His way instead of sin. Jesus gives us power to resist temptation. Discuss: What is temptation? When does temptation become sin?

RESPOND

PRAY: Jesus, thank You for giving me power to resist temptation.

HIGHLIGHT

OLDER KIDS: Romans 8:28
YOUNGER KIDS: Romans 8:28
MEMORY VERSE: Psalm 37:23

EXPLAIN

- Paul continued his letter to the Romans.
- Paul explained that through Jesus, Christians have the Holy Spirit's power to help live in a way that honors God.
- Paul shared that all things work together for the good of those who love God.
- Paul wanted Christians to understand that Jesus and the Holy Spirit give Christians the power to honor God with their lives, in both good and hard times.

APPLY

Believers are all part of God's family, and He makes all things work together for our good and His glory, even when we don't understand. Solve the puzzle by writing the first letter of each picture in the box above it.

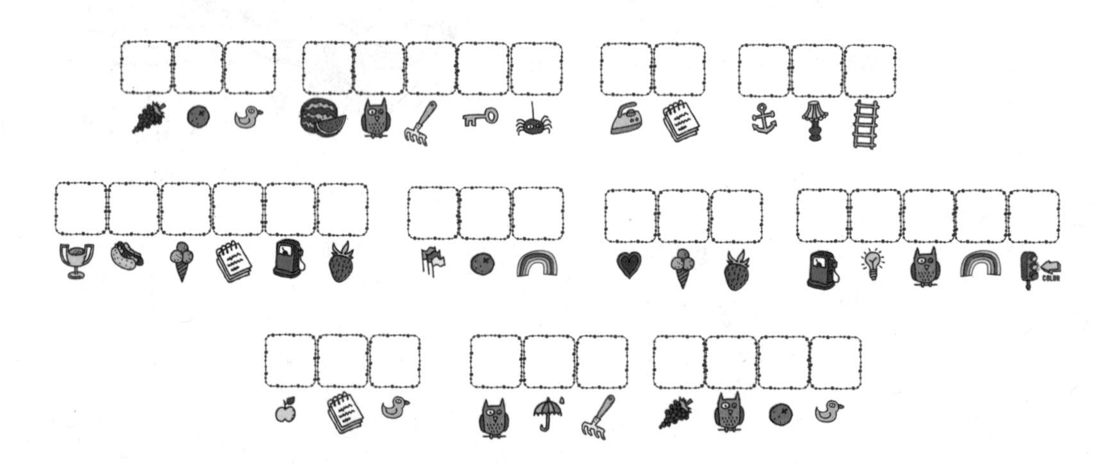

RESPOND

PRAY: God, thank You for working in all things for Your glory and my good.

HIGHLIGHT

OLDER KIDS: Romans 9:30-32
YOUNGER KIDS: Romans 9:30-32
MEMORY VERSE: Proverbs 16:9

EXPLAIN

- Paul wrote to teach the Roman Christians about God's character and people's responsibility.
- God is sovereign—in control of all things. He provides access for everyone to receive God's salvation—by faith.
- No one can save themselves by doing good things. Salvation comes through faith in Jesus alone. God is in control, and people are responsible to trust in Him for salvation.
- Paul reminded them that the Israelites had tried to save themselves through the law, but obeying the law will never bring salvation. Gentiles didn't have the law, but could be saved through faith—the same way Israelites are saved. Paul stressed that God does not have favorites and everyone is saved from their sin in the same way—faith in Jesus.

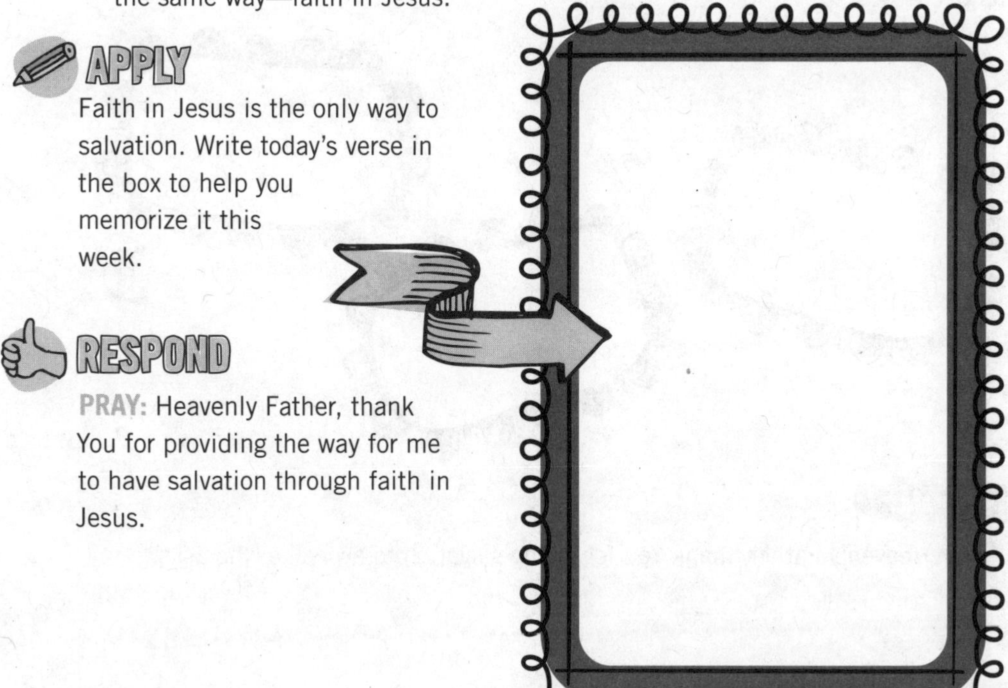

APPLY

Faith in Jesus is the only way to salvation. Write today's verse in the box to help you memorize it this week.

RESPOND

PRAY: Heavenly Father, thank You for providing the way for me to have salvation through faith in Jesus.

OLDER KIDS: Romans 10:9-13
YOUNGER KIDS: Romans 10:13
MEMORY VERSE: Proverbs 16:9

- Paul told the Romans that people are saved by faith in Jesus alone, not by anything they do.
- Paul explained that everyone who believes in Jesus with their hearts will be saved.
- God's salvation is for everyone who repents and trusts in Jesus.
- Paul wanted the Romans to understand that knowing about Jesus wasn't enough. We must truly believe in our hearts and ask Jesus to save us—and He will.

Everyone who asks Jesus for salvation will be saved from sin. Who do you know that you could tell about Jesus' forgiveness? List 3 people you could tell about Jesus' forgiveness.

PRAY: Heavenly Father, thank You for giving salvation to everyone who asks.

OLDER KIDS: Romans 11:33-36
YOUNGER KIDS: Romans 11:33-36
MEMORY VERSE: Proverbs 16:9

EXPLAIN

- Paul included a song of praise to God in his letter to the Roman Christians.
- Paul praised God because of His wisdom, His knowledge, and His creation of all things.
- God deserves all worship and praise.
- Paul reminded his readers that Israel had not been rejected by God, but that God had just made their family larger when He included the Gentiles through their belief in Jesus.

APPLY

God made a way for everyone to be forgiven of sin. He is worthy to be praised. Discuss: What does it mean to praise God? How can you praise God this week?

RESPOND

PRAY: Heavenly Father, thank You for being worthy of all praise.

HIGHLIGHT

OLDER KIDS: Romans 12:1-2
YOUNGER KIDS: Romans 12:1-2
MEMORY VERSE: Proverbs 16:9

EXPLAIN

- Paul explained how believers are to live in a way that gives glory to God.
- Paul taught the Christians in Rome that they respond to God's grace by living for Him and obeying Him with their whole hearts.
- Paul explained that Christians are called to live differently from others in the world—they are called to respond to God's grace by living for Him, not themselves.
- Believers are different from people who don't know Jesus, because God's love changes their hearts and minds to trust and follow Him.

APPLY

Unscramble each word to reveal the main point of today's reading.

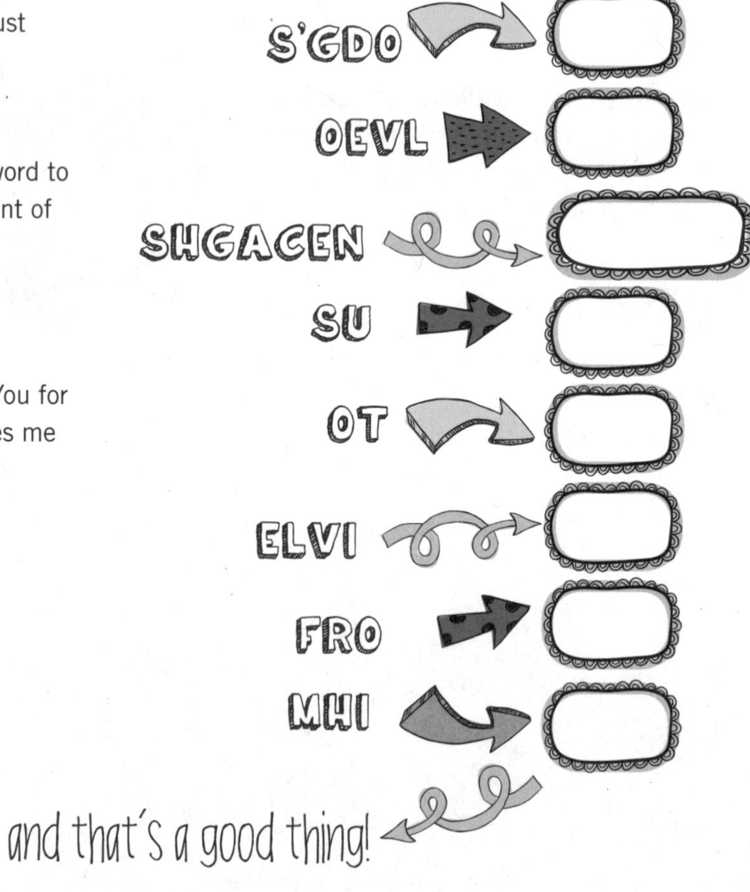

RESPOND

PRAY: God, thank You for Your love that makes me different.

OLDER KIDS: Romans 13:4-7
YOUNGER KIDS: Romans 13:7
MEMORY VERSE: Proverbs 16:9

EXPLAIN

- Paul wrote to the Romans to explain that God is in control of all things, including government leaders. He puts people in authority.
- One way to obey God is by obeying the rules and people in charge.
- Christians should live in obedience to God in all things, submitting to the leaders He has placed in their lives.
- Because God is sovereign and in control over everything, He is sovereign over who is in charge on earth. He allows leaders to be in charge here on earth. Christians honor God by honoring those in authority.

APPLY

We are to obey those in authority over us because we understand that God has placed them in our lives for His glory. Check any of the people in the list below who are authority figures in your life and write their names if you know them.

- [x] President ______________
- [ ] Coach ______________
- [ ] Teacher ______________
- [ ] Student Leader ______________
- [ ] Music Instructor ______________
- [ ] Bible Study Leader ______________
- [ ] Bus Driver ______________
- [ ] Principal ______________
- [ ] Babysitter ______________
- [ ] Parents ______________

PRAY: Heavenly Father, help me glorify You by honoring others.

HIGHLIGHT

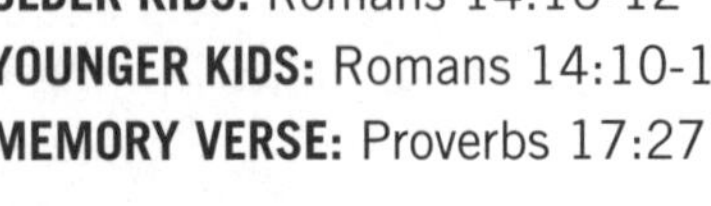

OLDER KIDS: Romans 14:10-12
YOUNGER KIDS: Romans 14:10-12
MEMORY VERSE: Proverbs 17:27

EXPLAIN

- In his letter, Paul asked the Roman believers why they were judging each other.
- Paul reminded them that all believers will bow before God and praise Him together.
- People are accountable, or responsible, to God for their actions.
- Paul explained that Christians should not judge each other for having different opinions. We should not do anything that causes someone else to sin.

APPLY

We are all accountable to God for our actions. When we love each other, we honor God with our actions. Use the maritime flags to decode the message.

When we love each other,

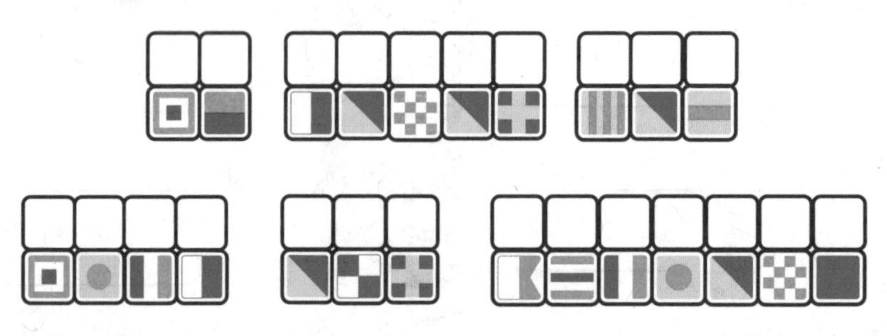

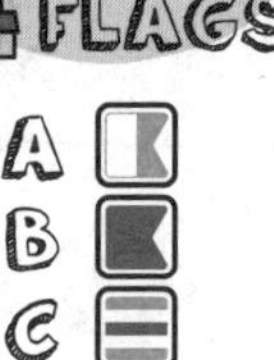

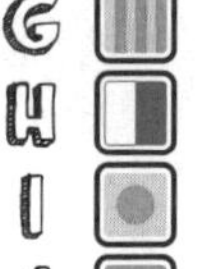
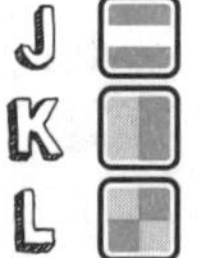

RESPOND

PRAY: Heavenly Father, help me love others like You love them.

OLDER KIDS: Romans 15:5-6
YOUNGER KIDS: Romans 15:5-6
MEMORY VERSE: Proverbs 17:27

EXPLAIN

- Paul reminded the Roman believers to continue following Jesus and loving others like He does.
- Paul explained that just as Christ gave Himself for others, believers are called to live in harmony, giving up their desires to serve others.
- Paul told the Romans that when they follow God's commands and love each other, they bring glory to God.
- Paul taught that followers of Jesus are to love each other because Jesus loved them. When believers love each other, they can focus their attention to bringing glory to God together.

APPLY

Write the letters for each picture in the boxes below to find another word and complete the sentence.

When we ____________ Jesus by loving each other, it gives glory to God.

RESPOND

PRAY: Heavenly Father, help me love others and bring glory to You.

HIGHLIGHT

OLDER KIDS: Romans 16:19
YOUNGER KIDS: Romans 16:19
MEMORY VERSE: Proverbs 17:27

EXPLAIN

- Paul heard reports about how the Roman church had been treating one another.
- He knew they were obeying God, so Paul rejoiced.
- Paul encouraged them to be wise and stay away from evil things.
- Paul closed his letter with some final words to the church at Rome. He wanted them to understand that their obedience was glorifying to God and an encouragement to others.

APPLY

When we obey, it affects people around us, encouraging others. Write Proverbs 17:27 in the box and work to memorize it this week.

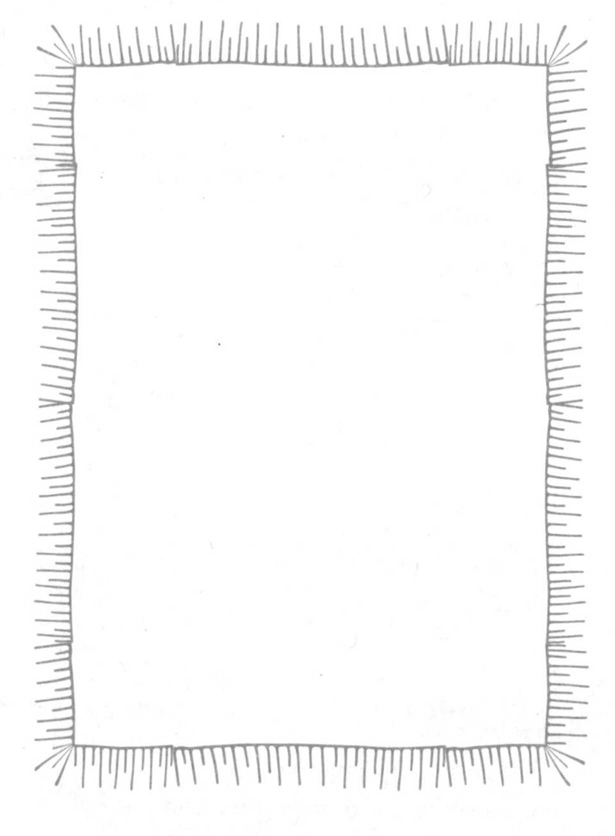

RESPOND

PRAY: Heavenly Father, help me obey You so You will be glorified and others will be encouraged.

OLDER KIDS: Acts 20:7-12
YOUNGER KIDS: Acts 20:9-10, 12
MEMORY VERSE: Proverbs 17:27

EXPLAIN

- Paul was in Troas preparing to leave. He wanted to preach to the people one more time.
- While Paul was preaching late one night, a young man who was sitting in the window fell asleep. The young man fell out of the window and died.
- Paul went down to the boy and wrapped his arms around him. God brought the boy back to life!
- Paul didn't just preach—he helped people, too. God allowed Paul to do miracles in order to bring glory to Himself.

APPLY

God works through people to point others to Jesus in many ways. If you are a follower of Jesus, He wants to use you to point others to Him too! Unscramble each word to reveal the secret message from today's reading.

RESPOND

PRAY: Heavenly Father, thank You for having power over death. Help me see different ways I can point people to You.

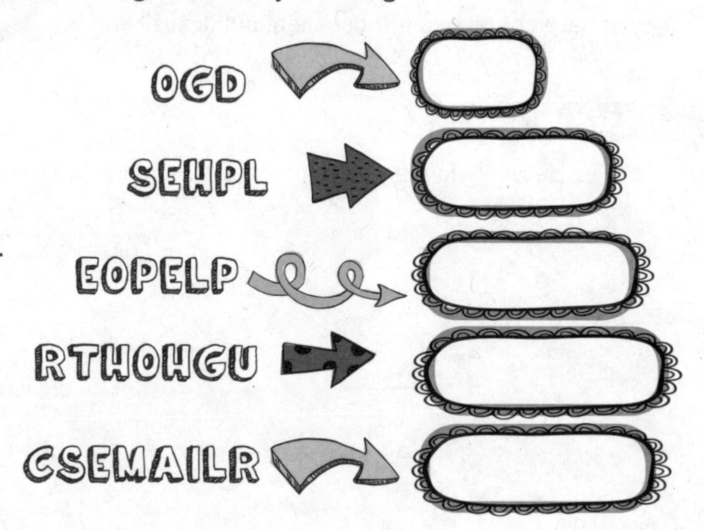

HIGHLIGHT

OLDER KIDS: Acts 21:30-36
YOUNGER KIDS: Acts 21:30-31
MEMORY VERSE: Proverbs 17:27

EXPLAIN

- Paul taught the good news of Jesus in Rome.
- People were mad at what Paul said, and they tried to hurt him. Soldiers protected him from the crowd.
- Paul would not let anyone stop him from telling others about Jesus.
- After the guards saved Paul from the crowd, he had an opportunity to defend himself. He told his story about becoming a follower of Jesus. He wanted everyone to know about Jesus.

APPLY

We should always be willing to tell others about Jesus, no matter the circumstances. Sometimes it takes courage to tell people about Jesus. Discuss: How did Paul have courage? How can you have courage to tell people about Jesus?

RESPOND

PRAY: Heavenly Father, help me always be ready to tell others about Jesus.

HIGHLIGHT

OLDER KIDS: Acts 22:15-16
YOUNGER KIDS: Acts 22:15-16
MEMORY VERSE: Proverbs 18:10

EXPLAIN

- Paul had been attacked and arrested in the temple.
- Paul told the people his own story about meeting Jesus, and how it changed his life.
- He told the people how to find forgiveness from their sins in Jesus.
- Paul shared his testimony, his story of how Jesus changed his life when he trusted in Him. Paul's story pointed others to Jesus and taught them how to become followers of Jesus.

APPLY

We can tell people about Jesus by sharing our own story of how He changed us. Use the words in the red box to complete the sentences below.

Before becoming a Christian, a person is ____________ of sin. As a Christian, a person's sin has been ____________. A person's life is ______ ______ because Jesus has changed their heart.

RESPOND

PRAY: Heavenly Father, help me to share my story with others.

HIGHLIGHT

OLDER KIDS: Acts 23:11
YOUNGER KIDS: Acts 23:11
MEMORY VERSE: Proverbs 18:10

EXPLAIN

- In Rome, some people wanted to hurt Paul because he was preaching about Jesus.
- Paul was a Roman citizen, which meant the Roman soldiers gave him special treatment.
- God told Paul to be courageous because it was God's plan for Paul to tell people the good news of Jesus in Rome, just like he shared the gospel in Jerusalem.
- The Roman soldiers took special care of Paul since he was a Roman citizen. God told Paul he would preach in Rome, even though people wanted to kill him there.

APPLY

God is always at work and will give us the strength we need to live for Him. Talk with your parents about ways God gives us strength.

RESPOND

PRAY: Heavenly Father, thank You for giving me strength to live for You.

OLDER KIDS: Acts 24:14-16
YOUNGER KIDS: Acts 24:14-16
MEMORY VERSE: Proverbs 18:10

EXPLAIN

- Paul was arrested and put in prison once again.
- The Roman governors didn't know what to do with Paul. They didn't think he had done anything wrong.
- Paul told people about Jesus no matter where he was—even in prison.
- Paul took every chance he had to share the good news about Jesus with other people. God allowed Paul to go to many different places and experience different situations so people could hear about Jesus.

APPLY

We can tell people about Jesus no matter what circumstances we are in. To find the answer, begin with the smiling face in the center and write the letter for each set of directions below. Begin in the center space each time.

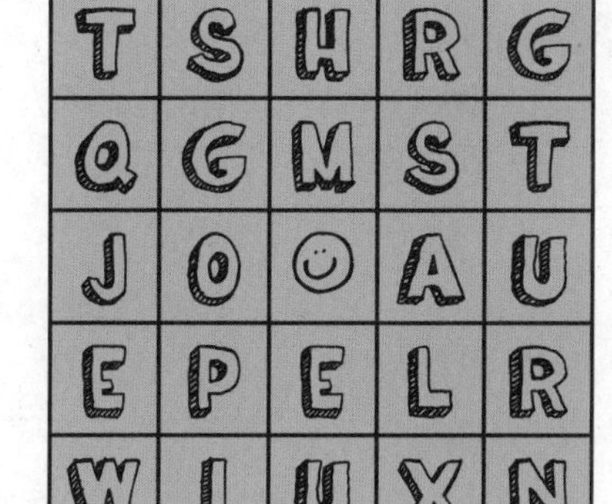

I can tell people about Jesus

___ ___   ___ ___ ___ ___ ___ ___   ___ ___ ___ ___

2↓2→ 1←   1↑ 1→ 2→1↑ 2↑2← 1↓ 1↓2→   2↓2← 2↑ 1↑ 2→1↑

PRAY: Heavenly Father, help me tell others about You.

OLDER KIDS: Acts 25:6-8
YOUNGER KIDS: Acts 25:7-8
MEMORY VERSE: Proverbs 18:10

EXPLAIN

- Paul was brought before a judge after he was arrested.
- Some Jews had accused Paul of doing wrong, but they could not prove anything.
- Paul said he had done nothing wrong according to anyone's laws.
- Paul shared the love of Jesus no matter what. Even when he was on trial and people were lying about him, he was brave and told others about the truth of the gospel.

The good news of Jesus is always something people need to hear. Fill in the blanks to complete Proverbs 18:10:

THE NAME OF THE LORD

______________________________;

THE RIGHTEOUS

______________________________.

PRAY: Heavenly Father, help me share the good news about You.

OLDER KIDS: Acts 26:12-15
YOUNGER KIDS: Acts 26:13-15
MEMORY VERSE: Proverbs 18:10

EXPLAIN

- Paul was on trial standing before King Agrippa.
- Paul was able to tell his own story. He told King Agrippa about how he had persecuted Christians before meeting Jesus on the road to Damascus.
- The reason Paul would not stop telling people about Jesus was because he loved Jesus, and he wanted everyone to know and follow Jesus.
- Paul told his story over and over again to whomever would listen. Even when he was in court, Paul shared the good news of Jesus with others with others because sharing the gospel was more important than what people thought of him.

Follow each octopus tentacle to place the letter in a flag and fill in the blank.

The __________ __________ of Jesus is for everyone and we should do our best to tell as many as we can about Him.

PRAY: Heavenly Father, help me tell everyone I can the good news about Jesus.

HIGHLIGHT

OLDER KIDS: Acts 27:20-26
YOUNGER KIDS: Acts 27:23-24
MEMORY VERSE: Psalm 51:10

EXPLAIN

- Paul was sailing on a ship as a prisoner, headed to Rome to go before Caesar, the ruler of Rome.
- The ship was caught in a terrible storm, and everyone was afraid they would die.
- God sent an angel to tell Paul that he and everyone on the ship would be safe.
- Paul was faithful to follow God. God was always with Paul. God stays faithful all the time.

APPLY

God never leaves us. He is always faithful to keep His promises. Find the highlighted words above in the word search.

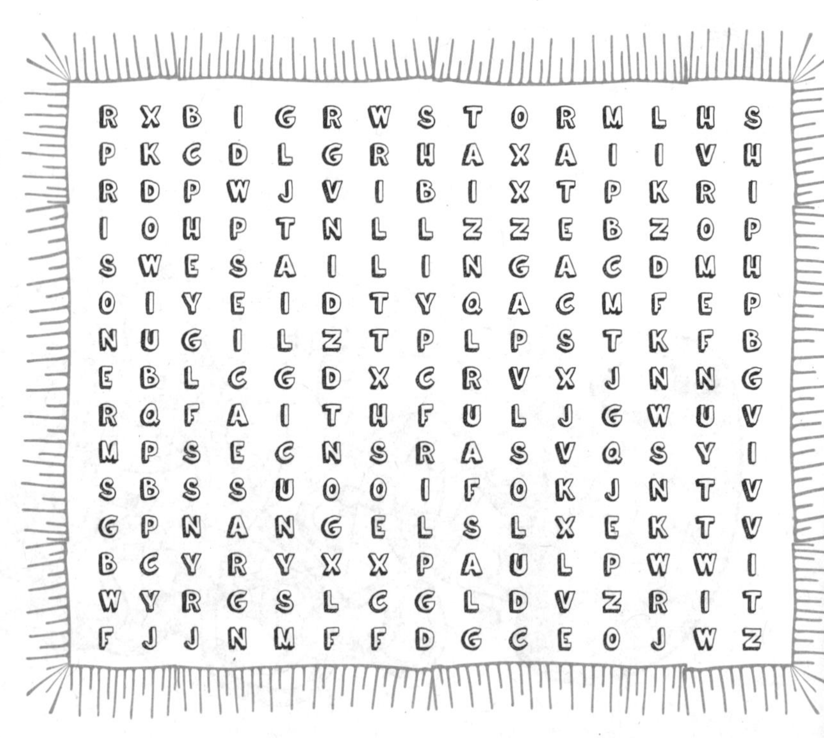

RESPOND

PRAY: Heavenly Father, thank You for never leaving me and always being faithful.

OLDER KIDS: Acts 28:23-24
YOUNGER KIDS: Acts 28:23-24
MEMORY VERSE: Psalm 51:10

EXPLAIN

- Paul's ship had finally arrived in Rome.
- Paul was allowed to live in a house as a prisoner, and people could come visit him.
- Even though he was a prisoner, Paul still told people the good news about Jesus.
- Paul endured some tough times, and he spent a lot of time as a prisoner. Even as a prisoner, he trusted God and never gave up. He told others about God's love with boldness every chance he had.

We should tell people about Jesus every chance we get. List 3 ways we can tell people about Jesus.

RESPOND

PRAY: Heavenly Father, help me tell people about Jesus.

OLDER KIDS: Colossians 1:9-10
YOUNGER KIDS: Colossians 1:9-10
MEMORY VERSE: Psalm 51:10

EXPLAIN

- Paul wrote a letter to the church in Colossae while he was in prison in Rome.
- Paul wanted the believers to be strong in their beliefs and know how to live.
- He let them know he was praying for them, even while he was in prison.
- Paul wanted the church in Colossae to grow in their faith and honor God in how they lived. He prayed they would be strengthened, have endurance, and have a spirit of joyful thankfulness to God.

We can show love and encouragement to others no matter where we are. Fill in the blanks to complete Psalm 51:10 to help you memorize it this week.

______________________________.

AND RENEW

______________________________.

PRAY: Heavenly Father, help me show love and encouragement to others.

OLDER KIDS: Colossians 2:6-7
YOUNGER KIDS: Colossians 2:6-7
MEMORY VERSE: Psalm 51:10

EXPLAIN

- Paul wrote a letter to the church in Colossae while he was in prison in Rome, encouraging them in their faith.
- Some people in Colossae were teaching wrong things about God, and Paul wanted the church to know the truth.
- Paul wanted them to understand that faith in Jesus is the only way to salvation. He encouraged them to continue in their faith and not to be confused by wrong teaching.
- Some teachers were teaching false things about worshiping God. Paul reminded the church to have faith in Jesus only. Believers should always follow Him and grow in their faith.

APPLY

Jesus is the source of our salvation, not other people or our actions. Solve the maze to discover which path leads to salvation.

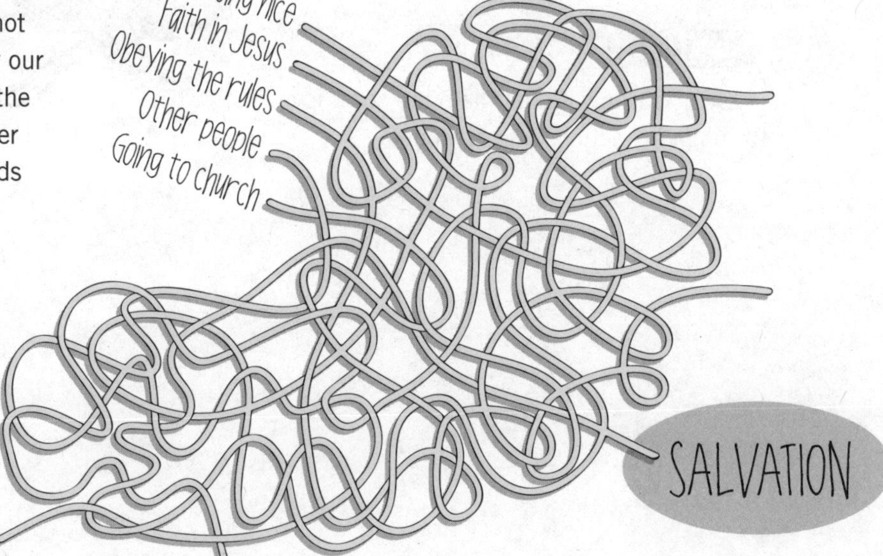

RESPOND

PRAY: Jesus, thank You for being the source of my salvation!

HIGHLIGHT

OLDER KIDS: Colossians 3:12-17
YOUNGER KIDS: Colossians 3:12-17
MEMORY VERSE: Psalm 51:10

EXPLAIN

- Paul helped believers know how they should act.
- Paul told believers that as followers of Christ, their behavior will show what they believe. Living a life of godliness sets believers apart from people who don't trust in Jesus.
- Paul said that everything we do should be for God's glory.
- Paul explained that salvation does not depend on someone's actions. At the same time, true followers of Christ will show others their faith by actions that come from a changed heart.

APPLY

If we love Jesus and follow Him, our actions will show it. Discuss: How we can show love to others?

RESPOND

PRAY: Heavenly Father, help me show love through my actions and attitudes.

HIGHLIGHT

OLDER KIDS: Colossians 4:2-6
YOUNGER KIDS: Colossians 4:6
MEMORY VERSE: Psalm 51:12

EXPLAIN

- Paul finished his letter to the Colossian believers with encouragement.
- He reminded them how they should live. He asked them to continue in prayer, to pray for him, and to be wise.
- Paul also taught the church to be loving with their words and how they treated others.
- The way people act shows what is in their hearts, including the words that come out of their mouths. When Christians are growing in their faith, their words will show it.

APPLY

How we treat others shows our love for Jesus. In the boxes below, write 5 ways you can treat other people well.

RESPOND

PRAY: God, help me show Your love to others.

HIGHLIGHT

OLDER KIDS: Ephesians 1:20-23
YOUNGER KIDS: Ephesians 1:22-23
MEMORY VERSE: Psalm 51:12

EXPLAIN

- While he was in prison, Paul wrote a letter to the church in Ephesus to remind them of God's grace.
- Paul told them that he remembered and prayed for them often, thanking God for their faith and their love for others.
- Paul reminded the believers in Ephesus that Jesus is the Messiah, and He is all-powerful. God has made Him head of His church.
- Jesus is all-powerful because He is the Son of God and ruler over everything.

APPLY

Jesus is ruler over everything! Discuss: What is everything? What does it mean to rule over everything?

RESPOND

PRAY: Jesus, thank You for being the ruler over everything.

OLDER KIDS: Ephesians 2:8-10
YOUNGER KIDS: Ephesians 2:8-10
MEMORY VERSE: Psalm 51:12

- Paul's letter reminded believers in Ephesus that all people are saved because of God's grace.
- He taught that salvation is not about what we do but what Jesus has done for us. Christians cannot boast in their salvation. It is God's gift to everyone who trusts in Jesus.
- Paul told the Ephesians that people are God's good creation, and He created us for a good purpose.
- Paul reminded the church that salvation is a gift from God. There is nothing for believers to be proud of—God deserves all the glory. He created everyone, and He has a good plan and purpose for His creation.

Write the first letter of each picture in the box above to solve the code.

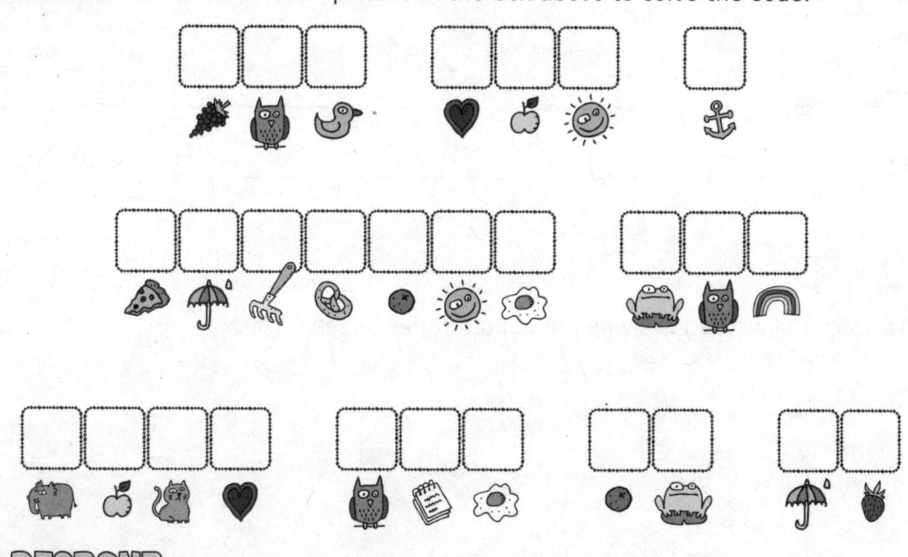

PRAY: Heavenly Father, thank You for Your gift of salvation.

OLDER KIDS: Ephesians 3:8-13

YOUNGER KIDS: Ephesians 3:11-13

MEMORY VERSE: Psalm 51:12

EXPLAIN

- Paul told the church at Ephesus that he had been given the task of telling the Gentiles about Jesus.
- Paul saw his time in prison as an opportunity to write to his friends, to encourage them, and to share the good news with anyone he could.
- Paul reminded them that Christians have boldness and confidence in their faith because of Jesus.
- Paul did not want the Ephesian church to feel bad for him. He wanted them to understand he was fulfilling God's purpose for his life, even while he was in prison.

God gives us opportunities to serve Him in many circumstances. Fill in the blanks to complete the memory verse, Psalm 51:12.

RESTORE ____ ,

AND ____ SPIRIT.

PRAY: God, thank You for giving me opportunities to serve You.

OLDER KIDS: Ephesians 4:25-32
YOUNGER KIDS: Ephesians 4:25-26
MEMORY VERSE: Psalm 51:12

EXPLAIN

- Paul wanted the church at Ephesus to know how they should act as followers of Jesus.
- Paul reminded the believers that before they knew Jesus, they acted one way. After Jesus changed them, their actions should reflect that change.
- Christians are called to remember the way Jesus loves and forgives, and they should love and forgive others in the same way.
- Paul reminded the church, that as followers of Jesus, their lives look different than others because Jesus has changed their hearts. Christians desire to honor God with their words, actions, and attitudes and reflect Jesus to those who don't trust in Him yet.

APPLY

Our actions should be different because of Jesus' love. Write 3 of your own actions that should be different because of Jesus' love.

PRAY: Heavenly Father, help me love and forgive others like Jesus.

OLDER KIDS: Ephesians 5:1-2
YOUNGER KIDS: Ephesians 5:1-2
MEMORY VERSE: Psalm 51:17

EXPLAIN

- Paul taught that Christians are called to imitate Christ, much like a child might imitate his parents.
- He reminded them that Christians are children of God. Everyone who trusts in Jesus is part of His family.
- Followers of Jesus are called to show love to others in the same way Jesus showed love by putting other before Himself.
- Paul gave instructions for how to live like Jesus, imitating Him by loving and serving others. Believers are to imitate Christ and His holiness in their actions, attitudes, and words.

APPLY

We should make the most of every chance we get to show others Jesus' love. In the circles below, write 3 ways you can show love to others.

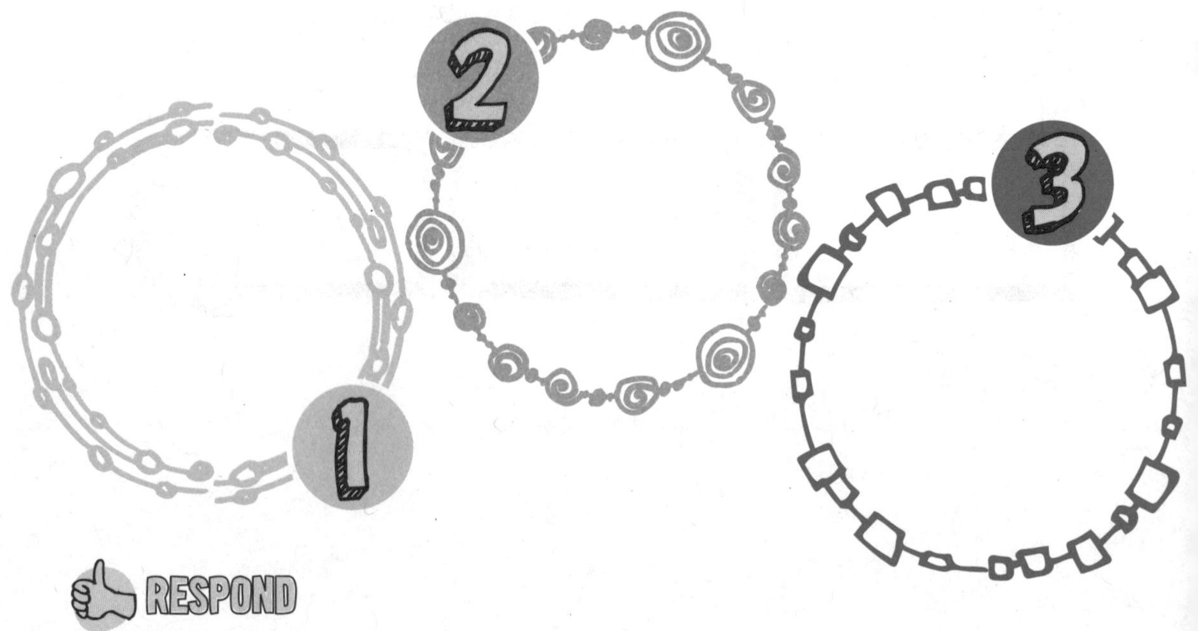

RESPOND

PRAY: Jesus, help me show others Your love every chance I get.

HIGHLIGHT

OLDER KIDS: Ephesians 6:1-4
YOUNGER KIDS: Ephesians 6:1-4
MEMORY VERSE: Psalm 51:17

EXPLAIN

- Paul continued encouraging the church in Ephesus about how they should treat others and submit to authority.
- Paul gave instructions to families about how to treat one another.
- Paul said that children should obey their parents just as they would obey God, and they will be blessed if they do.
- Paul explained how Christians should treat each other in family relationships, submitting to the authority God has planned for families. Husband and wives, children and parents—everyone is supposed to love and respect one another.

APPLY

As followers of Jesus, we are called to submit to those God puts in authority over us. Find the missing words by following the paths below.

We will be blessed when we _________ _________ _________.

RESPOND

PRAY: Heavenly Father, help me love and respect those around me.

OLDER KIDS: Philippians 1:20
YOUNGER KIDS: Philippians 1:20
MEMORY VERSE: Psalm 51:17

EXPLAIN

- Paul wrote to the church in Philippi from a Roman prison.
- Paul told them that he knew being in prison had given more people the chance to hear about Jesus.
- Paul's hope was that he would not be ashamed of the gospel, and Christ would be honored through him.
- Paul's life was not easy, but many people heard the good news because of his perseverance in the gospel and God's faithfulness. His life goal was to honor God, not to have an easy life.

APPLY

We can glorify God with our lives no matter where we are. Write Psalm 51:17 in the circle.

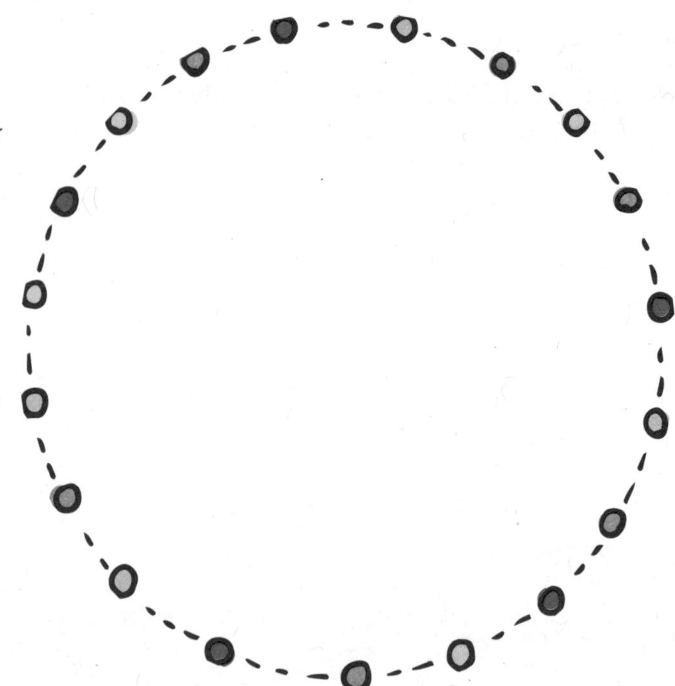

RESPOND

PRAY: Heavenly Father, help me glorify You no matter where I am.

HIGHLIGHT

OLDER KIDS: Philippians 2:1-4
YOUNGER KIDS: Philippians 2:3-4
MEMORY VERSE: Psalm 51:17

EXPLAIN

- Paul told the Philippian church they should be united with Jesus and His purpose.
- If believers are united with Jesus, they will be united with each other through their faith.
- Paul specifically encouraged the believers in Philippi to think of others as more important than themselves and to look out for others.
- Paul explained that Jesus is the perfect example of humility, and believers should have an attitude like His.

APPLY

God wants us to imitate Jesus and reflect Him to the people around us. Decode the message below to discover the main point from today's passage.

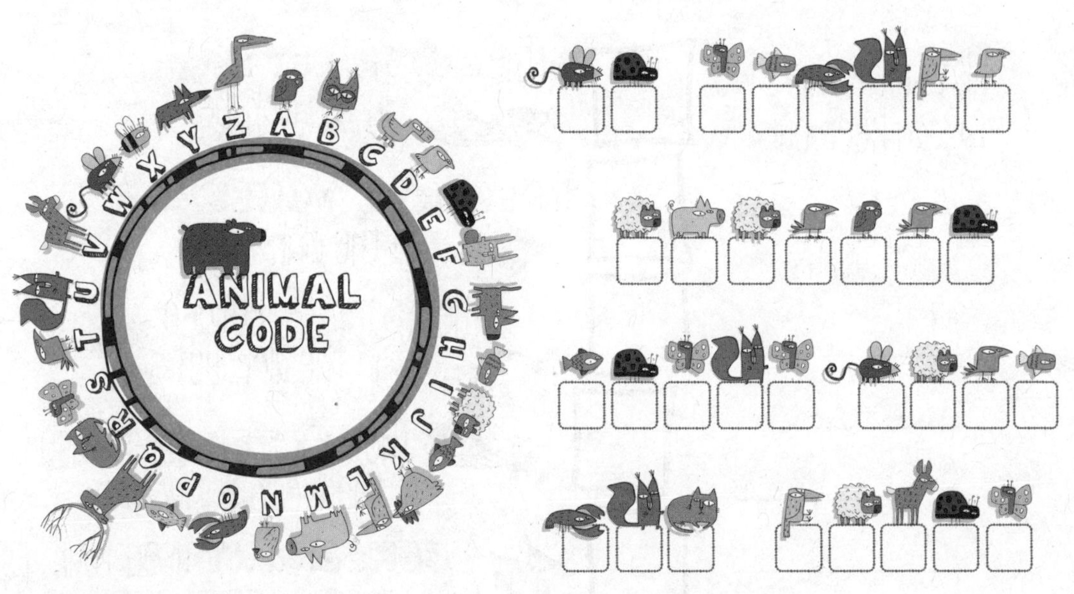

RESPOND

PRAY: God, help me imitate Jesus with my life so I can glorify You.

OLDER KIDS: Philippians 3:13-14
YOUNGER KIDS: Philippians 3:13-14
MEMORY VERSE: Psalm 51:17

- Sometimes Paul used analogies, or comparisons, to make a point. He compared the Christian life to a race to encourage the Philippian church to continue following Jesus.
- The prize Paul talked about at the end of the race was eternity with Jesus.
- Being focused on Jesus is what kept Paul going during hard times.
- Paul gave up a lot to follow Jesus and tell others about Him. He didn't regret giving those things up. The goal of his life was to follow Jesus.

Keeping our focus on Jesus helps us have joy in all things. Solve the clues to complete the sentence.

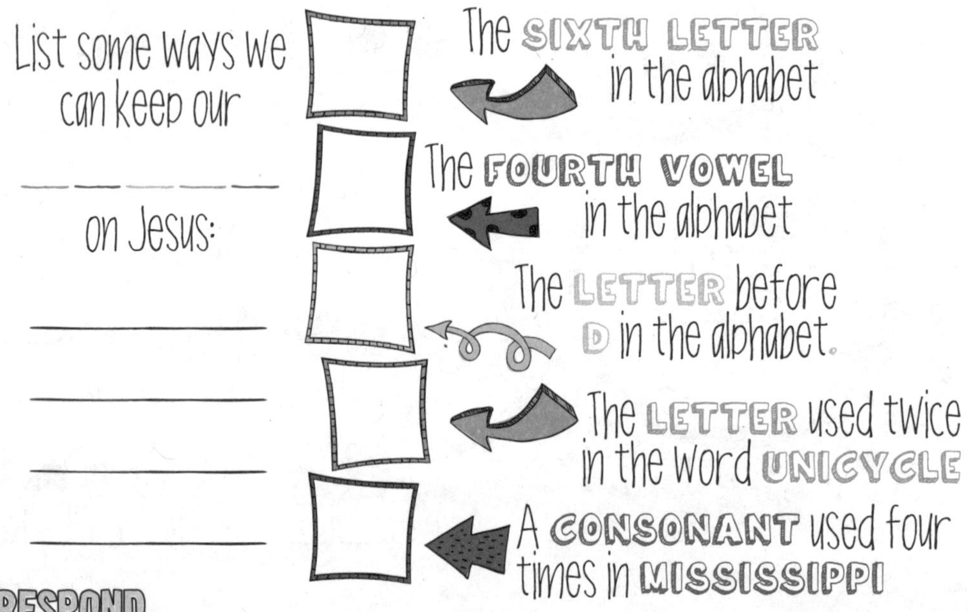

PRAY: Jesus, help me keep my focus on You.

HIGHLIGHT

OLDER KIDS: Philippians 4:11-13
YOUNGER KIDS: Philippians 4:13
MEMORY VERSE: Psalm 55:22

EXPLAIN

- Paul talked about trusting God in his letter to the Philippians.
- Paul told them he had learned to be satisfied with whatever he had in every circumstance.
- Paul explained that the secret to being content is knowing Christ will give you the strength to do what God wants you to do.
- Paul knew what it was like to have a lot of things and what it was like to have very few things. He learned he did not need material things to be happy because he knew God would provide him with the strength to do His will.

APPLY

In the box below, write what Paul said is the secret to being content.

RESPOND

PRAY: Heavenly Father, thank You for giving me the strength to follow You and do Your will.

HIGHLIGHT

OLDER KIDS: Philemon 1:8-10
YOUNGER KIDS: Philemon 1:8-10
MEMORY VERSE: Psalm 55:22

EXPLAIN

- Paul wrote a letter to a man named Philemon to remind him that the gospel has the power to change lives.
- Philemon's servant, Onesimus, ran away. After he ran away, he met Paul in Rome and became a Christian.
- Paul asked Philemon to forgive Onesimus and welcome him back just as he would welcome Paul.
- Christians should remember that the gospel is powerful to change and transform hearts. We should do everything we can to forgive others and make sure our friendships are healthy.

APPLY

We should forgive others because Jesus forgives us. Discuss: What does it mean to forgive?

RESPOND

PRAY: Jesus, thank You for forgiving me. Help me forgive others.

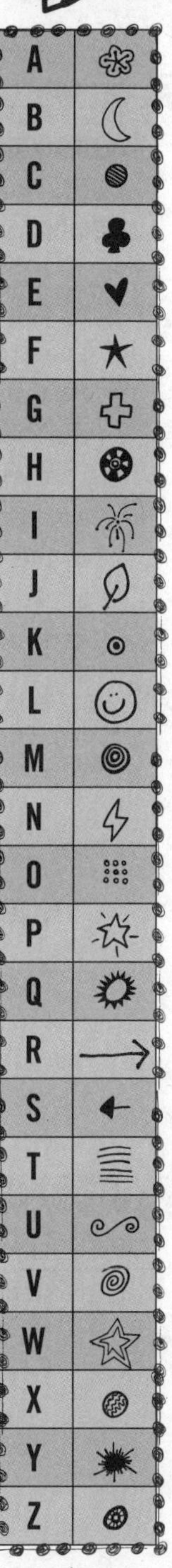

HIGHLIGHT

OLDER KIDS: Hebrews 1:1-4
YOUNGER KIDS: Hebrews 1:1-2
MEMORY VERSE: Psalm 55:22

EXPLAIN

- We don't know who wrote the book of Hebrews, but we know that the writer wanted to encourage Jewish Christians.
- The writer reminded the people that in the past, God spoke through prophets, but now He speaks through Jesus.
- Jesus is the Son of God, and He sits at the right hand of God.
- The writer of Hebrews lists attributes of Jesus and quotes the Old Testament. Jesus is the Son of God!

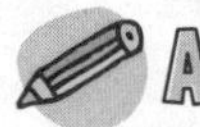

APPLY

Decode the message to reveal the main point of today's reading.

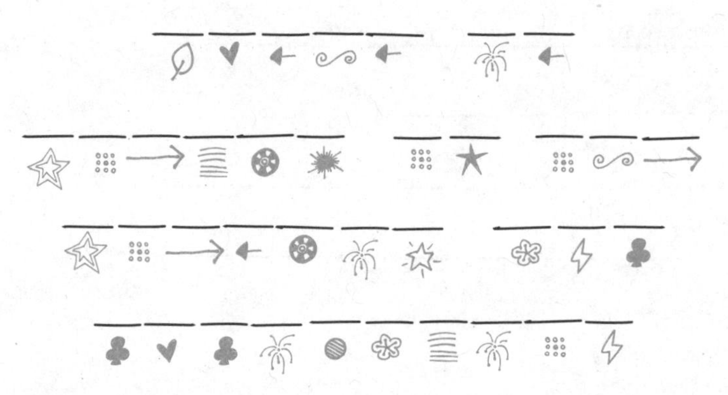

RESPOND

PRAY: Heavenly Father, thank You for speaking through Jesus.

OLDER KIDS: Hebrews 2:18
YOUNGER KIDS: Hebrews 2:18
MEMORY VERSE: Psalm 55:22

EXPLAIN

- The writer of Hebrews encouraged Christians to keep following Jesus.
- He wanted believers to understand why Jesus became a man and died for us—so that people could be saved from sin and live forever with God.
- The writer explained that Jesus understood suffering and temptation. He is sympathetic and merciful to those who endure suffering and temptation.
- In the Old Testament God spoke through prophets. When God sent Jesus, God spoke through Him. Jesus knew what it's like to be a man on earth—He came to earth to pay the price for sin.

Jesus came to save us from our sin. Fill in the blanks to complete Psalm 55:22.

CAST ______________________________,

AND ______________________________.

HE ______________________________

______________________________.

PRAY: Jesus, thank You for enduring suffering and temptation on earth so You can understand what I am going through.

HIGHLIGHT

OLDER KIDS: Hebrews 3:1-6
YOUNGER KIDS: Hebrews 3:5-6
MEMORY VERSE: Psalm 55:22

EXPLAIN

- The writer of Hebrews wrote about faithfulness and used Moses as an example.
- The Jews would have studied and been familiar with the stories of Moses.
- The writer pointed out that while Moses was a faithful servant in God's household, Jesus is the Son of God who is over God's household.
- The Jewish people studied a lot about their history. The writer of Hebrews used Moses as an example when discussing Jesus because he knew that the Jewish Christians would understand what he meant. Moses was faithful as a servant, but Jesus was the faithful Son of God.

APPLY

Jesus is the Son of God. He is always faithful and trustworthy. Cross out every other circle to solve the puzzle.

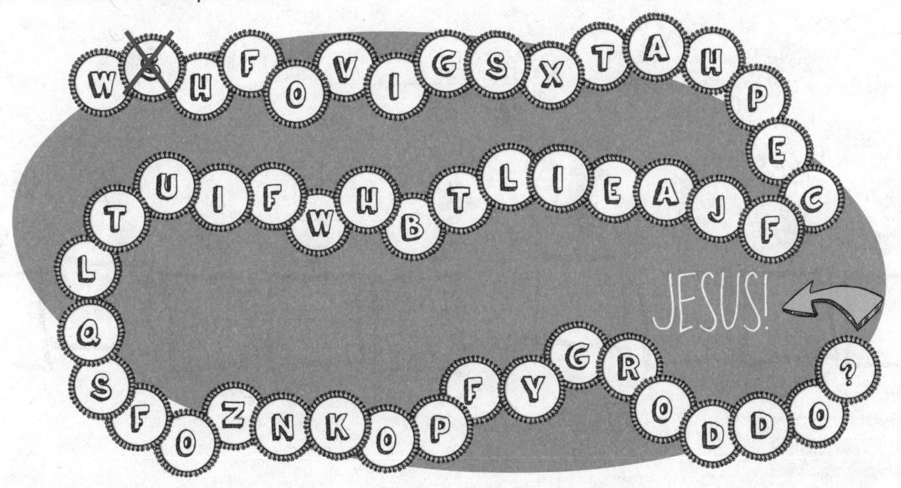

___ ___ ___ ___ ___ ___ ___?

RESPOND

PRAY: Jesus, thank You for being the faithful Son of God.

HIGHLIGHT

OLDER KIDS: Hebrews 4:12-13
YOUNGER KIDS: Hebrews 4:12-13
MEMORY VERSE: Proverbs 19:21

EXPLAIN

- The writer of Hebrews reminded people that God's Word is powerful.
- Hebrews says that God's Word is true and speaks to the hearts and every part of the Christian's life.
- God's Word teaches that no one can hide anything from God. He knows the truth about everything, even the thoughts and intentions of people.
- The writer explained that Christians will have to answer to God for their actions. God knows everything about people, and He loves them anyway. To be forgiven from sin, you just have to ask Him. He will forgive anyone who asks and confesses Jesus as Lord.

APPLY

We can trust that the Bible is powerful and true. Decode the words to fill in the blanks:

God's __________ and its __________ are for everyone.

X−1 L+3 Q+1 B+2

Z−6 R+2 Z−5 P+4 C+5

RESPOND

PRAY: Heavenly Father, thank You for Your Word and its truth.

OLDER KIDS: Hebrews 5:1-6
YOUNGER KIDS: Hebrews 5:5-6
MEMORY VERSE: Proverbs 19:21

EXPLAIN

- The writer of Hebrews wrote about how priests were called by God.
- Jesus was set apart by God to be the High Priest.
- Jesus is not like other high priests, because He never sinned.
- Jesus is the ultimate High Priest because He never needed to offer animal sacrifices to pay for sin. He gave His own life for us, and that sacrifice will last forever.

According to today's reading, who is Jesus to us? To discover the answer, begin with the H in the center and follow the directions below, writing each new letter in the box.

T	S	H	R	G
Q	E	I	S	T
J	G	H	A	U
E	P	E	H	R
W	I	U	X	N

[H] Start in the center.
[ ] Go ↑ up one space.
[ ] Go ← left one space and ↓ down one space.
[ ] Go ↓ down one space and → right two spaces.

[ ] Go ← left two spaces.
[ ] Go → right three spaces.
[ ] Go ↑ up two spaces and ← left two spaces.
[ ] Go ← left one space.
[ ] Go → right two spaces.
[ ] Go ↑ up one space and ← left three spaces.

PRAY: Jesus, thank You for being our High Priest.

OLDER KIDS: Hebrews 6:10-12
YOUNGER KIDS: Hebrews 6:10-12
MEMORY VERSE: Proverbs 19:21

EXPLAIN

- The writer of Hebrews encouraged believers to keep growing in their faith.
- Hebrews says that Christians can't just hope to grow in their faith in God—they must work at it with purpose.
- The writer suggested that followers of Jesus can look to people who are good examples of strong Christians and learn from them.
- It is important to continue following Jesus and growing in your faith. If believers don't purposely try to grow, they will stay like spiritual babies instead of growing up in their faith.

APPLY

Growing in our faith is important. In the space below, draw or write the names
of people you know who are strong Christians.
How can you learn from them?

RESPOND

PRAY: Heavenly Father, help me grow in my faith.

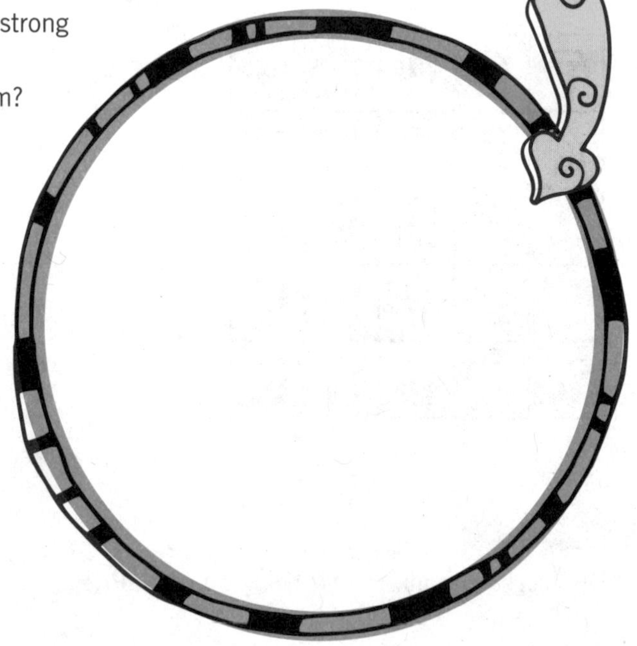

OLDER KIDS: Hebrews 7:24-25
YOUNGER KIDS: Hebrews 7:24-25
MEMORY VERSE: Proverbs 19:21

- The writer of Hebrews compared the high priest from the tribe of Levi to Jesus, the ultimate High Priest.
- Jesus is the Son of God, and His work as High Priest is forever, not like the priests of the Old Testament.
- The sacrifice Jesus made when He died to take the punishment for sin lasts forever.
- The sacrifices the Old Testament high priests made for people's sin didn't last. These sacrifices pointed ahead to Jesus' sacrifice. Because Jesus never sinned and He is the Son of God, His sacrifice lasts forever.

The salvation Jesus gives us never fades or goes away. Starting with the first box (J), place all the letters in along the path into the blue boxes in order. Then do the same with each color.

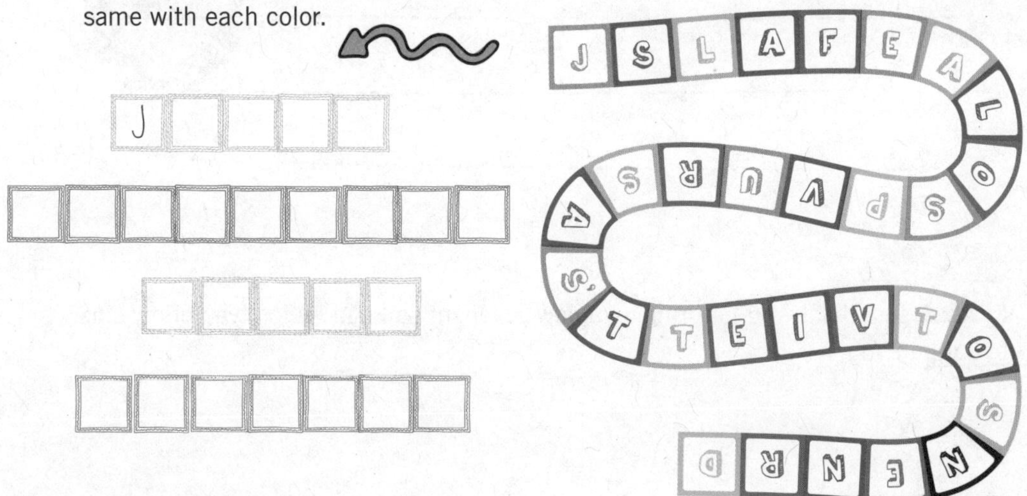

PRAY: Jesus, thank You for salvation that lasts forever.

OLDER KIDS: Hebrews 8:7,13
YOUNGER KIDS: Hebrews 8:7,13
MEMORY VERSE: Proverbs 19:21

EXPLAIN

- Hebrews explains that the "old covenant" was the law that God gave to Moses.
- God used this law to tell His people how to live before Jesus came.
- No one can follow the law without making mistakes. The law was intended to show us our need for a perfect Savior. That is why God sent Jesus to establish a new covenant for His people.
- The new covenant Jesus established is not about following rules, but about a changed heart.

APPLY

Jesus brought a new covenant so we can have salvation through faith in Him. Write Proverbs 19:21 to help you memorize this week's verse.

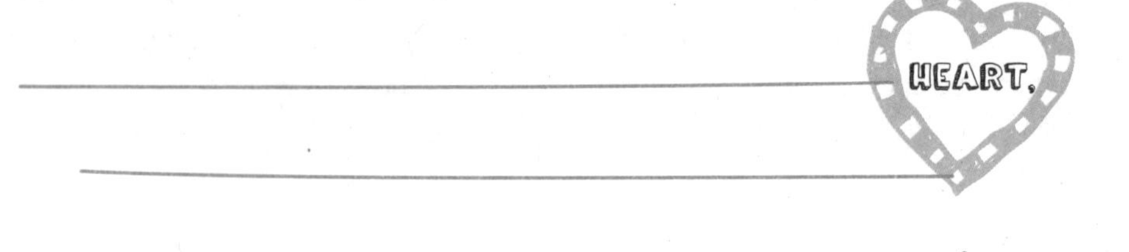

PRAY: Jesus, thank You for bringing a new covenant so I can be forgiven of my sins by faith in You.

HIGHLIGHT

OLDER KIDS: Hebrews 9:11-12
YOUNGER KIDS: Hebrews 9:11-12
MEMORY VERSE: Psalm 67:1

EXPLAIN

- The writer of Hebrews explained the difference between God's Old Testament law and the tabernacle during Moses' time and Jesus' sacrifice.
- During Moses' time, the priests would sprinkle blood from the animal sacrifices, following God's instructions for the sacrifices.
- The priests had to make sacrifices again and again. Their imperfect sacrifices were pointing ahead to Jesus' perfect sacrifice that lasts forever.
- We can see the difference between the sacrifice of animals and the sacrifice Jesus gave—Himself. The animal sacrifices didn't last, but Jesus' sacrifice of His own innocent blood lasts forever. When Jesus forgives, He forgives forever.

APPLY

Because He is perfect, Jesus' sacrifice lasts forever. Discuss: What does it mean that Jesus' sacrifice lasts forever?

RESPOND

PRAY: Jesus, thank You for Your sacrifice for me.

HIGHLIGHT

OLDER KIDS: Hebrews 10:23-25
YOUNGER KIDS: Hebrews 10:23-25
MEMORY VERSE: Psalm 67:1

EXPLAIN

- The Book of Hebrews addressed the church and explained that, because Jesus is the High Priest, Christians in the church can be sure that He will forgive sin.
- Christians can trust in God's promises and focus on loving others and honoring God.
- People in the church are called to encourage each other and spend time together in fellowship on a regular basis.
- The church is called to hold onto and depend on the promises of God. Because Christians have hope in Jesus for salvation, they can encourage one another even when things are hard.

APPLY

Write the first letter of each picture in the circle below it to complete the sentence.

We can be sure of God's promises and Jesus'...

RESPOND

PRAY: Jesus, thank You for the people You've put in my life to encourage me. Help me encourage them, too.

OLDER KIDS: Hebrews 11:1-3
YOUNGER KIDS: Hebrews 11:1-3
MEMORY VERSE: Psalm 67:1

- The Book of Hebrews teaches that having faith means trusting God and His promises, even if you may not get to see all of God's promises happen.
- God wants His children to have faith in Him and His promises.
- The writer of Hebrews gave many examples of people in the Bible who lived by faith.
- Practicing real faith means obeying God and trusting Him no matter what. It takes faith to obey God and follow Him.

We can believe God, even when we don't see all His promises happen. That's faith. List 3 ways we can have faith in God.

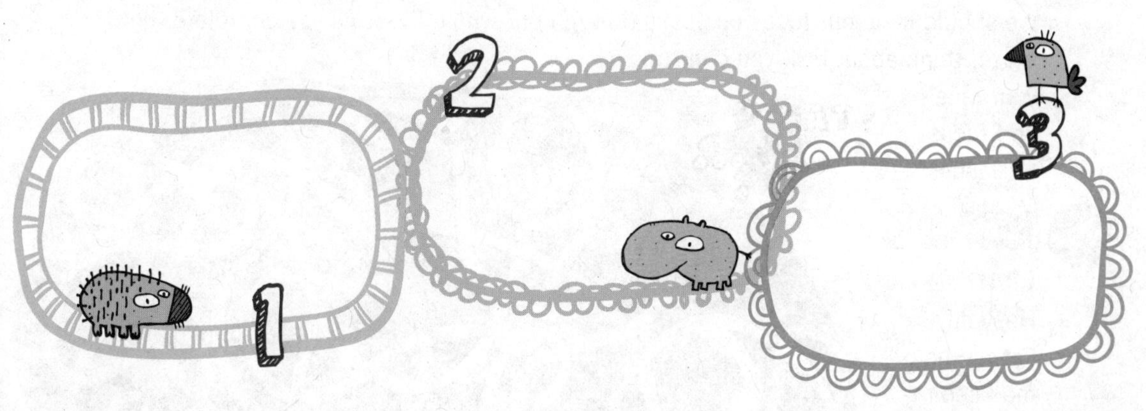

PRAY: Heavenly Father, help me live by faith and trust You no matter what.

OLDER KIDS: Hebrews 12:1-2
YOUNGER KIDS: Hebrews 12:1-2
MEMORY VERSE: Psalm 67:1

EXPLAIN

- The writer of Hebrews taught that life is like a race—a long race.
- Running a long race takes endurance (strength for a long time). Christians keep running their race by focusing on Jesus.
- The writer encouraged the people to remember Jesus and how He endured the cross.
- To run with endurance means Christians keep going and depend on God for strength. Jesus is the source of salvation. His followers can continue to live by faith with confidence, because Jesus has changed our hearts and is working to make us more like Him.

APPLY

We should keep our focus on Jesus through our whole lives. As you complete the maze, think about how you can run your race and focus on Jesus.

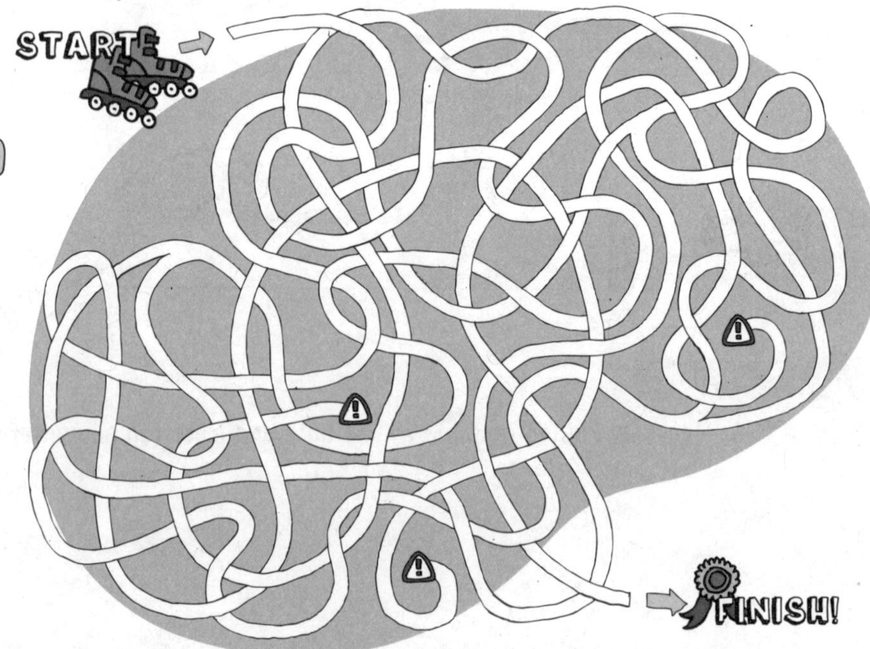

RESPOND

PRAY: Heavenly Father, help me keep my focus on You all the time.

OLDER KIDS: Hebrews 13:20-21
YOUNGER KIDS: Hebrews 13:20-21
MEMORY VERSE: Psalm 67:1

EXPLAIN

- The writer of Hebrews closed the letter by reminding Christians to live in a way that shows Jesus to others.
- The writer encouraged believers that God was giving them everything needed to follow His will.
- Disciples of Jesus should live in a way that honors God and gives glory to Him.
- God has high expectations, and no one could never fulfill them on their own. We trust Jesus' perfection to meet God's expectations.

How you live shows Jesus' work in your life. Fill in the blanks to complete this week's memory verse.

________________________________ BLESS US,

____________________ HIS FACE

________________________.

PRAY: Jesus, help me follow God's will and give glory to Him.

HIGHLIGHT

OLDER KIDS: 1 Timothy 1:3-4
YOUNGER KIDS: 1 Timothy 1:3-4
MEMORY VERSE: Psalm 68:5

EXPLAIN

- Paul wrote a letter to Timothy to encourage him.
- Timothy began spending time with Paul while he was still a young man, and they remained friends for a long time.
- Paul began his letter by warning Timothy about people who taught wrong things about Jesus and God's plan.
- Paul's letters to Timothy instructed him in how to minister to others so he could be a good leader in the church.

APPLY

It is important to listen to leaders who mentor and encourage us in our faith. Find the highlighted words in the word search below.

Y	N	T	S	O	H	H	R	W	A	R	N	I	N	G	A
O	G	E	N	T	I	M	O	T	H	Y	X	R	E	X	N
U	F	R	I	E	N	D	S	C	M	U	P	M	A	L	T
N	M	C	L	E	A	D	E	R	J	A	A	R	D	K	A
G	S	H	C	Y	I	F	I	U	E	S	U	V	E	D	U
G	E	U	V	H	N	A	H	B	W	R	L	W	D	B	G
T	C	R	W	G	J	L	E	T	T	E	R	X	I	N	H
R	C	H	R	W	R	T	M	I	N	I	S	T	E	R	T
I	N	S	T	R	U	C	T	E	D	C	H	U	R	C	H

RESPOND

PRAY: Heavenly Father, help me listen to others who encourage me in my faith.

OLDER KIDS: 1 Timothy 2:1-4
YOUNGER KIDS: 1 Timothy 2:1-4
MEMORY VERSE: Psalm 68:5

- Paul taught Timothy about the importance of prayer.
- Paul said Christians should pray for everyone, including people who are in authority.
- The mission of every believer is to spread the gospel. The Holy Spirit gives strength, boldness, and peace through prayer to share the good news of Jesus.
- Praying along with other believers is an important part of following Jesus and worshiping with others.

APPLY

Praying is an important part of following Jesus. Decode the message by placing the first letter of each object in the box above it.

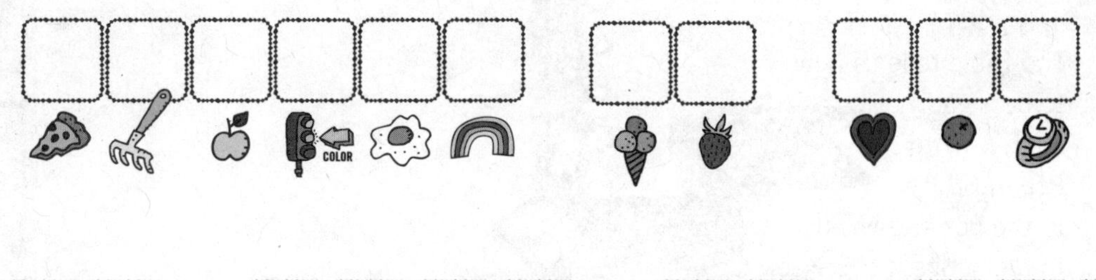

PRAY: Heavenly Father, thank You for giving us prayer so we can talk to You.

HIGHLIGHT

OLDER KIDS: 1 Timothy 3:1-4
YOUNGER KIDS: 1 Timothy 3:1-4
MEMORY VERSE: Psalm 68:5

EXPLAIN

- Paul wrote a letter to his friend Timothy to teach and encourage him in his ministry.
- Paul gave Timothy instructions for being a godly leader.
- Paul stated that a good leader should be kind, fair, honest, and faithful.
- Timothy was leading a church, and Paul wanted to help him be a godly leader. The qualities Paul taught Timothy to look for in leaders in the church are qualities all Christians should to model in their lives.

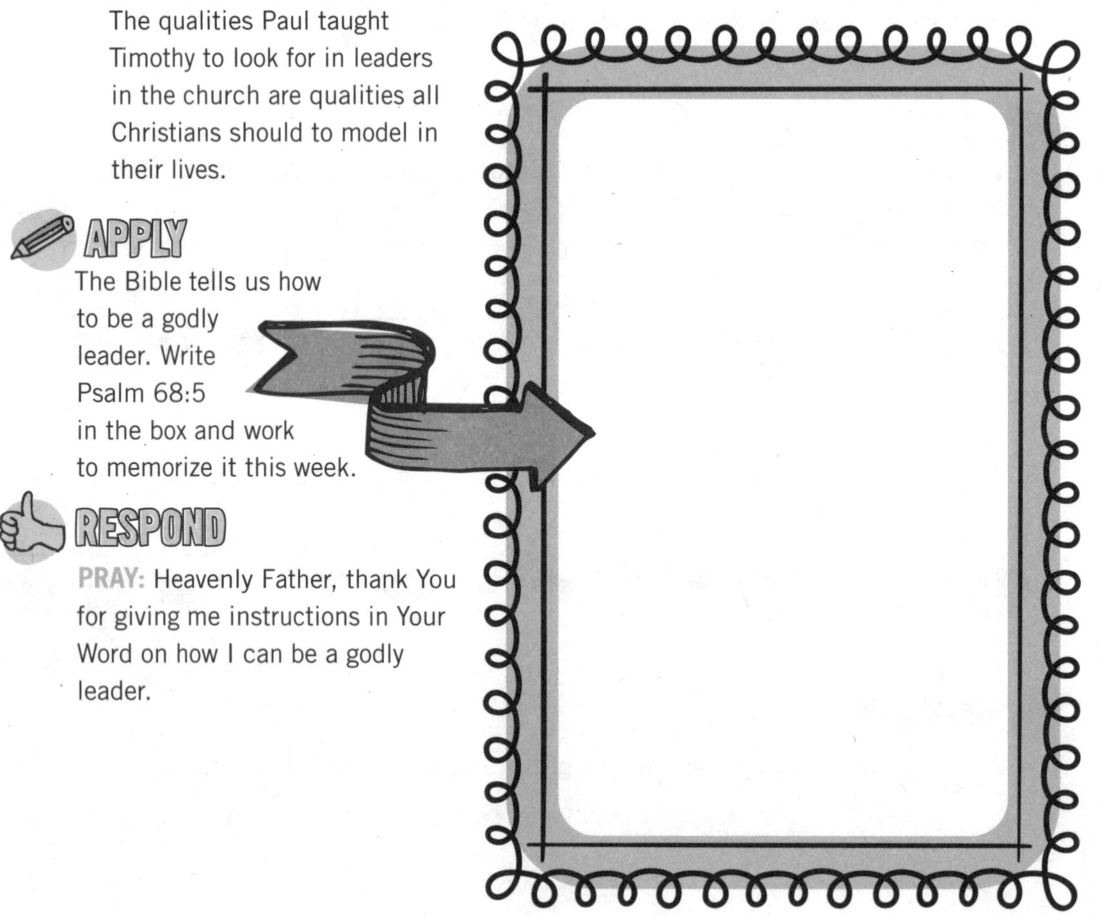

APPLY

The Bible tells us how to be a godly leader. Write Psalm 68:5 in the box and work to memorize it this week.

RESPOND

PRAY: Heavenly Father, thank You for giving me instructions in Your Word on how I can be a godly leader.

OLDER KIDS: 1 Timothy 4:11-12
YOUNGER KIDS: 1 Timothy 4:12
MEMORY VERSE: Psalm 68:5

EXPLAIN

- Paul continued giving Timothy instructions for leading the church well.
- Paul wanted Timothy to know that, even if he was young, he could make a difference for Jesus.
- Every Christian can be a good example to others through both speech and actions.
- Paul wanted Timothy to be a good leader in his church. He gave Timothy instructions for leading and teaching others to be good leaders, too. Paul wanted to make sure Timothy understood how to act and treat others so he would be a good leader for the church.

APPLY

We don't have to wait until we grow up to serve God and point others to Him. Draw a line from each skill at the top and match it to a way that we can serve God using that skill.

RESPOND

PRAY: Heavenly Father, help me to serve You and point others to You.

OLDER KIDS: 1 Timothy 5:1-2
YOUNGER KIDS: 1 Timothy 5:1-2
MEMORY VERSE: Psalm 68:5

EXPLAIN

- Paul continued his letter by giving Timothy instructions on getting along with people in the church.
- Paul wanted Timothy to understand that believers should respect others who are older and younger than them.
- Paul also wanted Timothy to understand how to show compassion to those who need it.
- Paul gave Timothy detailed instructions on taking care of people in the church who needed help and holding leaders in the church accountable. Christians can be respectful in offering compassion and in holding others accountable.

APPLY

We should have respect for all people. List 3 ways we can be respectful of others.

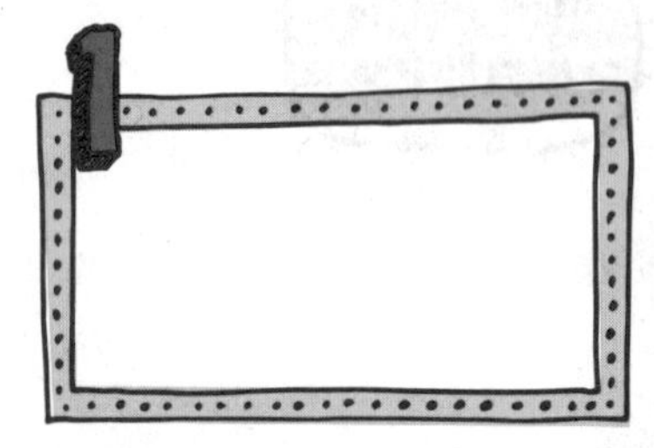

PRAY: Heavenly Father, help me be respectful of all people.

HIGHLIGHT

OLDER KIDS: 1 Timothy 6:17-19
YOUNGER KIDS: 1 Timothy 6:18-19
MEMORY VERSE: Proverbs 20:27

EXPLAIN

- As he closed his letter, Paul discussed handling money God's way.
- Paul wanted Timothy to understand that greed is not godly.
- Those whom God blesses with riches are expected to use it for God's glory.
- Paul wanted Timothy to understand that money is not bad, but that people's attitude about money can be sinful. He didn't want Timothy to be worried about getting more money, but to spend his time focused on following God.

APPLY

Following God is more important than anything else. Go through the maze to find the most important thing.

RESPOND

PRAY: God, help me follow Your plan.

OLDER KIDS: 2 Timothy 1:13-14
YOUNGER KIDS: 2 Timothy 1:13-14
MEMORY VERSE: Proverbs 20:27

EXPLAIN

- Paul wrote a second letter to Timothy to teach him about helping others grow in their faith.
- Paul reminded Timothy that discipleship should be an important part of his ministry.
- Paul meant that teaching others Scripture and helping them grow in their faith is a very important part of ministry, and Paul had prepared Timothy to do those things.
- Paul used himself as an example because he had discipled Timothy. He knew Timothy was able to disciple others, and it would be important to his ministry.

APPLY

Everyone who follows Jesus can disciple someone else. Decode the message by placing the first letter of each object in the box above it.

PRAY: Heavenly Father, help me disciple others.

OLDER KIDS: 2 Timothy 2:15
YOUNGER KIDS: 2 Timothy 2:15
MEMORY VERSE: Proverbs 20:27

EXPLAIN

- Paul encouraged Timothy to be strengthened by God's grace and teach others the gospel.
- Paul reminded Timothy to keep growing in his faith and following God.
- Paul didn't want Timothy to get discouraged, but instead, to keep teaching others how to understand and teach God's Word.
- Paul was in prison in Rome and thought this might be his last chance to send a message to Timothy. He encouraged Timothy to be strong in his faith in God and always to teach others about Jesus.

We should always live in a way that honors God and teaches others about Him. List 3 ways you can teach others about Jesus.

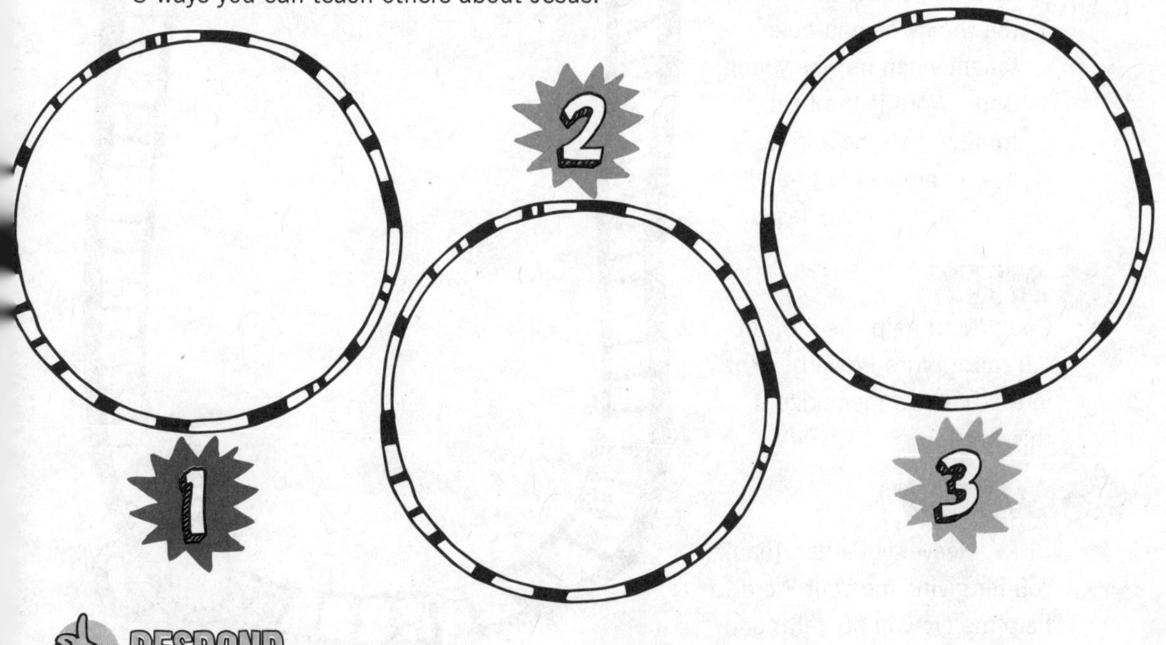

RESPOND

PRAY: Heavenly Father, thank You for people who encourage me to follow You.

HIGHLIGHT

OLDER KIDS: 2 Timothy 3:13-17
YOUNGER KIDS: 2 Timothy 3:16-17
MEMORY VERSE: Proverbs 20:27

EXPLAIN

- Paul told Timothy he would meet people who were deceiving others and confusing what is true with what is not.
- Paul encouraged Timothy to remember what he had been taught when he was a child—the Word of God.
- Paul reminded Timothy that Scripture is the Word of God. Timothy needed it to help others to live like Jesus.
- Paul warned Timothy to be careful of evil people. Paul told Timothy not to participate in wrong behavior, but to remember the things he had been taught when he was young. God's Word is the best thing to help people learn how to grow in faith and become more like Jesus.

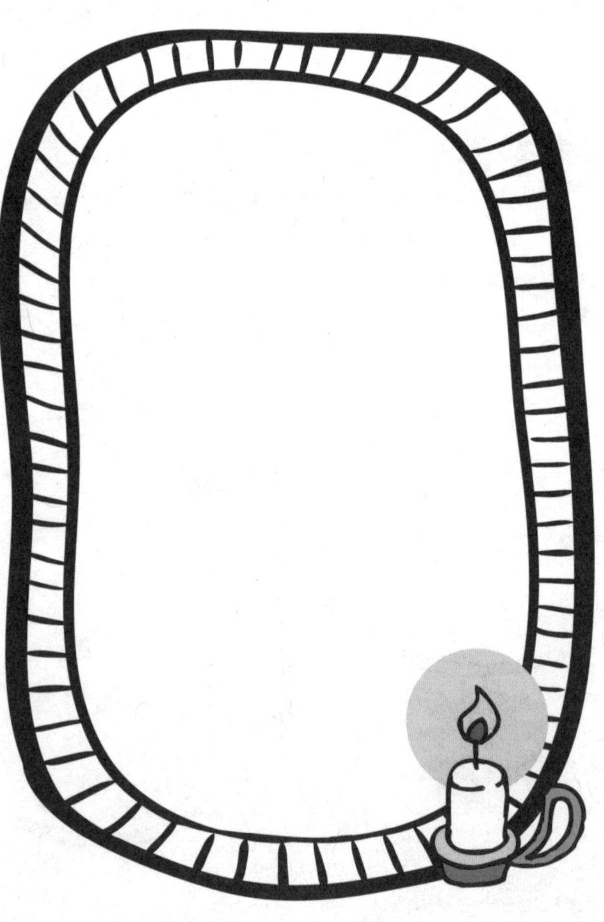

APPLY

God's Word helps us grow in our faith. Write Proverbs 20:27 in the box and memorize it this week.

RESPOND

PRAY: Heavenly Father, thank You for giving me Your Word to help me grow in my faith and be more like You.

HIGHLIGHT

OLDER KIDS: 2 Timothy 4:1-5
YOUNGER KIDS: 2 Timothy 4:2
MEMORY VERSE: Proverbs 20:27

EXPLAIN

- Paul closed his letter to Timothy by reminding him to be faithful in preaching God's Word.
- Paul knew people would be tempted by sin and would stray away from following God.
- He wanted Timothy to remain strong in his faith no matter what others did.
- Paul knew Timothy would have challenges, and he wanted Timothy to be prepared to continue to lead. He encouraged Timothy to continue on and fulfill his ministry.

APPLY

We all have the opportunity to tell others the truth of God's Word. Complete the sentence about today's reading by using the clues provided.

RESPOND

PRAY:
Heavenly Father, help me be strong and tell others Your truth.

HIGHLIGHT

OLDER KIDS: Titus 1:5-9
YOUNGER KIDS: Titus 1:5-6
MEMORY VERSE: Proverbs 21:1

EXPLAIN

- Paul wrote a letter to Titus, a Greek man who had ministered with Paul. Titus was at a church in Crete.
- Paul gave Titus instructions on appointing leaders at the church in Crete.
- Leaders in the church must be strong and help the believers in the church grow in their faith.
- Paul never forgot his friends, and he continued to help them grow even when he couldn't be with them. That is why he wrote to Titus, Timothy, and others—to help them stay strong in their faith.

APPLY

Strong leaders who follow Jesus can help others grow in their faith. Discuss: How can we help others grow in their faith?

RESPOND

PRAY: Heavenly Father, use me help others grow in their faith.

OLDER KIDS: Titus 2:11-15
YOUNGER KIDS: Titus 2:11
MEMORY VERSE: Proverbs 21:1

EXPLAIN

- Paul wrote to Titus about specific groups of people and how they should behave as followers of Jesus.
- All believers should behave in a godly way because Christians know God and reflect Him to others.
- When disciples of Jesus follow Him and grow in their faith, their lives will look different from the world around them.
- While Paul has specific instructions for different groups of believers, some things apply to everyone, like self-control, integrity, and commitment to truth.

APPLY

As our lives look more like Jesus, people will see Him in our lives. Write Proverbs 21:1 in the box to help you memorize it this week.

RESPOND

PRAY: Jesus, help me to live like You.

HIGHLIGHT

OLDER KIDS: Titus 3:1-3
YOUNGER KIDS: Titus 3:1-3
MEMORY VERSE: Proverbs 21:1

EXPLAIN

- Paul finished his letter to Titus by discussing how believers should act.
- Paul explained that believers should have an attitude of obedience, kindness, peace, and humility.
- Following Jesus changes a person's life, and that should be seen in her attitude and behavior.
- Paul encouraged Titus to remind people in the church that they had been changed by Jesus, and their lives should reflect it.

APPLY

When Jesus changes our lives, our attitudes and behaviors should change as well. Crack the code and fill in the box below.

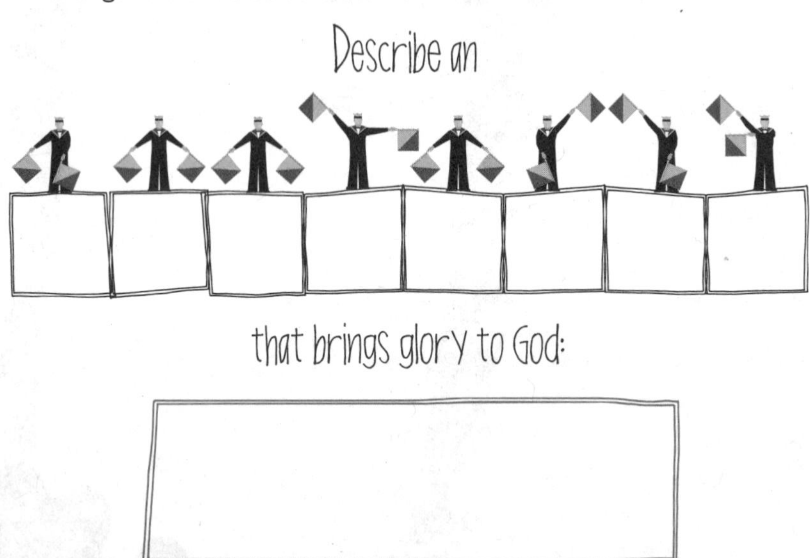

RESPOND

PRAY: Heavenly Father, help me bring glory to You with my attitude and behavior.

HIGHLIGHT

OLDER KIDS: 1 Peter 1:13-16
YOUNGER KIDS: 1 Peter 1:13-16
MEMORY VERSE: Proverbs 21:1

EXPLAIN

- Peter wrote a letter to Christians who were being persecuted (treated badly) for their belief in Jesus.
- Peter reminded them their hope is in Christ, not their circumstances.
- Peter told them that believers are called by God to be holy.
- Christians were being persecuted all over the Roman empire. Peter wrote to encourage them to be faithful even during persecution. He wanted them to understand that their faith and hope was in God, not their circumstances.

APPLY

Peter taught that we are called by God to be holy and to continue trusting Him no matter our circumstances. Use the decoder to the right to solve the flag puzzle about today's Bible reading.

We should follow God even during __________ __________.

RESPOND

PRAY: God, help me always follow You, even in tough times.

HIGHLIGHT

OLDER KIDS: 1 Peter 2:1-3
YOUNGER KIDS: 1 Peter 2:1-3
MEMORY VERSE: Proverbs 21:1

EXPLAIN

- Peter explained how believers should act as disciples of Jesus.
- He used the example of a baby who wants milk to explain how believers should want to study God's Word.
- Christians experience the goodness of God and want to know more about Him.
- When a believer follows Jesus by studying God's Word and growing in faith and discipleship, God gives that person power to get rid of behaviors that do not honor Him and cultivate behaviors that do honor Him.

APPLY

As we grow in our faith, God gives us power to live in a way that glorifies Him. Draw something you can do today that glorifies God!

RESPOND

PRAY: Heavenly Father, help me live in a way that glorifies You.

HIGHLIGHT

OLDER KIDS: 1 Peter 3:8-9
YOUNGER KIDS: 1 Peter 3:8-9
MEMORY VERSE: Psalm 84:10

EXPLAIN

- In this letter, Peter gave instructions for how Christians are to show love to others.
- Peter told believers that they should get along with one another in grace and humility.
- Followers of Jesus are called to be compassionate, humble, and bless one another.
- Peter gave instructions for Christians to live in unity and to care for one another. Disciples of Jesus are called to live differently, pointing others to Him in words, actions, and attitudes.

APPLY

Our behavior can point people toward Jesus. Use Morse code to solve the message below.

What can my behavior do?

___ ___ ___ ___ ___
.--. --- .. -. -

___ ___ ___ ___ ___ ___
--- - .... . .-. ...

___ ___   ___ ___ ___ ___ ___
- ---   .--- . ... ..- ...

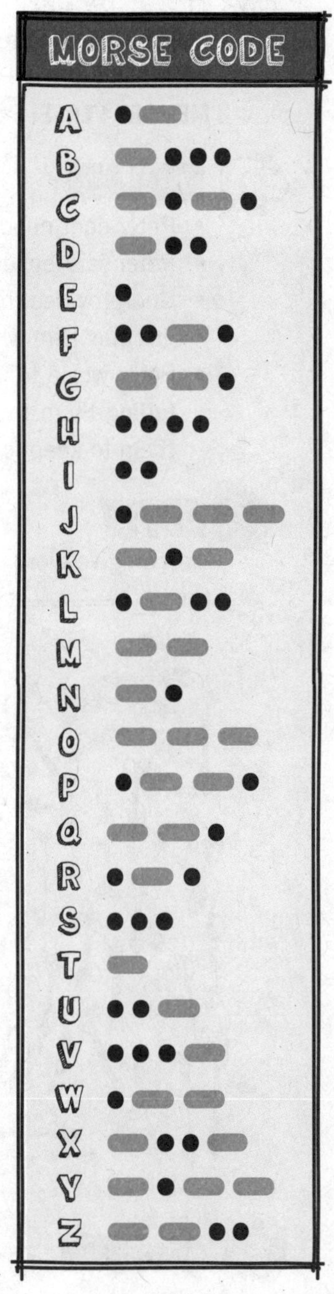

RESPOND

PRAY: Jesus, help me to point others to You with my words, actions, and attitude.

HIGHLIGHT

OLDER KIDS: 1 Peter 4:8-11
YOUNGER KIDS: 1 Peter 4:8-11
MEMORY VERSE: Psalm 84:10

EXPLAIN

- Peter continued his letter by telling Christians how to treat others.
- Peter said believers should love and care for each other without complaining.
- God provides the strength and ability for His followers to care for others, and it glorifies Him when the church takes care of each other.
- Peter wrote to Christians who were being persecuted for their faith. Instead of telling them to hide, Peter told them to keep following Jesus. He also wanted them to keep loving and caring for others so they could glorify God.

APPLY

We can give glory to God by caring for others. Color in all the arrows that look like this: [arrow] What are we to show to others to glorify God?

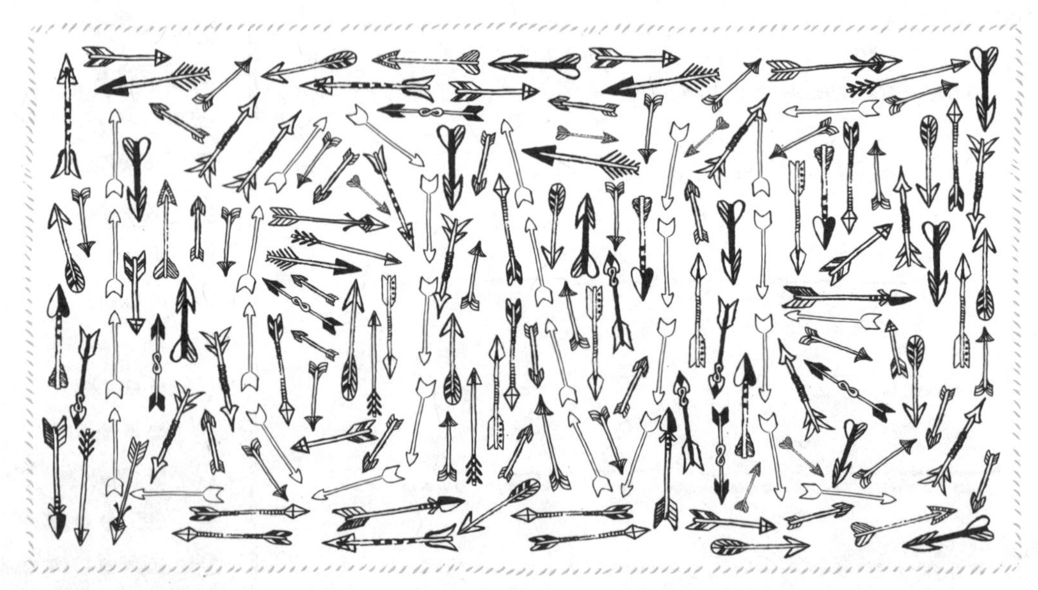

RESPOND

PRAY: Heavenly Father, help me glorify You by loving and caring for other people.

HIGHLIGHT

OLDER KIDS: 1 Peter 5:5-7
YOUNGER KIDS: 1 Peter 5:5-7
MEMORY VERSE: Psalm 84:10

EXPLAIN

- Peter finished this letter to the church by telling believers to be humble.
- He said being humble means not thinking about yourself and putting the needs of others before your own.
- Peter wrote that humility (putting others before yourself) helps Christians depend on God and be thankful for how He provides.
- Peter wanted believers to be humble. He knew that, as Christians were being persecuted, humility would be an important part of helping them depend on God.

APPLY

Putting others' needs before our own with a happy heart brings glory to God. Write Psalm 84:10 in the box and work to memorize it this week.

RESPOND

PRAY: God, help me be humble and depend on You. Show me how I can put others before myself today.

HIGHLIGHT

OLDER KIDS: 2 Peter 1:5-8
YOUNGER KIDS: 2 Peter 1:5-7
MEMORY VERSE: Psalm 84:10

EXPLAIN

- Peter wrote a second letter to believers to remind them that the grace of God changes their lives.
- He described how God's power changes the lives of believers to live for Him.
- The Holy Spirit brings characteristics of godliness to the life of every believer. Exercising those godly characteristics brings glory to God.
- When Christ followers pursue godliness and godly characteristics, God is glorified and the church is useful to the kingdom of God.

APPLY

We can be useful to God's kingdom and bring glory to Him by growing in our faith and treating others like God says we should. Follow the paths to see how God's power changed each person's life.

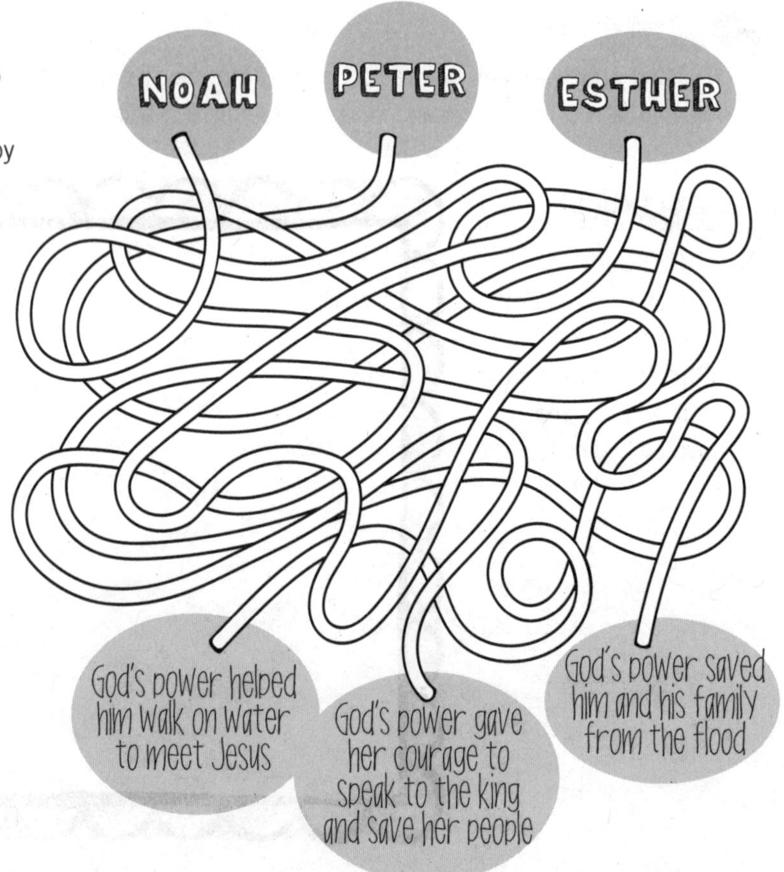

RESPOND

PRAY: Heavenly Father, help me bring glory to You.

OLDER KIDS: 2 Peter 2:1-3
YOUNGER KIDS: 2 Peter 2:1
MEMORY VERSE: Psalm 84:10

EXPLAIN

- Peter warned the church about people who would teach wrong things about Jesus. These people were called false prophets or false teachers.
- Peter explained that the lies of false teachers would bring destruction, and many people would be tricked by them.
- False teachers wanted to trick people for their own benefit, not for God's glory.
- Peter gave examples of God's judgment against people who went against Him in the Old Testament. Just like there were false teachers during those times, there would also be false teachers that come and try to mislead the church from the truth of God's Word.

APPLY

It is important to stay true to God and His Word. Discuss: What does it mean to stay true to God's Word?

RESPOND

PRAY: Heavenly Father, help me stay true to You and Your Word.

HIGHLIGHT

OLDER KIDS: 2 Peter 3:17-18
YOUNGER KIDS: 2 Peter 3:17-18
MEMORY VERSE: Proverbs 21:23

EXPLAIN

- Peter encouraged the believers to grow in their faith and to watch out for false teachers.
- Peter warned them about people who would try to teach wrong things about Jesus. The church should be on guard and remain faithful to God's Word.
- Peter wanted everyone to grow in their faith and be ready for Jesus when He returns.
- Peter encouraged believers to grow in their relationship with God. He alerted them to watch out for people who would try to trick them into believing wrong things. He challenged them to be ready for Jesus to return and to continue growing in grace and knowledge of Jesus.

APPLY

As we wait for Jesus to return, we should continue to grow in our faith. Color the word to help you remember to grow in your faith.

PRAY: Heavenly Father, help me grow in my faith and be ready for Jesus to return.

HIGHLIGHT

OLDER KIDS: John 1:1-5, 14
YOUNGER KIDS: John 1:1-2, 14
MEMORY VERSE: Proverbs 21:23

EXPLAIN

- Jesus is called the Word. He was with God, and He is God.
- Jesus was present during the creation of the world.
- He became a man and lived on earth in order to rescue sinners from their sin.
- Jesus never sinned. He was, is, and always has been perfect. He died on the cross and rose again to fulfill God's plan for the forgiveness of sin.

APPLY

Jesus came to live on earth because He loves us. Keeping the letters in order, fill in the letters from the path to the correct color boxes below.

RESPOND

PRAY: Jesus, thank You for loving me and for coming to earth to pay the penalty for my sin.

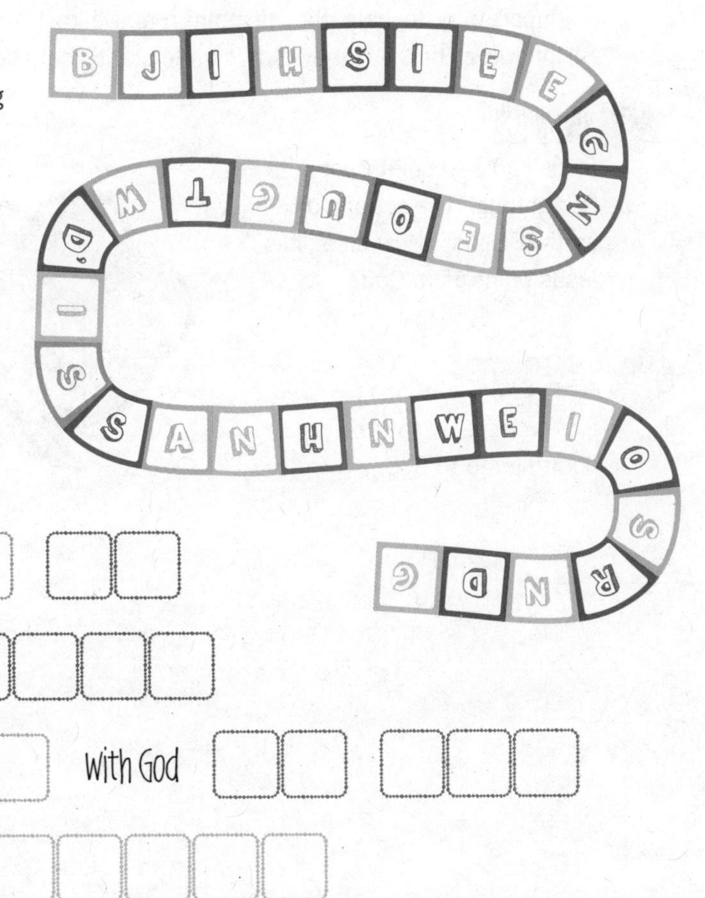

OLDER KIDS: John 2:6-11
YOUNGER KIDS: John 2:7-8, 11
MEMORY VERSE: Proverbs 21:23

EXPLAIN

- Jesus and His disciples were at a wedding where they ran out of wine.
- Jesus' mother, Mary, asked Him to help. Jesus turned water into wine for the guests.
- Jesus did this miracle so the disciples would see His glory and understand He is the Messiah.
- Jesus wasn't quite ready to show His glory to everyone yet, but He used this opportunity to help the disciples believe in Him. The disciples were already following Him, but they didn't understand that He was the true Messiah.

APPLY

Jesus came to point people to God through His actions on earth. Discuss: How else does Jesus point us to God?

RESPOND

PRAY: Jesus, thank You for pointing me to God.

OLDER KIDS: John 3:16-18
YOUNGER KIDS: John 3:16
MEMORY VERSE: Proverbs 21:23

- Nicodemus, a religious leader, was curious about Jesus and went to see Him one night.
- Jesus explained to Nicodemus that God loves everyone, and He sent His Son, Jesus, to save people from sin.
- He explained that God wants every person to believe in Jesus.
- Nicodemus did not believe Jesus was the Messiah, but he knew Jesus had been sent from God. Jesus explained being "born again" means letting the Holy Spirit change your life through faith in Jesus.

Jesus is the Son of God. He came to save people from sin. Decode the question and write the answer in the blank below.

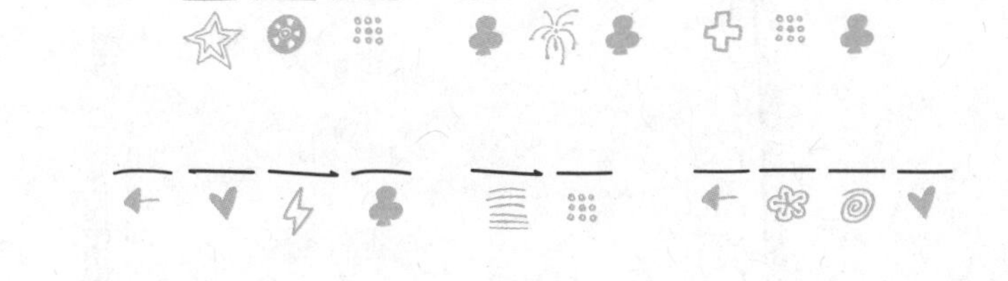

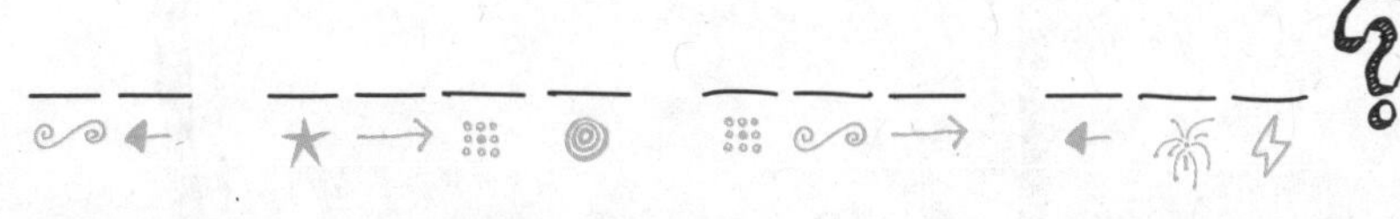

____

PRAY: Jesus, thank You for coming to save me from my sin.

OLDER KIDS: John 4:13-15
YOUNGER KIDS: John 4:13-15
MEMORY VERSE: Proverbs 21:23

EXPLAIN

- Jesus spoke to a Samaritan woman who was getting water from a well.
- He told the Samaritan woman that He could give her living water.
- The living water Jesus was talking about is the Holy Spirit.
- Jesus met a Samaritan woman at a well. Jews and Samaritans did not get along very well, but Jesus showed love toward the woman. He told her about the Holy Spirit and faith that leads to eternal life.
  She recognized Jesus as the Messiah.

APPLY

When we trust in Jesus and have faith in Him, He gives us the living water of the Holy Spirit. Write Proverbs 21:23 in the box to help you memorize it this week.

RESPOND

PRAY: Jesus, thank You for sending the Holy Spirit.

HIGHLIGHT

OLDER KIDS: John 5:37-40
YOUNGER KIDS: John 5:37
MEMORY VERSE: Psalm 86:5

EXPLAIN

- Jesus healed a sick man on the Sabbath day, and the religious leaders were angry with Him.
- Jesus made it clear that He was sent by God, so He follows God's instructions.
- Jesus also told the people that the Scriptures tell about Him, so they should believe in Him.
- Religious leaders tried to convince everyone Jesus was disobeying God. Jesus always followed God's instructions and lived in obedience to God's commands.

APPLY

Jesus is the Son of God and fulfilled His instructions and commands. Fill in the boxes with the correct letters to spell out who God sent to be our example of obedience.

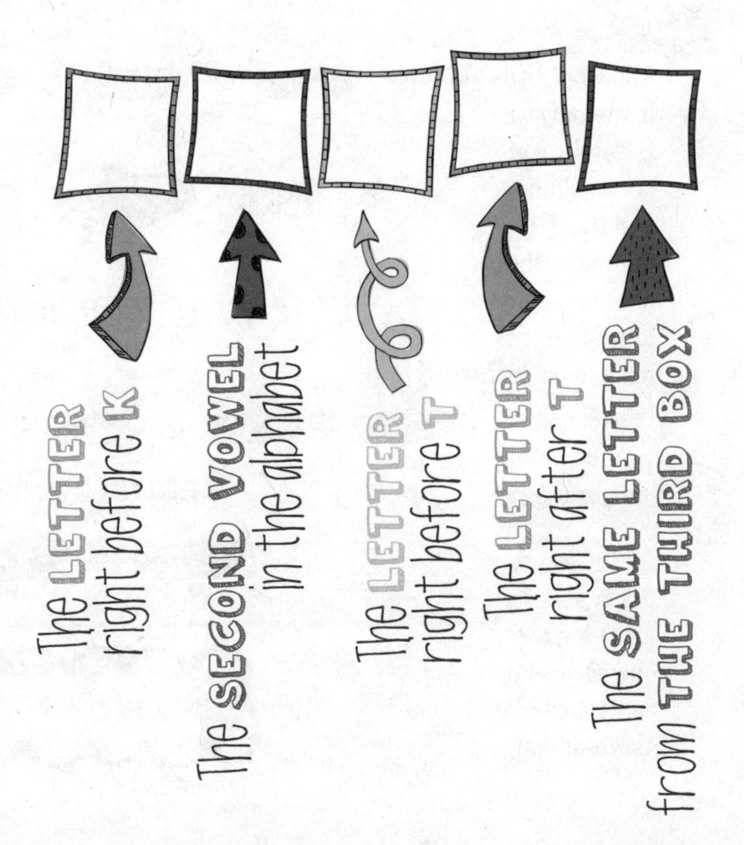

RESPOND

PRAY: Jesus, thank You for fulfilling God's instructions and commands.

HIGHLIGHT

OLDER KIDS: John 6:35
YOUNGER KIDS: John 6:35
MEMORY VERSE: Psalm 86:5

EXPLAIN

- A large crowd crossed the sea to find Jesus. They wanted to see another miracle.
- Jesus told the people that He is the bread of life.
- Jesus meant that He is the only one who can satisfy spiritual hunger.
- Jesus fed over 5,000 people with one small meal—5 loaves of bread and 2 fish. The next day the people followed Him on boats to Capernaum. They wanted Jesus to perform another great miracle. Jesus knew they were more interested in seeing wonderful things than understanding His eternal gift. The people wanted food, but Jesus told them that He alone could satisfy their soul.

APPLY

Knowing Jesus is the only way to satisfy your spiritual hunger and thirst. Complete the number sentence to find out how many men Jesus fed.

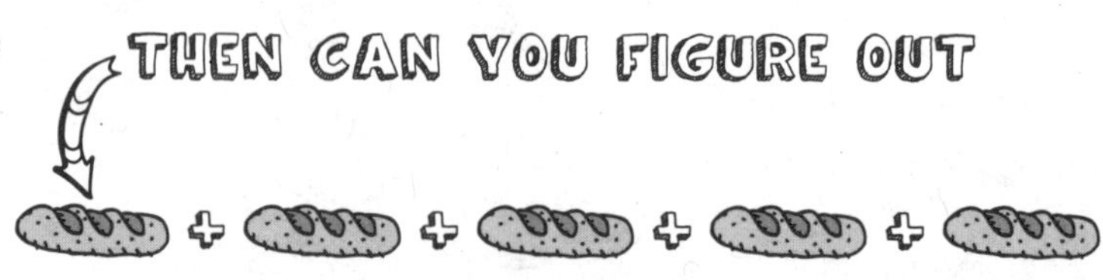

RESPOND

PRAY: Jesus, thank You for being the only One who can satisfy my spiritual hunger.

HIGHLIGHT

OLDER KIDS: John 7:28-29
YOUNGER KIDS: John 7:28-29
MEMORY VERSE: Psalm 86:5

EXPLAIN

- John wrote about how people responded to Jesus during His ministry.
- Jesus used His time teaching in the temple to point people to God and let them know God had sent Him.
- Jesus proclaimed that He was from God, the promised Messiah.
- Even Jesus' brothers did not believe He was the Messiah at first. Many people were confused about who He was and why He was there.

APPLY

Jesus always points people to God. Use the box to write your memory verse to help you memorize it this week.

RESPOND

PRAY: Jesus, thank You for always pointing me to God.

HIGHLIGHT

OLDER KIDS: John 8:12
YOUNGER KIDS: John 8:12
MEMORY VERSE: Psalm 86:5

EXPLAIN

- Jesus said He is the light of the world.
- Jesus used examples like light and dark because it is something everyone understands.
- By calling Himself the light of the world, Jesus helped people understand that He is the Messiah.
- Jesus uses light to describe Himself because it's something everyone can see. Jesus came to provide light and hope for people to have a relationship with God and not live in the darkness of sin.

APPLY

Jesus' salvation is for everyone who follows Jesus by faith. Discuss: What does it mean that Jesus is the light of the world?

RESPOND

PRAY: Jesus, thank You for providing salvation for everyone who trusts in You.

HIGHLIGHT

OLDER KIDS: John 9:1-5
YOUNGER KIDS: John 9:3-5
MEMORY VERSE: Psalm 86:5

EXPLAIN

- Jesus and the disciples saw a man who had been born blind.
- The disciples asked Jesus whose sin caused the man to be blind.
- Jesus explained that the man had been born blind so God's glory could be shown through his healing.
- It was common in that time for people to believe that physical sickness or suffering was caused by sin. Jesus made it clear that this man's blindness was not directly caused by a person's sin.

APPLY

God uses all kinds of circumstances to show His glory. Use the braille decoder to find a question, then write your thoughts in the box below!

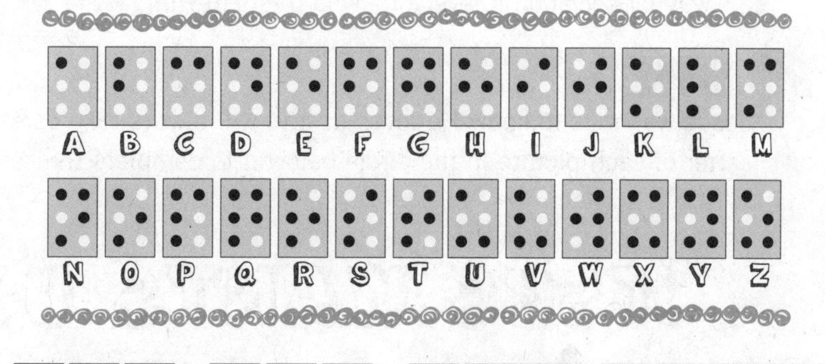

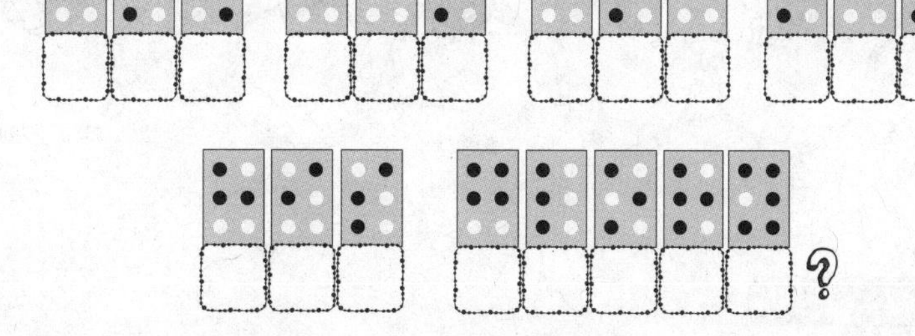

RESPOND

PRAY: Heavenly Father, thank You for showing Your glory in many different ways.

OLDER KIDS: John 10:14-18
YOUNGER KIDS: John 10:14-15
MEMORY VERSE: Psalm 90:12

- Jesus describes Himself as the Good Shepherd.
- Shepherds care for, protect, and provide for their sheep.
- Sheep recognize their shepherd's voice and obey him because they know and trust him to take care of them.
- Jesus used shepherds and sheep as an illustration to teach the people that He is the Messiah. Jesus laid down His life when He was crucified and took it up again when He was resurrected. Jesus is the Son of God who came to provide a way for salvation to everyone who trusts in Him.

Jesus wants us to know He loves us and will always take care of us. Write the first letter of each picture in the circle below it to complete the sentence.

JESUS WANTS US TO

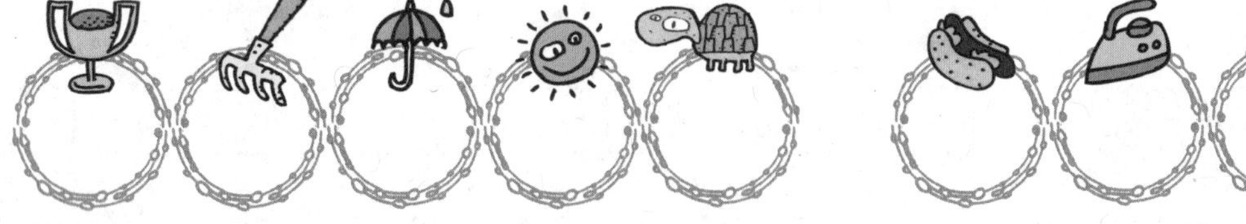

PRAY: Jesus, help me trust You to always take care of me.

OLDER KIDS: John 11:17, 39-44
YOUNGER KIDS: John 11:43-44
MEMORY VERSE: Psalm 90:12

- Lazarus was Jesus' friend. Lazarus became sick and died.
- Lazarus had been dead for four days when Jesus visited Lazarus' family.
- Jesus called Lazarus to come out from his tomb, and Lazarus did. Jesus raised Lazarus from the dead.
- Lazarus' sister, Martha, told Jesus that if He'd been there, Lazarus would not have died. Jesus told Martha that He is the resurrection and the life. Martha confessed her belief that Jesus is the Messiah, who has ultimate power over life and death.

Jesus has total power over death. Discuss: Why do you think Jesus waited four days before visiting Lazarus' family?

PRAY: Jesus, thank You that You are all-powerful, even more powerful than death. Help me always remember that You are the Messiah.

OLDER KIDS: John 12:44-50
YOUNGER KIDS: John 12:46
MEMORY VERSE: Psalm 90:12

- Jesus explained to everyone He is the light of the world.
- Jesus made it clear that He was sent by God, and believing in Him is believing in God.
- Jesus told everyone He came to save them from their sin.
- Jesus wanted everyone to understand that He was sent by God and He was following God's commands.

Jesus came to save us from our sins. Circle all the green letters and use the clue to answer the question.

K D L V B J L G H J K L B H I J Q K E
V H K G R I O U I O I C H O A P I C K
L I D B J I F L G Q H F B C K N L T Z
B V O L A H J K F L G A E H K T B R
W G U I E W G C H J S K D B G E R H
F B W A X C N S K D L I G J O P Q R
W L Y O Q P D U S A B C M X C K V

Who do the letters above describe? ______________________

PRAY: Jesus, thank You for coming to save me from my sins.

HIGHLIGHT

OLDER KIDS: John 13:34-35
YOUNGER KIDS: John 13:34-35
MEMORY VERSE: Psalm 90:12

EXPLAIN

- Jesus and His disciples were sharing a meal together during Passover.
- Jesus gave a new command to His disciples to love each other just as He loved them.
- Jesus said people will know they are His disciples by the way they show love. This is true for Christians today, too.
- In the final days before Jesus' crucifixion, Jesus shared a final meal with His disciples. He washed His disciples' feet and taught them that, just as Jesus—their Savior and Lord—washed their feet, so everyone should wash each other's feet, or serve others. Jesus commanded His disciples to help people through loving and serving them.

APPLY

Jesus shows us how to love others. We should love each other because Jesus loves us. Write Psalm 90:12 below and work on memorizing it this week.

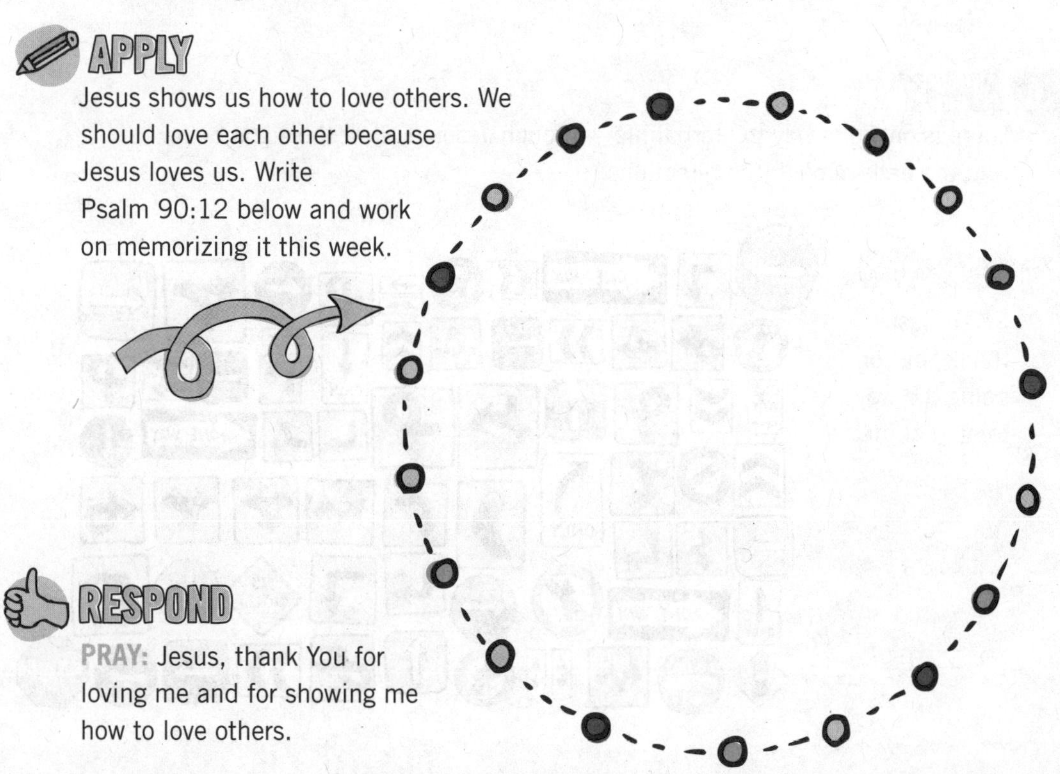

RESPOND

PRAY: Jesus, thank You for loving me and for showing me how to love others.

HIGHLIGHT

OLDER KIDS: John 14:5-6
YOUNGER KIDS: John 14:5-6
MEMORY VERSE: Psalm 90:12

EXPLAIN

- After explaining His new command, Jesus told His disciples about heaven. He said He would be going away to prepare a place for them, and that the disciples would know the way.
- Thomas asked Jesus how to find heaven.
- Jesus answered Thomas that He (Jesus) is the only way to heaven.
- Jesus had already predicted His death, and now—during the last supper—He told His disciples that He would have to go away. Thomas grew anxious. Jesus had said that they would know the way, but Thomas didn't know where Jesus was going...so how would he know the way? Jesus assured Thomas that He (Jesus) alone is the way. Trusting in Jesus is the only way to life with God forever.

APPLY

There is only one way to eternal life—through Jesus. Follow the signs below to find the path through the directions.

RESPOND

PRAY: Jesus, thank You for being the way to eternal life.

OLDER KIDS: John 15:9-13
YOUNGER KIDS: John 15:12-13
MEMORY VERSE: Psalm 96:2

- Jesus explained to His disciples that He loves like God does.
- Jesus wants His followers to love each other like God loves.
- When Christians love each other like Jesus loves, they will make sacrifices for others.
- Jesus taught the disciples how to live by loving one another. This is how they knew to teach other believers.

Loving others is an important way to show Jesus' love. Place a heart in the box next to each sentence if it describes a way to show love to others.

PRAY: Jesus, help me to show others Your love.

HIGHLIGHT

OLDER KIDS: John 16:33
YOUNGER KIDS: John 16:33
MEMORY VERSE: Psalm 96:2

EXPLAIN

- Jesus taught the disciples a lot of things, some of which they did not understand.
- Jesus wanted the disciples to understand and believe His teachings so they would have peace in Him.
- Jesus warned His disciples that they would suffer, but they should have courage because He has already conquered the world.
- As Jesus neared His final hours before His crucifixion, He told His disciples a day would come when He would talk about God plainly and they would understand. Before that time, though, there would be challenges. Jesus assured them that He has already conquered the world, so they should not fear.

APPLY

When we find ourselves alone and in trouble, we can have hope and peace in the promise of a victorious Savior. Jesus has given us hope and peace because He has already conquered the world. Complete the crossword using the highlighted words.

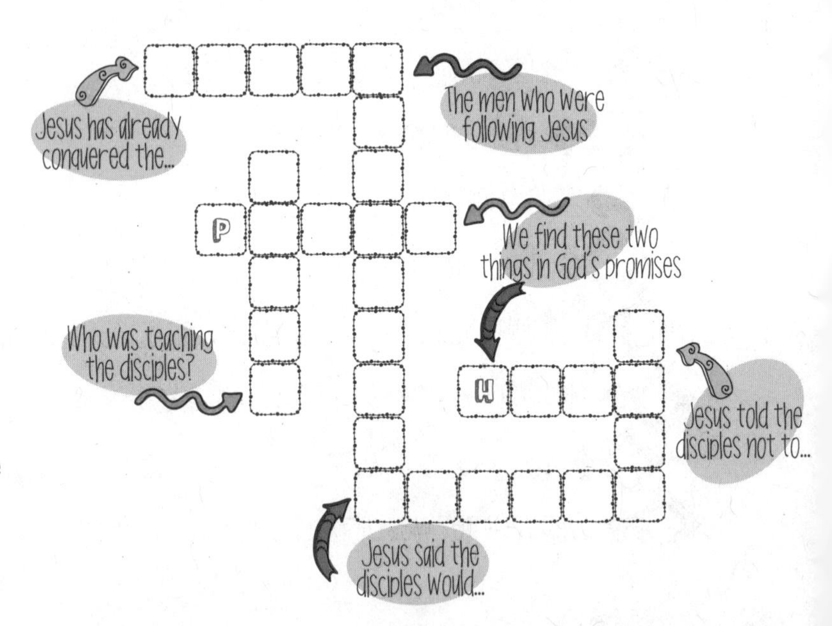

RESPOND

PRAY: Jesus, thank You for giving me hope and peace because You have already conquered the world.

HIGHLIGHT

OLDER KIDS: John 17:1-5
YOUNGER KIDS: John 17:1-5
MEMORY VERSE: Psalm 96:2

EXPLAIN

- Jesus talked to God through prayer. He knew the time for His death was coming.
- Jesus prayed that He would bring glory to God so that He could give the gift of eternal life.
- Jesus told God that He had glorified Him by completing His work on earth and was ready to be glorified in His presence as He was before creation.
- When Jesus finished praying for God to be glorified in His perfect plan, He prayed for His disciples and for all believers.
- The passionate prayer of Christ should urge everyone to seek to glorify God, like Jesus, in everything we do.

APPLY

We should strive to glorify God in everything we do. Write Psalm 96:2 in the box to help you memorize it this week.

RESPOND

PRAY: Heavenly Father, give me a heart to glorify You in everything I do.

HIGHLIGHT

OLDER KIDS: John 18:4-9
YOUNGER KIDS: John 18:4-6
MEMORY VERSE: Psalm 96:2

EXPLAIN

- John wrote about Jesus in the Garden of Gethsemane with the disciples.
- Judas betrayed Jesus and brought soldiers to arrest Him.
- Jesus knew everything that was about to happen and did not stop it.
- As the Son of God, Jesus is always in control. He knew Judas would betray Him, and He knew He would be arrested, beaten, and crucified. Jesus' crucifixion, burial, and resurrection were necessary parts of God's plan for the forgiveness of sin.

APPLY

Jesus sacrificed Himself so we could be saved from our sins. Use the decoder to solve the message below.

A
B
C
D
E
F
G
H
I
J
K
L
M
N
O
P
Q
R
S
T
U
V
W
X
Y
Z

RESPOND

PRAY: Jesus, thank You for giving Your life for me.

HIGHLIGHT

OLDER KIDS: John 19:38-42
YOUNGER KIDS: John 19:41-42
MEMORY VERSE: Psalm 96:2

EXPLAIN

- Nicodemus and Joseph of Arimathea took care of Jesus' body after He died.
- Nicodemus and Joseph wrapped Jesus' body in cloth and used spices on His body.
- Jesus' friends laid His body in a tomb. There was a garden outside the tomb, and the tomb had never been used before.
- Nicodemus, one of the men who assisted with Jesus' burial, was a member of the Sanhedrin, the Jewish council that had plotted against Jesus. Even some people among Jesus' enemies had become believers and followed Him

APPLY

Jesus died on the cross and rose again to save you from sin. When you trust in Jesus for salvation, you can have confidence that you will have eternal life with God. Unscramble the words in the phrases below to read what happened after Jesus was crucified.

RESPOND

PRAY: Jesus, thank You for dying for me. Help me remember that You died and rose again for me to have eternal life.

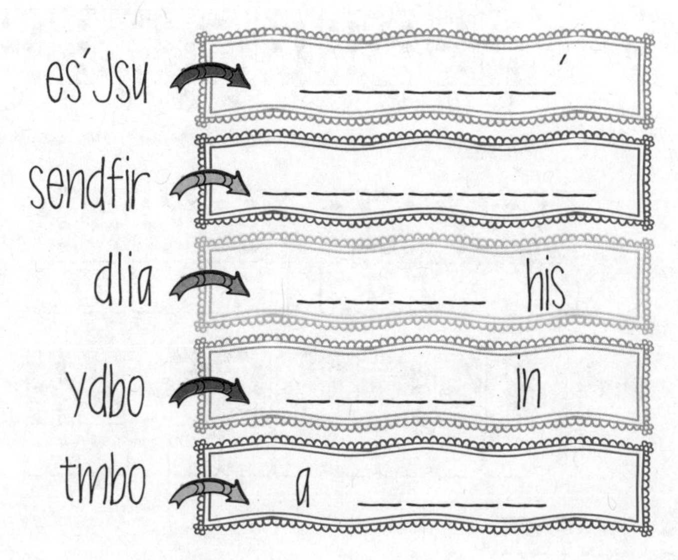

HIGHLIGHT

OLDER KIDS: John 20:24-29
YOUNGER KIDS: John 20:24-29
MEMORY VERSE: Psalm 100:4

EXPLAIN

- Thomas, one of the disciples, did not believe the other disciples had really seen Jesus after His resurrection.
- Jesus appeared to the disciples in a locked room.
- When he saw Jesus, Thomas believed it was really Him.
- Jesus made it clear there would be many people who would never see Him with their own eyes who would be blessed because they believe in Him.

APPLY

Jesus appeared to the disciples after His resurrection. Solve the braille code to find the secret message.

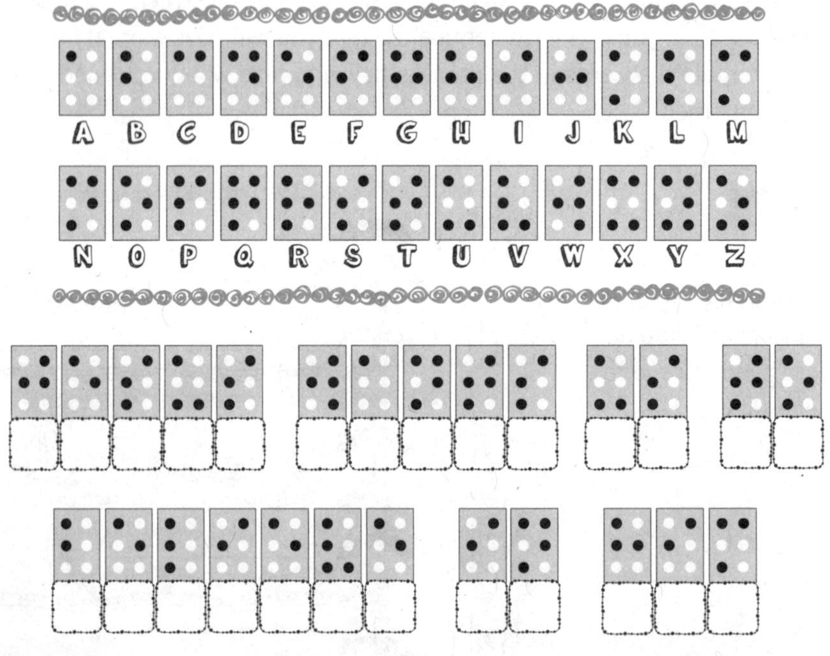

RESPOND

PRAY: Jesus, help me trust You in all things.

OLDER KIDS: John 21:15-17
YOUNGER KIDS: John 21:15
MEMORY VERSE: Psalm 100:4

EXPLAIN

- During the time Jesus was being crucified, Peter denied knowing Jesus three times, just like Jesus said he would.
- After His resurrection, Jesus asked Peter three times if he loved Him.
- Each time Peter said that he loved Jesus, Jesus told him to take care of and love others.
- Love is an important part of being a faithful disciple. Peter would show his love for Jesus by loving God's people and teaching them about God.

We show our love for Jesus by caring for others and teaching others about Him. List 3 ways you can show your love for Jesus.

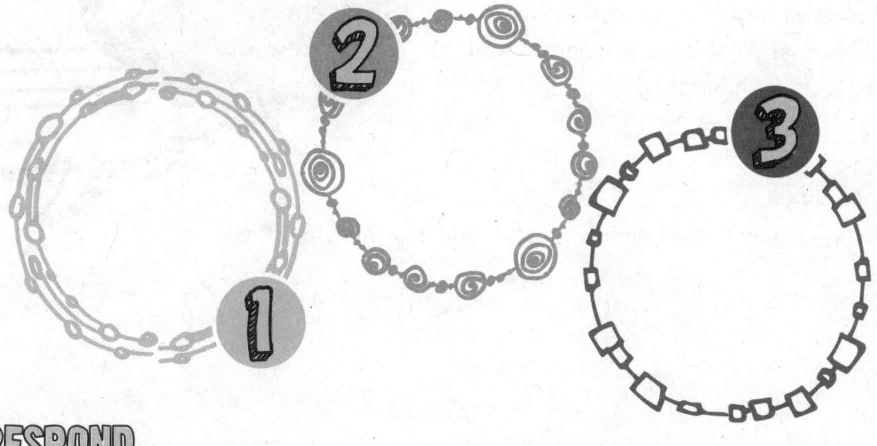

RESPOND

PRAY: Jesus, help me show Your love to others.

HIGHLIGHT

OLDER KIDS: 1 John 1:5-9
YOUNGER KIDS: 1 John 1:9
MEMORY VERSE: Psalm 100:4

EXPLAIN

- John wrote this letter to help believers understand that Jesus really is the Son of God.
- John used the examples of light and dark to help believers understand what having a relationship with Jesus is like as opposed to living in sin.
- John reminds Christians that if they confess their sin to God, He will forgive them.
- John was an apostle of Jesus who wrote to help believers understand who Jesus is. Christians show belief in Jesus by obeying Him and loving others like He did.

APPLY

God is faithful to forgive our sin when we ask. Discuss: What does it mean to walk in the light as a Christian?

RESPOND

PRAY: Heavenly Father, thank You for forgiving me when I ask.

OLDER KIDS: 1 John 2:3-6
YOUNGER KIDS: 1 John 2:3
MEMORY VERSE: Psalm 100:4

- John continued to explain to the church how disciples of Jesus are called to live.
- John said that when you truly know Jesus, you will want to keep His commands.
- John explained that anyone who claims to know Jesus but doesn't show it in the way he lives is a liar.
- John taught that when someone trusts in Jesus, she will want to follow His commands because Jesus has changed her heart. When someone becomes a follower of Jesus, He changes her heart to want to follow Jesus instead of following after sin.

When we love Jesus, we will follow His commands. Based on what you read today, match the IF statements on the left with the correct THEN statements on the right.

 we truly know Jesus,

 we should forgive others

 we say we love Jesus but don't follow His truth,

 we will want to keep His commands.

 we've been forgiven,

 we are liars.

PRAY: Jesus, help me follow Your commands.

OLDER KIDS: 1 John 3:1-3
YOUNGER KIDS: 1 John 3:1
MEMORY VERSE: Psalm 100:4

EXPLAIN

- John reminded Christians in his letter that when people trust in Jesus, they are called children of God.
- As God's children, believers are not like the world, who follow after sin and do whatever they want.
- God's love shapes Christians to look more like Him.
- Believers are children of God, and all believers are part of God's family.

APPLY

As we grow to be more like God, we will look different from the rest of the world and strive to sin less. Write Psalm 100:4 in the box to help you memorize it this week.

RESPOND

PRAY: Heavenly Father, thank You for making me part of Your family.

HIGHLIGHT

OLDER KIDS: 1 John 4:7-12
YOUNGER KIDS: 1 John 4:11
MEMORY VERSE: Psalm 103:1

EXPLAIN

- John talked about God's love. He told the early Christians that they should love each other because God loves them.
- John said that love is from God because God is love.
- God loved us first, and He sent Jesus to die for people.
- John reminded the believers that before they loved God, He loved them. He planned His own Son to be the sacrifice for sin. John reminded them to be obedient to God, love God, and love others.

APPLY

Because God loves us, we should love others. Look at each picture and think creatively about how you can show love to others in some way that relates to the picture. Write your ideas on the lines.

RESPOND

PRAY: Heavenly Father, thank You for loving me. Help me find ways to show Your love to others.

OLDER KIDS: 1 John 5:14-15
YOUNGER KIDS: 1 John 5:14-15
MEMORY VERSE: Psalm 103:1

EXPLAIN

- John finished his letter to believers by calling them to love and obey.
- John explained that disciples of Jesus can have confidence (trust) that when they ask anything according to God's will, He hears.
- God wants people to talk to Him.
- Prayer is a way to talk and listen to God. God wants people to communicate with Him through prayer.

God hears us when we pray. Use the first letter of each picture to solve the code.

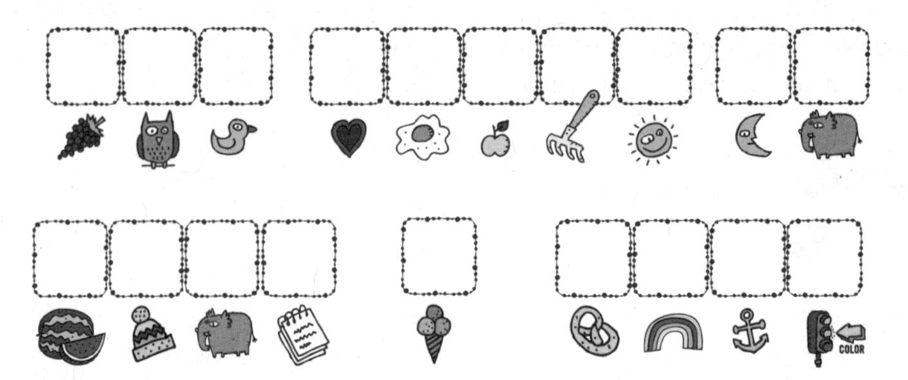

PRAY: Heavenly Father, thank You for hearing me when I pray.

OLDER KIDS: 2 John 1:6
YOUNGER KIDS: 2 John 1:6
MEMORY VERSE: Psalm 103:1

EXPLAIN

- John wrote a second letter to a church, reminding them to love all people.
- John wanted believers to live according to God's commands and love one another.
- Christ followers are called to walk in obedience to God's Word, continuing to obey Him and love those around them.
- Knowing and following God's commands are important to believers because of what God has done for us through Jesus.

When we focus on following God's commands, we can easily see when someone tries to teach something different. Place a check mark next to the things that are God's commands.

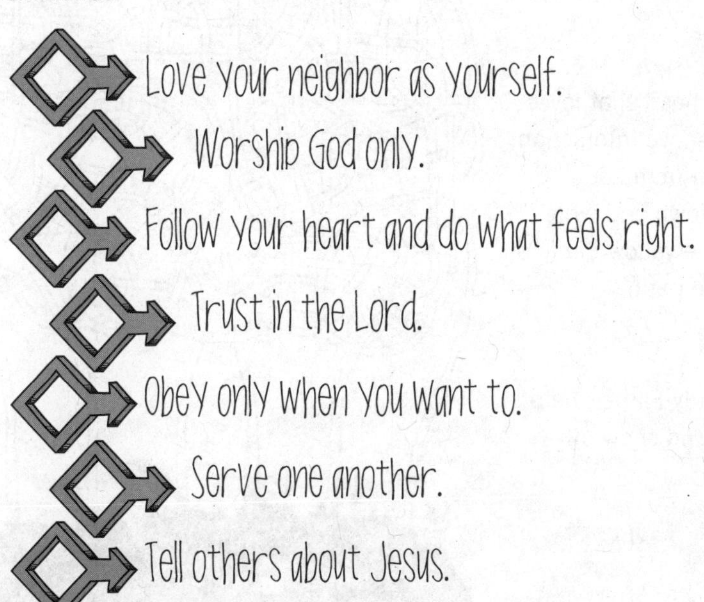

PRAY: Heavenly Father, help me know and follow Your commands.

HIGHLIGHT

OLDER KIDS: 3 John 1:5-8
YOUNGER KIDS: 3 John 1:5
MEMORY VERSE: Psalm 103:1

EXPLAIN

- John wrote this letter to his friend, Gaius, to encourage him to remain steadfast and faithful during hard times.
- John was happy that Gaius was showing faithfulness in following Jesus.
- Gaius was supporting people who were preaching the gospel by showing hospitality and friendship to them while they were in his town.
- John praised Gaius for his example to other believers.

APPLY

God values a heart that loves Him and puts love into action. Trace the path from each home in the town and write its letter in the yellow circle at the end of the path.

Gaius was putting his love into action when he showed hospitality and friendship to the people who were sharing the...

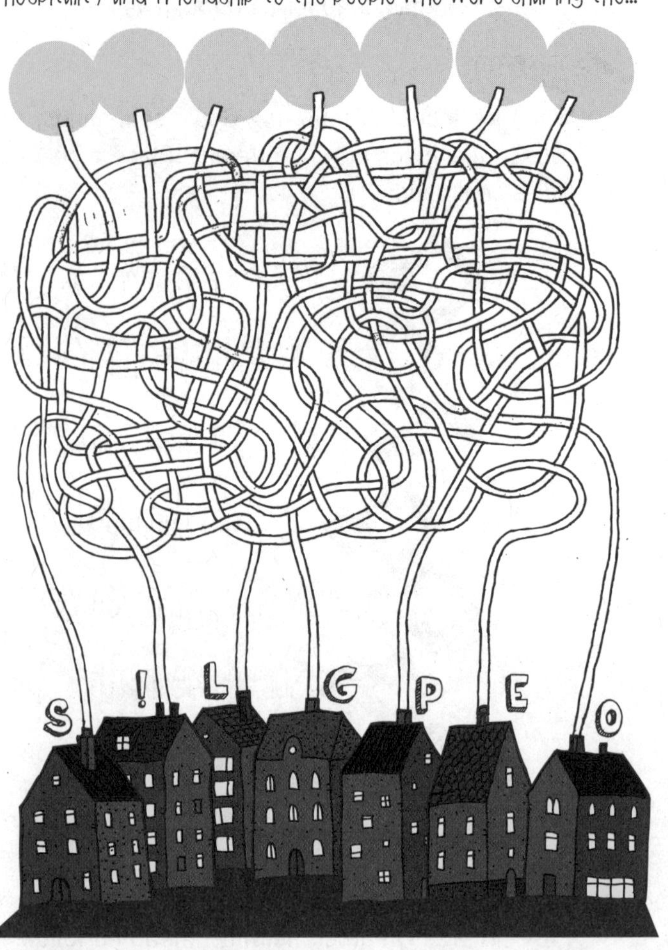

RESPOND

PRAY: Heavenly Father, help me love You and show others Your love.

HIGHLIGHT

OLDER KIDS: Jude 1:20-25
YOUNGER KIDS: Jude 1:20-21
MEMORY VERSE: Psalm 103:1

EXPLAIN

- Jude, the brother of Jesus and James, wrote a letter to Jewish Christians.
- Jude encouraged the believers to stand firm in their faith and help others do the same.
- He said Christians should seek holiness and try to be more like Jesus.
- Jude warned them about false teachers and people who said sin is not a big deal. He encouraged believers to follow Jesus and be obedient to the way He said we should live.

APPLY

Becoming more like Jesus is an important part of following Jesus. There is a big word that means becoming more like Jesus. Find out what the word is by using the decoder.

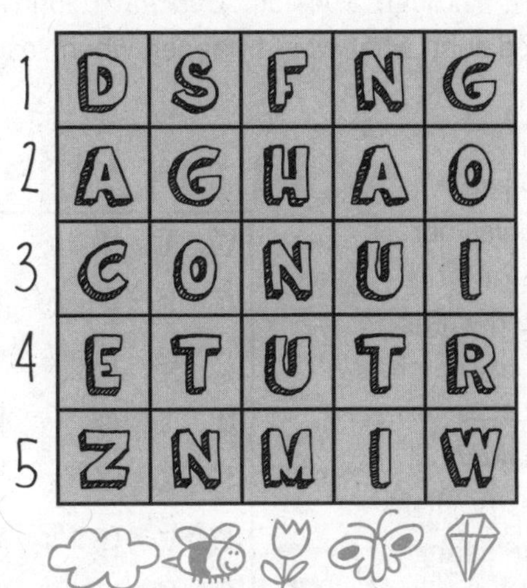

RESPOND

PRAY: Heavenly Father, help me become more like Jesus every day.

OLDER KIDS: Revelation 1:17-19
YOUNGER KIDS: Revelation 1:17-19
MEMORY VERSE: Proverbs 26:20

EXPLAIN

- The apostle John wrote Revelation to tell believers about the vision he had from God.
- Jesus is alive today, and He has conquered death.
- God sent a special message through John about what will happen when Jesus returns.
- John was living on the island of Patmos in exile (he was forced to leave his home). Through a vision, God gave John a message for seven churches and showed John what would happen when Jesus comes back.

APPLY

Jesus is alive and deserves our worship. Find the highlighted words in the word search.

W	T	Y	D	T	Y	U	J	E	K	I	N	U
A	S	P	A	T	M	O	S	D	X	F	G	H
X	C	F	P	V	G	H	Y	U	W	I	J	K
M	I	C	O	N	Q	U	E	R	E	D	L	U
E	G	Y	S	Z	G	H	J	K	V	I	Y	E
S	F	G	T	V	Y	U	I	O	K	L	M	B
S	E	R	L	W	G	Y	U	I	N	C	E	R
A	J	R	E	V	E	L	A	T	I	O	N	M
G	K	H	J	G	Y	S	U	J	K	S	L	A
E	T	R	O	E	W	W	P	O	D	E	V	L
V	K	I	H	U	G	Y	T	Q	I	V	Y	I
E	K	G	N	R	T	Y	U	O	M	E	O	V
Y	G	F	C	V	I	S	I	O	N	N	M	E

RESPOND

PRAY: Jesus, thank You for defeating death. Help me continue following You as I wait for You to return.

OLDER KIDS: Revelation 2:7
YOUNGER KIDS: Revelation 2:7
MEMORY VERSE: Proverbs 26:20

EXPLAIN

- Jesus gave John messages to seven different churches.
- The messages Jesus gave for the seven churches are for all Christians, too.
- The message for each church was different, but Jesus called them all to be strong in their faith.
- Jesus wanted His followers to pay attention to the messages He gave to the seven churches. He wanted Christians to stay faithful in following Him no matter how we feel or how hard or easy our lives are.

APPLY

Jesus wants us to stay faithful to follow Him no matter what. Write the name of each picture in the column below it.

RESPOND

PRAY: Jesus, help me to hear Your message and be faithful to You.

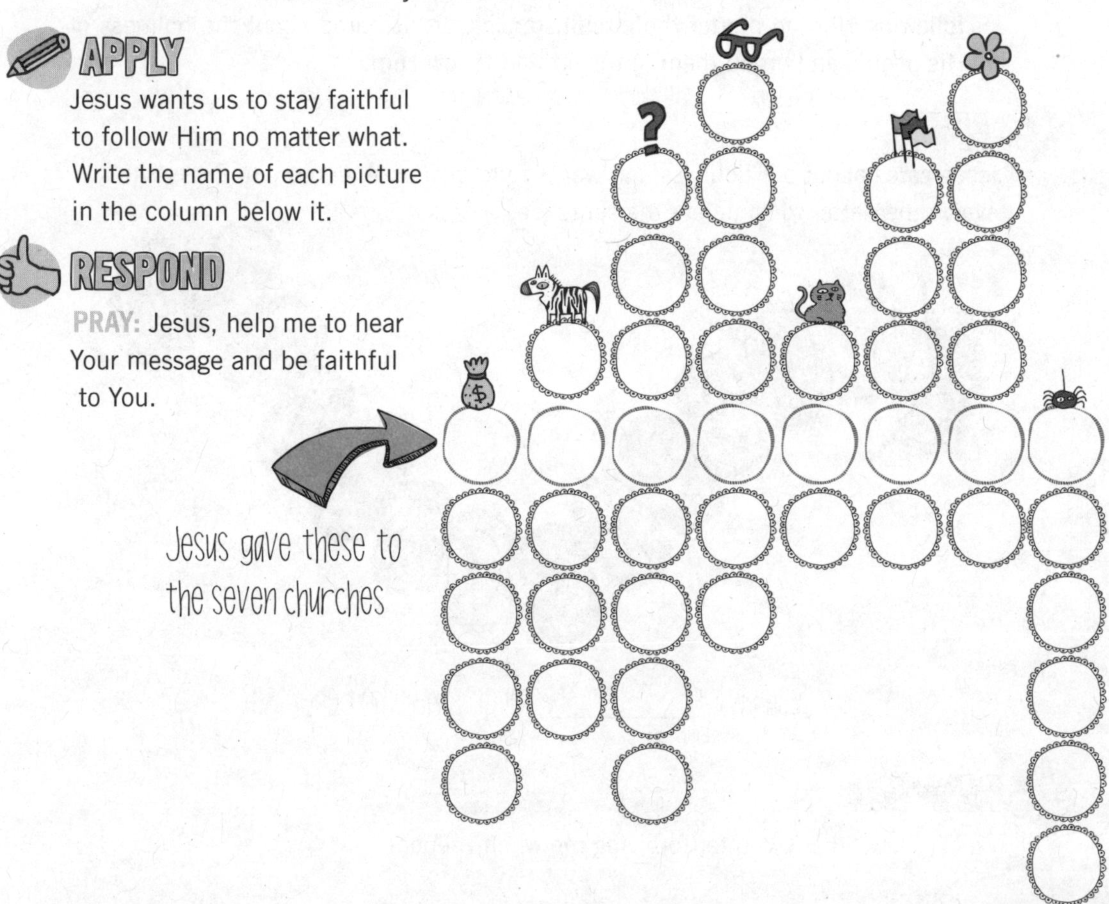

HIGHLIGHT

OLDER KIDS: Revelation 3:19-22
YOUNGER KIDS: Revelation 3:19-20
MEMORY VERSE: Proverbs 26:20

EXPLAIN

- John wrote God's words to the church in Laodicea to discipline their disobedience and call them to repent.
- Jesus rebuked Laodicea (tell them they've done something wrong) for not loving Him like they should.
- Jesus says that He corrects those He loves, and He will forgive anyone who repents (turns from sin and turns to God).
- The theme of the letters to the seven churches is staying true to Jesus and following Him no matter the circumstances. Jesus cared about the holiness of His people and urged them to repent and follow Him.

APPLY

Jesus cares about our holiness and wants to forgive us when we sin. Cross out every other letter to complete the sentence.

Jesus will __________ everyone who repents.

RESPOND

PRAY: Jesus, thank You for forgiving me when I repent.

HIGHLIGHT

OLDER KIDS: Revelation 4:11
YOUNGER KIDS: Revelation 4:11
MEMORY VERSE: Proverbs 26:20

EXPLAIN

- John described what he saw in God's throne room in his vision.
- John saw many people and creatures worshiping God.
- God created all things, and He is worthy of our praise.
- John saw many things in his vision; one was the throne of God surrounded by continuous worship. John may not have understood everything he saw, but he did understand that God is worthy of worship—praise, glory, and honor.

APPLY

God is worthy of our worship. Discuss: What does it mean to give God praise, glory, and honor?

RESPOND

PRAY: Heavenly Father, thank You for being worthy of worship. Help me to praise, glorify, and honor You.

HIGHLIGHT

OLDER KIDS: Revelation 5:5
YOUNGER KIDS: Revelation 5:5
MEMORY VERSE: Proverbs 26:20

EXPLAIN

- In his vision John saw Jesus, in His glory, at the right hand of God.
- God is the only One worthy of all worship.
- Jesus is victorious over sin and death and is worthy to sit at God's right hand.
- Jesus is described as the Lion of Judah and the Root of David. He is described this way in other places in the Bible as well.

APPLY

Jesus is victorious! Find the letter on each kid's shirt and follow the string up to the correct balloon. Then write that letter in the balloon to complete the statement.

RESPOND

PRAY: Jesus, You are victorious and worthy of my praise!

OLDER KIDS: Revelation 6:1-2
YOUNGER KIDS: Revelation 6:1-2
MEMORY VERSE: Proverbs 27:17

EXPLAIN

- John saw Jesus begin to open God's scroll. Each seal Jesus opened represents different judgments on the earth from God because of sin. God's judgment is righteous.
- Through the events of this vision, God was showing John that He would one day demonstrate His final act of victory of Satan.
- The events John saw in his vision are similar to the things Daniel wrote about and Jesus taught while on earth.
- The Bible describes different judgments that will happen on earth during what is called "end times." We can trust these things will happen because we trust the Bible is God's truth.

God will defeat Satan and sin forever. God's victory will last forever. Use the highlighted words above to complete the crossword puzzle.

RESPOND

PRAY: Heavenly Father, thank You for telling us You are more powerful than Satan and sin.

HIGHLIGHT

OLDER KIDS: Revelation 7:9-10
YOUNGER KIDS: Revelation 7:9-10
MEMORY VERSE: Proverbs 27:17

EXPLAIN

- Even in the middle of great judgment, God cares for and protects His people.
- After the judgment, a great multitude from every tribe and people and nation will worship God together.
- There is hope for everyone who is a follower of Jesus, even during difficult times.
- God is holy, so He must judge sin and hold Satan accountable for leading people away from God. But God loves and cares for people, and He wants every person to trust in Jesus as Savior.

APPLY

God loves and cares for everyone, and He wants every person to trust in Jesus as Savior. As you follow along the path on this map, thank God that after the judgment, a great multitude from every tribe and people and nation will worship God together.

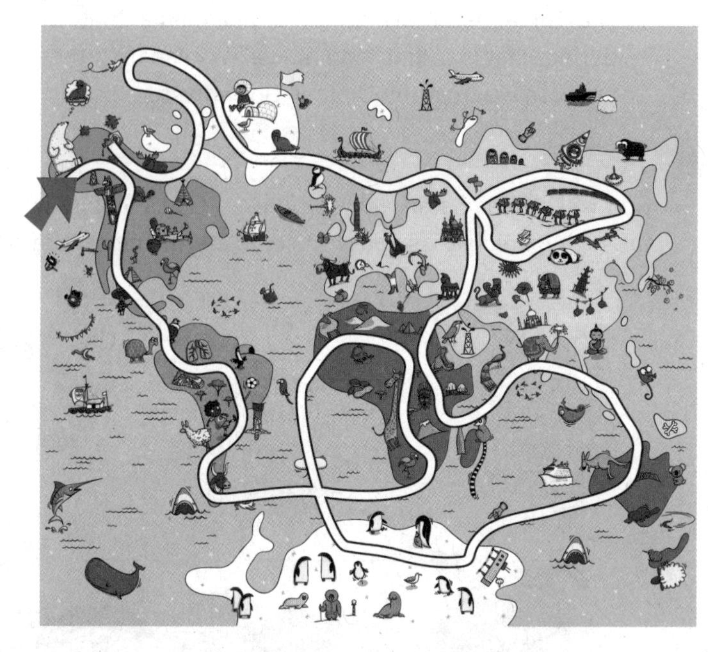

RESPOND

PRAY: God, You are worthy of all worship and praise. Thank You for loving and caring for people and making a way for us to live with You forever.

HIGHLIGHT

OLDER KIDS: Revelation 8:1-2
YOUNGER KIDS: Revelation 8:1-2
MEMORY VERSE: Proverbs 27:17

EXPLAIN

- John recorded the final seal of God's righteous judgment being opened.
- Seven angels were given trumpets to announce the next phases of judgment.
- God heard the prayers of His people who asked for justice during His judgment.
- Even during the middle of judgment, God hears the prayers of His people.

APPLY

God always hears us when we talk to Him. Starting in the center each time, follow the directions to find each letter and complete the sentence.

God always hears my ________ .

D	S	F	Y	G
A	G	H	A	O
C	O	⏰	U	W
E	P	U	L	R
Z	N	M	X	W

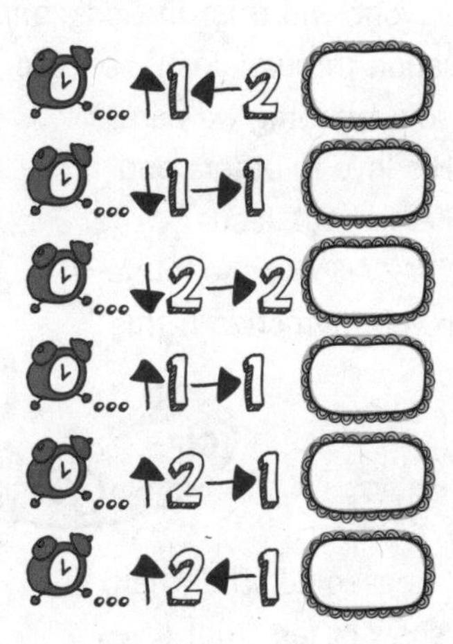

RESPOND

PRAY: Heavenly Father, thank You for always hearing my prayers.

OLDER KIDS: Revelation 9:20-21
YOUNGER KIDS: Revelation 9:20-21
MEMORY VERSE: Proverbs 27:17

- John saw God's righteous judgment continue in his vision.
- John explained that even with terrible things happening, some people will not turn away from their sin and ask God for forgiveness.
- Followers of Jesus are called to share the good news of Jesus with everyone. We are part of God's mission to rescue people from sin by telling others the gospel.
- Even today, many people refuse to receive God's gift of salvation and follow Jesus. God wants believers to show His love through words and actions so that others can see His hope and love.

APPLY

Not everyone will trust in God's gift of salvation through Jesus, but we must do everything we can to show His love to others and tell others about Jesus. Write Proverbs 27:17 in the circle to help you memorize it this week.

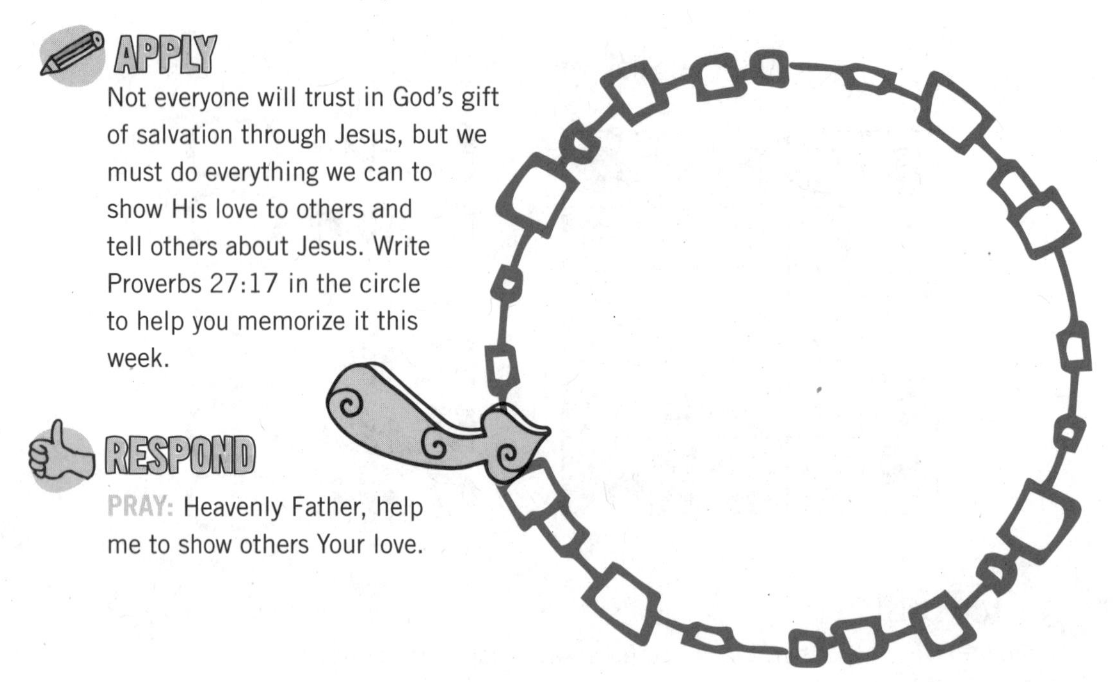

RESPOND

PRAY: Heavenly Father, help me to show others Your love.

HIGHLIGHT

OLDER KIDS: Revelation 10:4
YOUNGER KIDS: Revelation 10:4
MEMORY VERSE: Proverbs 27:17

EXPLAIN

- John continued to write down the vision God gave him for things that will happen one day.
- God gave John specific instructions to not write down some events.
- God shared some things, but there are some things God will not tell ahead of time.
- When Christians cannot know all the details about God's plans for the future, we should still trust that He is good and in control of all things.

APPLY

We should trust God even when we don't know everything. When should we trust God? Unscramble the word below to find the answer.

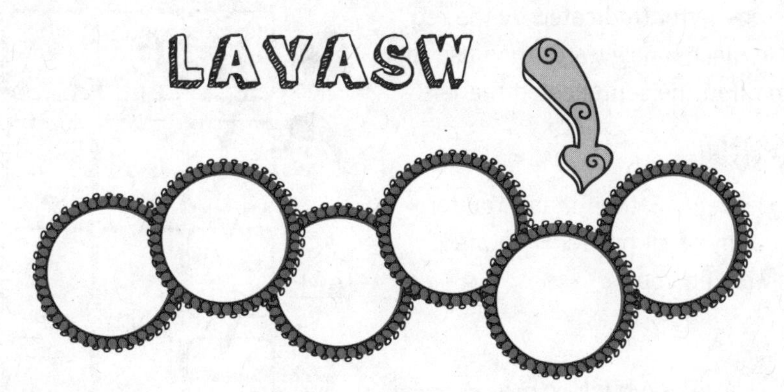

RESPOND

PRAY: Heavenly Father, help me trust You all the time.

HIGHLIGHT

OLDER KIDS: Revelation 11:15
YOUNGER KIDS: Revelation 11:15
MEMORY VERSE: Psalm 106:1

EXPLAIN

- John saw many things that will happen on earth because of God's righteous judgment, and those things will show God's power and glory.
- The seventh trumpet will sound, God will be praised, and it will be time for God's final judgment to begin.
- God will be worshiped because He is worthy of all praise.
- Revelation is a book of hope, teaching that God is in control of all things. One day Jesus will return and establish God's kingdom forever and ever.

APPLY

God is always worthy of our praise, no matter the circumstances. In each row, change one letter (indicated by the red arrow) to make a new word, then use that word to fill in the sentence on the left.

RESPOND

PRAY: Heavenly Father, thank You for being worthy of all praise. Help me always worship You.

The 7th trumpet will sound, and it will be ________ for God's final judgment to begin.

HIGHLIGHT

OLDER KIDS: Revelation 12:10-12
YOUNGER KIDS: Revelation 12:10
MEMORY VERSE: Psalm 106:1

EXPLAIN

- John heard a loud voice in heaven talking about Satan's defeat.
- Jesus, the Messiah, conquered Satan through His death and resurrection.
- Satan will continue to cause trouble on earth until God stops him forever.
- Although Satan was defeated through the resurrection of Jesus, God still allows him to have limited power today. Jesus will return and be victorious forever.

APPLY

Jesus conquered sin and death through His resurrection so we can have a relationship with Him. Transfer each set of letters from the path to the boxes below of the same color to reveal the statement below about today's passage.

RESPOND

PRAY: Jesus, thank You for dying for my sins and defeating Satan through Your resurrection.

OLDER KIDS: Revelation 13:6-10
YOUNGER KIDS: Revelation 13:6-8
MEMORY VERSE: Psalm 106:1

EXPLAIN

- God gave John a vision of Satan's limited reign.
- John saw Satan and two of Satan's followers, described as beasts, who trick people into following them instead of God.
- John explained that those who fight against God will be conquered in the end, and believers can have hope and must stay faithful.
- Satan and his helpers are able to trick people into following them because they try to look as powerful as God, but Satan and his helpers will never be as powerful as God!

APPLY

God is the one true God, and no one is as powerful as Him. Write Psalm 106:1 in the box to help you memorize it this week.

RESPOND

PRAY: Heavenly Father, thank You for being the one true God. You are more powerful than anyone!

HIGHLIGHT

OLDER KIDS: Revelation 14:6-7
YOUNGER KIDS: Revelation 14:6-7
MEMORY VERSE: Psalm 106:1

EXPLAIN

- In his vision, John saw an angel calling everyone on the earth to follow God and worship Him.
- Even during God's righteous judgment, He wants people to repent and follow Him.
- God wants all people to trust in Jesus as Savior and have a relationship with Him.
- The book of Revelation reminds believers that God will make all things new. God calls Christians to be faithful and persevere, even during hard times.

APPLY

John's letter teaches us that God loves all people and wants everyone to know and follow Him. Follow the path of each letter to discover the hidden message from today's passage.

and He wants everyone to follow Him.

RESPOND

PRAY: Heavenly Father, thank You for loving me and providing Jesus so I can follow you when I repent.

HIGHLIGHT

OLDER KIDS: Revelation 15:1
YOUNGER KIDS: Revelation 15:1
MEMORY VERSE: Psalm 106:1

EXPLAIN

- John saw the preparation for God's final righteous judgments on the earth.
- John saw people worshiping God, reminding him of God's glory and holiness.
- God is right to judge the evil in the world because He is the Creator of everything.
- Ever since the world was broken by sin, God has been planning to defeat sin and death forever, and that includes His judgment against evil.

APPLY

God is both loving and just. Because He is holy and just, He punishes sin, and because He loves us, He sent Jesus to take the punishment for sin. Unscramble the words to complete the main point from today's Bible reading.

RESPOND

PRAY: Heavenly Father, thank You for being holy, just, and good.

HIGHLIGHT

OLDER KIDS: Revelation 16:17-18
YOUNGER KIDS: Revelation 16:17
MEMORY VERSE: Psalm 119:10

EXPLAIN

- John saw what he called the last seven plagues, which will finish God's righteous judgment on the earth.
- These judgments affect both creation and people.
- Even though people will suffer during this time, they will still refuse to turn to God and worship Him.
- John explained that people living during this time will curse God and realize the things happening are His judgments. Sadly, that still will not make them want to turn to Him.

APPLY

We should do all we can to share God's love with everyone we can. Solve the word puzzle to complete the sentence.

RESPOND

PRAY: Heavenly Father, help me share Your good news with everyone.

HIGHLIGHT

OLDER KIDS: Revelation 17:14
YOUNGER KIDS: Revelation 17:14
MEMORY VERSE: Psalm 119:10

EXPLAIN

- In John's vision, an angel showed him a woman and a beast. This is called symbolism because it tells a story with pictures.
- The woman represents people who are tempted away from God, and the beast represents Satan.
- Even though in this vision the woman and the beast are strong, they are no match for the Lamb (Jesus), and God is still in charge of everything.
- John needed to use symbolic language to describe things that were hard to understand. We know this is symbolism because the angel explained to John the meaning of what he saw.

APPLY

Revelation calls Jesus the Lion of Judah and the Lamb of God. Jesus is more powerful than Satan, and God is always in charge. Complete the second half of the face of each animal below.

RESPOND

PRAY: Jesus, You are powerful! Help me to remember You are in control of all things.

HIGHLIGHT

OLDER KIDS: Revelation 18:1-2
YOUNGER KIDS: Revelation 18:1-2
MEMORY VERSE: Psalm 119:10

EXPLAIN

- John saw an angel sing a victory song, and the entire earth was lit up by God's glory.
- The angel was announcing God's final victory, which has been prophesied throughout Scripture.
- Babylon represents selfishness and idolatry, or the worship of things that are not God. God is forever, but things are not.
- God has all authority over everything. John saw God's glory fill the earth in his vision. God has ultimate victory over everything. He is worthy of all glory and worship.

APPLY

This victory over the things of the world reminds us that none of the things here—money or things we have—will last forever. Solve the maze to help you remember what lasts forever.

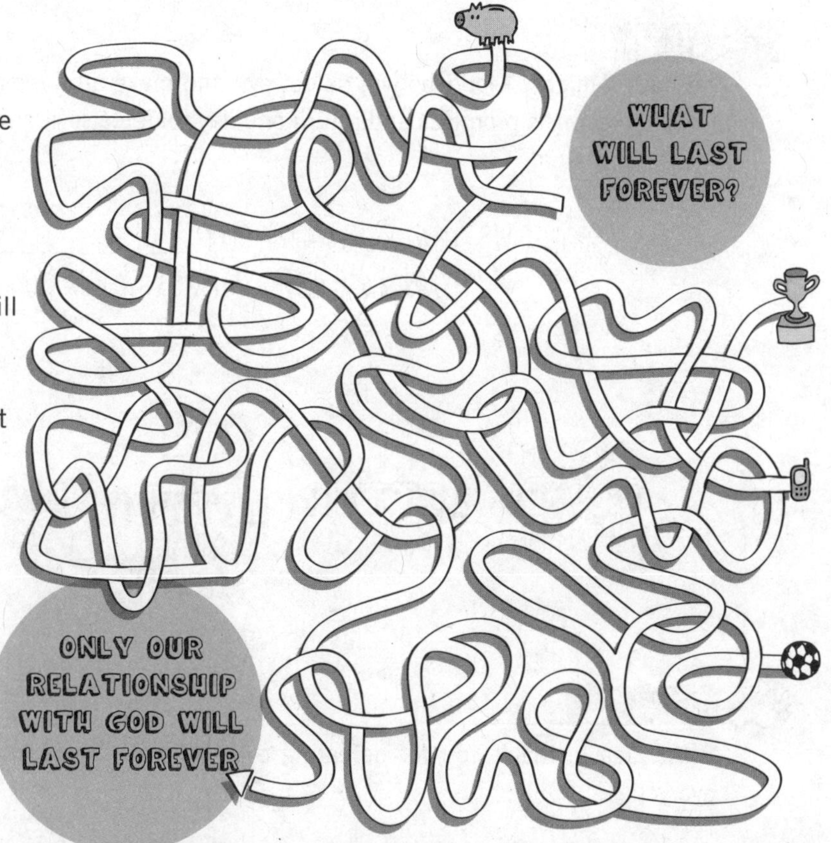

RESPOND

PRAY: Heavenly Father, thank You for a relationship with You that will last forever.

OLDER KIDS: Revelation 19:11-13
YOUNGER KIDS: Revelation 19:11-13
MEMORY VERSE: Psalm 119:10

EXPLAIN

- John wrote about Jesus returning as a mighty King who will defeat evil once for all.
- John described Jesus as riding a white horse. He gave descriptions of Jesus' power and character.
- Jesus is faithful, true, and righteous.
- Jesus came to earth the first time as a baby. When He returns, He will come as a mighty King, ready to battle against Satan and his army. Jesus will defeat Satan and the forces of evil because He is all-powerful.

APPLY

We have a mighty King who will defeat evil and make all things new. We can trust Jesus to keep His promises and return one day to defeat evil and sin forever. Fill in the missing word:

Because we know Jesus will win over ____ ____ ____ ____,
we should share His good news with everyone.

THE SECOND **VOWEL** IN THE ALPHABET	THE **LETTER** BEFORE **W**	THE **LETTER** THAT FOLLOWS **H**	THE **LETTER** BEFORE **M**

PRAY: Jesus, thank You for defeating evil. Help me share Your good news with everyone.

OLDER KIDS: Revelation 20:1-3
YOUNGER KIDS: Revelation 20:1-3
MEMORY VERSE: Psalm 119:10

EXPLAIN

- John wrote about a time when Satan will be locked away.
- During this time, Jesus will reign on earth.
- After that time is over, Satan will again try to defeat God, but God will defeat Satan and send him away forever.
- After Satan's final defeat, John wrote that God will judge all people. Those who have faith in Jesus stay with God for eternity. Those who do not will join Satan forever.

APPLY

God is sovereign and has ultimate victory over sin and death. Write Psalm 119:10 in the circle.

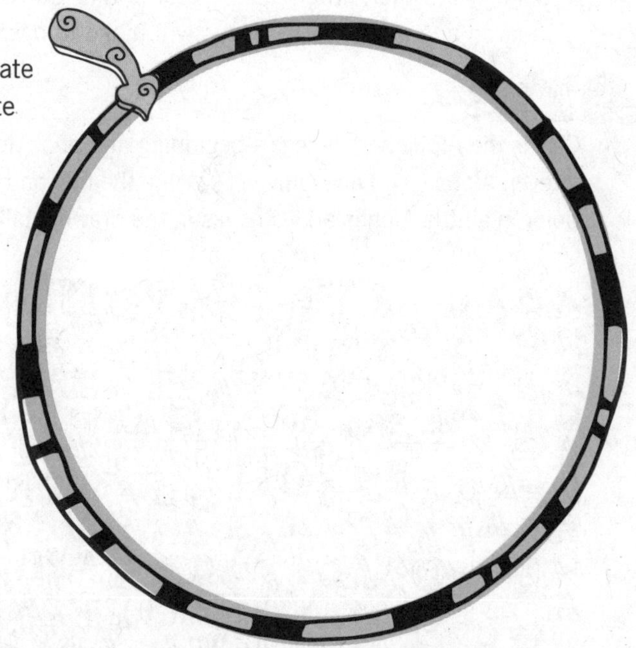

RESPOND

PRAY: Heavenly Father, thank You for having victory over sin and death.

HIGHLIGHT

OLDER KIDS: Revelation 21:5-7
YOUNGER KIDS: Revelation 21:5-7
MEMORY VERSE: Psalm 119:11

EXPLAIN

- John saw a vision of a new heaven and a new earth.
- In John's vision, Satan, death, and evil were judged and sent away. People who chose not to believe in Jesus were sent to eternal punishment away from God forever.
- God is the Alpha and Omega—the beginning and end. God was at the beginning, and He will be here forever. He wants everyone to know about Him, so He wants His followers to tell people about Him.
- John wrote that, when Jesus returns and defeats all evil, there will be a new heaven and a new earth. Jesus will make things new.

APPLY

God is the Alpha and Omega—beginning and end. He has defeated evil and will reign forever. Alpha (Α) and Omega (Ω) are the first and last letters of the Greek alphabet. Color in all the Alphas and Omegas in the drawing below to complete the sentence.

Jesus will reign ________ .

RESPOND

PRAY: Heavenly Father, thank You for being the Alpha and Omega.

HIGHLIGHT

OLDER KIDS: Revelation 22:1-5
YOUNGER KIDS: Revelation 22:1-5
MEMORY VERSE: Psalm 119:11

EXPLAIN

- The final part of the vision God gave John described a river flowing from God's throne.
- The place described is beautiful, peaceful, free from sin and death, and will last forever.
- God's faithfulness is clear throughout the entire Bible, and all people should trust Him and He can be trusted when He declares what will happen.
- The Bible began with a description of Eden—a paradise of God's perfect world. The new paradise will be a city that will continue forever because Jesus' defeated of sin and death.

APPLY

God is faithful and true, and everything He does is working toward when those who follow Him can finally live with Him forever. Find the highlighted words in the word search.

F	A	I	T	H	F	U	L	N	E	S	S	E	Y
R	P	O	I	E	U	O	H	N	K	S	Y	P	R
E	A	S	D	F	D	G	R	Y	H	N	F	A	Y
E	K	J	H	P	G	E	T	E	F	T	Y	R	B
F	E	R	R	T	Y	G	N	H	V	X	C	A	H
R	Z	I	R	A	T	Y	T	Y	R	E	Z	D	N
O	M	V	N	B	V	C	R	F	G	O	R	I	I
M	P	E	A	C	E	F	U	L	U	T	N	S	G
S	C	R	T	E	Y	H	S	J	N	N	C	E	Z
I	Y	T	R	F	V	B	T	J	K	K	B	V	E
N	T	I	V	I	S	I	O	N	K	L	R	A	S
S	T	D	E	F	E	A	T	E	D	F	S	E	Y
D	B	E	A	U	T	I	F	U	L	Z	O	Z	T
F	W	W	E	T	Y	I	O	S	L	J	H	G	D

RESPOND

PRAY: Heavenly Father, thank You for Your faithfulness and for providing a way for me to be with You forever.

OLDER KIDS: Matthew 1:20-21, 24
YOUNGER KIDS: Matthew 1:20-21
MEMORY VERSE: Psalm 119:11

EXPLAIN

- Matthew began his book by talking about Jesus' family, all the way back to Abraham.
- This was important to the Jewish people because it fulfilled Old Testament prophecies or promises about the Messiah.
- At first Joseph was afraid to marry Mary, but an angel told him in a dream not to be afraid.
- Joseph was faithful to do what the angel told him, and he showed faithfulness to Mary as well. Matthew wanted to make sure that Christians understood God's faithfulness to His promise all the way from Abraham.

APPLY

God is faithful and true, and He will do what He says.
Write Psalm 119:11 in the box to help you memorize it this week.

RESPOND

PRAY: Heavenly Father, thank You for being faithful and true.

HIGHLIGHT

OLDER KIDS: Matthew 2:1-2, 9-12
YOUNGER KIDS: Matthew 2:1-2, 9-12
MEMORY VERSE: Psalm 119:11

EXPLAIN

- Wise men came looking for Jesus. They followed a star in the sky.
- King Herod was jealous of Jesus and told the wise men to report back to him about Jesus later.
- The wise men fell to their knees, worshiped Jesus, and gave Him gifts of gold, frankincense, and myrrh.
- Herod wanted to know where the King of the Jews was because he was threatened—he did not want there to be another king. The wise men did not help Herod. Instead, they praised Jesus, gave Him gifts, and avoided Herod on their way home.

APPLY

Jesus is our Savior, and He is worthy to be praised. The wise men worshiped Jesus and made wise decisions to honor Him and protect Him from Herod. Discuss: How can we make wise decisions and honor Jesus?

RESPOND

PRAY: Jesus, thank You for coming to earth as our Savior.

HIGHLIGHT

OLDER KIDS: Matthew 3:1-3
YOUNGER KIDS: Matthew 3:1-3
MEMORY VERSE: Psalm 119:11

EXPLAIN

- Matthew wrote about John the Baptist, Jesus' cousin, who prepared the way for Jesus.
- John the Baptist called people to turn away from their sins.
- John's ministry was the fulfillment of the prophecy in Isaiah 40:3 that said someone would come to prepare the way for the Messiah.
- Matthew helped people understand that John and Jesus fulfilled what was written about them in the Old Testament. John prepared the way for Jesus to begin His ministry.

APPLY

Jesus is the Messiah who was promised by God in the Old Testament. Write 3 facts you remember from today's reading.

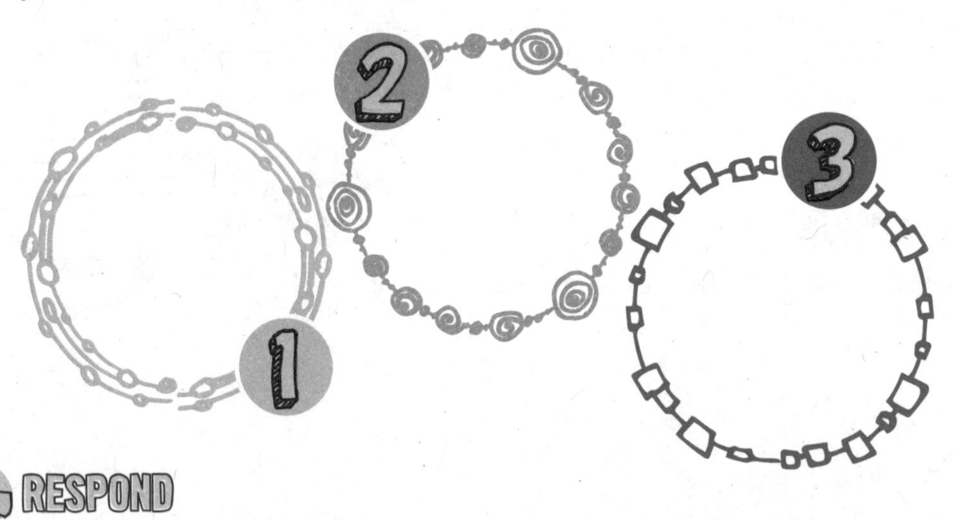

RESPOND

PRAY: Heavenly Father, thank You for sending Jesus just like You promised.

OLDER KIDS: Matthew 4:1, 10-11
YOUNGER KIDS: Matthew 4:1, 10-11
MEMORY VERSE: Psalm 119:105

EXPLAIN

- After Jesus was baptized, He was led by the Holy Spirit into the wilderness to be tempted.
- The devil tried to tempt Jesus and cause Him to sin three times.
- Each time Jesus was tempted, He used Scripture to defeat Satan.
- Jesus was led into the wilderness by the Holy Spirit where Satan tempted Him three times. Jesus resisted Satan's temptations using God's Word, and Jesus won!

Jesus understands what it is like to be tempted to sin. When we are tempted to sin, we can remember Jesus and follow His example to fight temptation with God's Word. Complete this sentence by writing the first letter of each picture in the box above it.

Jesus was a perfect sacrifice for our sin because...

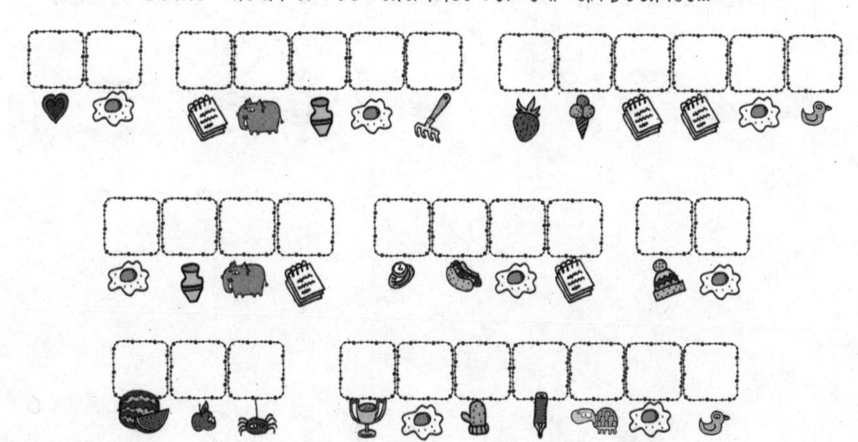

PRAY: Heavenly Father, help me follow Christ's example and not sin when I am tempted.

HIGHLIGHT

OLDER KIDS: Matthew 5:43-48
YOUNGER KIDS: Matthew 5:43-48
MEMORY VERSE: Psalm 119:105

EXPLAIN

- Jesus began His ministry by choosing twelve disciples and preaching to crowds of people.
- Jesus' Sermon on the Mount taught God's people what life in His kingdom would look like.
- Jesus told His followers to love all people, even their enemies.
- Jesus instructed His followers to practice loving and praying for their enemies. His teachings in the Sermon on the Mount show believers what the life of someone who follows Jesus could look like.

APPLY

Jesus is our perfect example. He gives us instructions on how to honor God with our actions by loving others. Draw a straight line from the picture at the top to the picture that matches it at the bottom. Then write the letter you crossed over in the box.

RESPOND

PRAY: Jesus, thank You for teaching me how to honor God and love others.

OLDER KIDS: Matthew 6:9-15
YOUNGER KIDS: Matthew 6:9-15
MEMORY VERSE: Psalm 119:105

- Jesus continued preaching to the people and commanded them not to pray to be seen by others but to pray with a sincere heart.
- Jesus taught His disciples how to pray by showing them what to pray. Prayer is talking to God and expressing trust in His control.
- Jesus told His followers they should have the right reasons for doing things. They should not worry or be anxious, but trust God in all things.
- Jesus criticized the hypocrisy (deceiving others to believe they are someone they are not) of people who pray to be seen. He taught people to pray with pure motives, not to bring attention to themselves.

APPLY

When we pray, we should pray with a pure heart and our words should be honest. Write Psalm 119:105 in the box to help you memorize it this week.

RESPOND

PRAY: Jesus, thank You for teaching me how to pray and trust You for all things

HIGHLIGHT

OLDER KIDS: Matthew 7:13-14
YOUNGER KIDS: Matthew 7:13-14
MEMORY VERSE: Psalm 119:105

EXPLAIN

- Matthew wrote about Jesus' Sermon on the Mount. Jesus told believers to ask, search, and knock. Jesus meant that believers should pray to God about everything.
- Jesus taught that the gate that leads to God's kingdom is narrow. The road that leads to eternal life is difficult. Not many people choose to follow God.
- Jesus taught that the wide gate and easy road lead to destruction. Believers should obey God, even when it is difficult.
- Jesus urged His followers to be seekers—to ask, search, and knock continually—and they would learn more about God. Many people will choose the easy way, but believers must trust in the Lord. His way is challenging, but it is worth it.

APPLY

It is not always easy to love God and put our trust in Him, but it is always worth it. Starting in the middle room, which door would you knock on to find your way to the arrow?

RESPOND

PRAY: Heavenly Father, help me put my trust in You, even when it is not easy.

HIGHLIGHT

OLDER KIDS: Matthew 8:14-17
YOUNGER KIDS: Matthew 8:14-17
MEMORY VERSE: Psalm 119:105

EXPLAIN

- Jesus performed many miracles. He healed a soldier's servant, Peter's mother-in-law, and many other people who were sick or possessed by demons.
- Isaiah had written that the Messiah would carry our weakness and pain.
- Jesus was the Messiah prophesied by Isaiah (Isaiah 53:4). He changed the lives of many, and He continues to work in people's lives in miraculous ways today.
- After His Sermon on the Mount, Jesus cared for people. He healed the sick and the demon-possessed, just as Isaiah had prophesied hundreds of years before. The crowds increased, and Jesus continued to teach and heal as news of His ministry spread.

APPLY

Jesus fulfilled Isaiah's words and changed many people's lives through miracles. Jesus changes us, too, by forgiving our sin and working His plan in our lives. Discuss: How does Jesus change our lives?

RESPOND

PRAY: Jesus, thank You for changing my life in an amazing way by forgiving my sin. Help me to trust and follow Your plans for my life.

HIGHLIGHT

OLDER KIDS: Matthew 9:35-38
YOUNGER KIDS: Matthew 9:35-38
MEMORY VERSE: Proverbs 29:22

EXPLAIN

- Jesus taught people in many different towns and synagogues during His ministry.
- He felt compassion for the people because He knew their greatest need would be found by loving God with all their heart and believing in Him.
- When Jesus said to His disciples that the harvest is plentiful but the workers are few, He meant there are a lot of people who need to hear about His good news and not enough people to share it with them.
- Jesus calls all of His followers to discipleship (helping others grow in their faith) and missions (sharing the gospel everywhere you go) so that others can learn about His good news, believe in Him, and grow in their faith.

APPLY

It is our job to tell others about Jesus and His good news. In the boxes below write the names of some people you can tell about the good news on the left. In the boxes on the right, write what you can tell each person about who Jesus is.

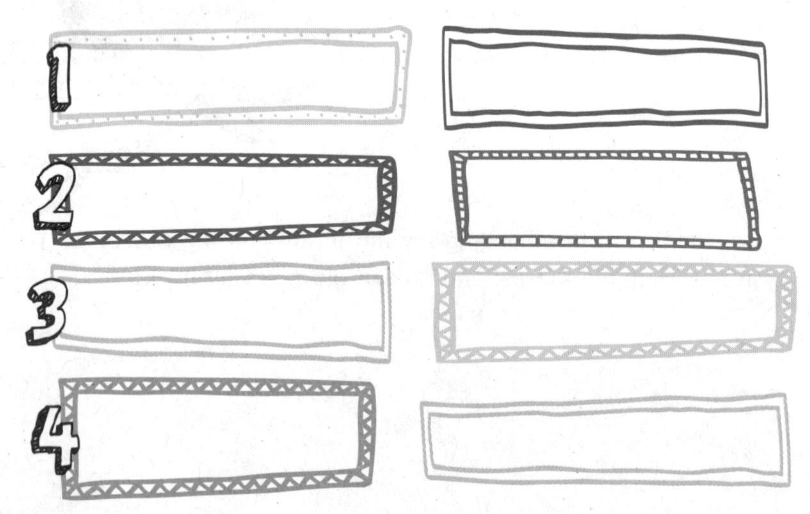

PRAY: Jesus, help me tell others about Your good news.

OLDER KIDS: Matthew 10:5-8
YOUNGER KIDS: Matthew 10:5-7
MEMORY VERSE: Proverbs 29:22

EXPLAIN

- After explaining how many people needed to hear His good news, Jesus sent His disciples out to tell others, beginning with the Jews.
- The disciples learned from Jesus during His ministry. He prepared them for the work He was sending them out to do.
- Jesus gave His disciples instructions on how to act as they went to different places to share His good news.
- Jesus trained the disciples for the purpose of sending them out to share the good news of salvation with people. He encouraged them to continue in the ministry they had learned from Him, and to make more disciples.

APPLY

Everyone who trusts in Jesus is called to make disciples by sharing His good news with others. If you are a Christian, you are called to be a disciple-maker. God wants to use you to tell others people about Jesus. Write Proverbs 29:22 in the space below to help you memorize it this week.

RESPOND

PRAY: Jesus, thank You for preparing me to share Your good news. Please help me tell others about You.

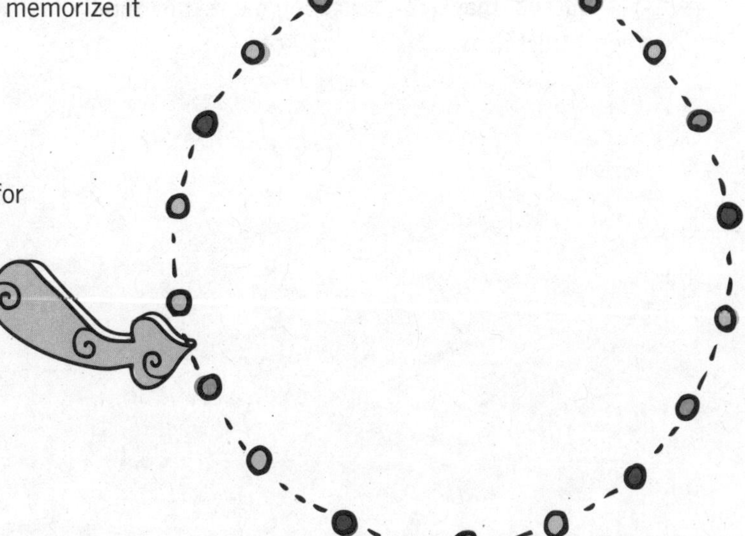

OLDER KIDS: Matthew 11:28-30
YOUNGER KIDS: Matthew 11:28
MEMORY VERSE: Proverbs 29:22

- Even though Jesus had been teaching in many towns, lots of people did not believe in Him.
- Jesus invited the people to come to Him and trust Him for their salvation.
- Jesus explained that for those who believe in Him, He provides rest. Jesus gives rest and freedom from the burden of guilt and sin to everyone who repents.
- Jesus loves everyone, and He wants everyone to love Him. He wants all people to trust in Him for salvation and receive Him.

Those who have faith in Jesus and follow Him will have rest in Him. Discuss: What does it mean to rest in Jesus?

PRAY: Jesus, thank You for giving me rest in You when I trust in You.

OLDER KIDS: Matthew 12:33-35
YOUNGER KIDS: Matthew 12:33-35
MEMORY VERSE: Proverbs 29:22

EXPLAIN

- Jesus used a tree as an example to teach the Pharisees about what matters most.
- He explained that just like a good tree gives good fruit and a bad tree gives bad fruit, a person's actions (their fruit) will reveal what is in his heart.
- Jesus made it clear that what's in a person's heart is what matters most, because what's in his heart will come out of his mouth and show in his actions.
- Jesus taught the Pharisees that following the law without having a changed heart did not make them good. In fact, He said they were like a bunch of snakes because they pretended to be good by what they said but their hearts had not been changed by God.

Our words and actions show what's in our heart. Look over the Explain points above and complete the statements in the green boxes by matching them with the statements in the blue boxes.

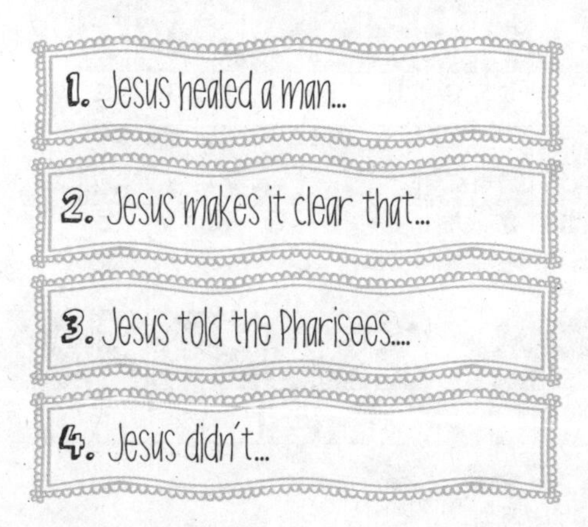

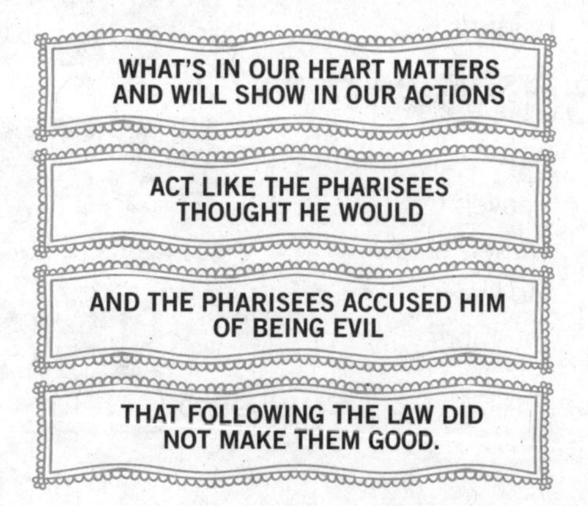

PRAY: Heavenly Father, help my thoughts, attitudes, and actions reflect my changed heart so others see You in my life.

HIGHLIGHT

OLDER KIDS: Matthew 13:34-35
YOUNGER KIDS: Matthew 13:34-35
MEMORY VERSE: Proverbs 29:22

EXPLAIN

- Matthew shared a lot of Jesus' parables.
- Jesus explained why He used parables to teach people. Jesus would use familiar people, places, and things in His parable. He often explained to His disciples what a parable meant.
- He taught the people that His parables were fulfillment of Old Testament prophecy. He wanted them to understand that He was the promised Messiah.
- Jesus didn't just tell fun stories—His stories were all meant to help His disciples understand more about Him and God's kingdom.

APPLY

Jesus helps us understand more about Him through reading and understanding His Word, the Bible. Decode the message below using the dominoes to reveal what is true based on today's reading.

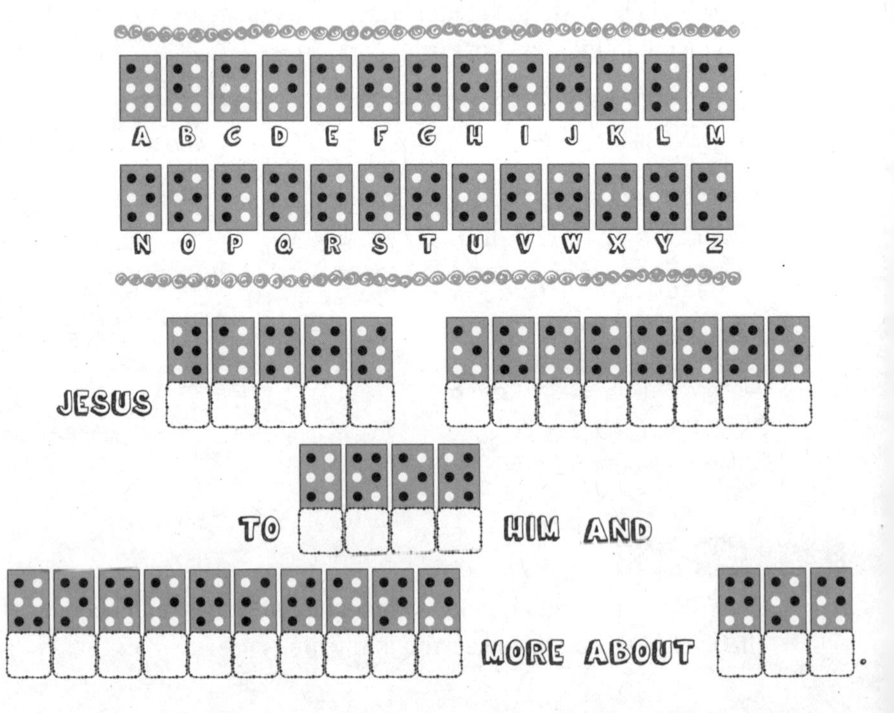

RESPOND

PRAY: Heavenly Father, help me know You more.

HIGHLIGHT

OLDER KIDS: Matthew 14:25-33
YOUNGER KIDS: Matthew 14:26-30
MEMORY VERSE: Proverbs 30:5

EXPLAIN

- The disciples were on a boat, and Jesus walked out to them on top of the water!
- Peter wanted to go out to Jesus, and Jesus told him to come.
- Peter became afraid and started to sink into the water, but he called out to Jesus, and Jesus saved him. Peter's faith was not perfect, and Jesus knew that.
- Jesus again showed the disciples His power as the Son of God as He walked on the water, and He even had Peter come to Him.

APPLY

Jesus helps us trust and follow Him, even when we mess up sometimes. Write the name of each item in the column below it to reveal the missing word.

We do not have to be __________ to follow Jesus.

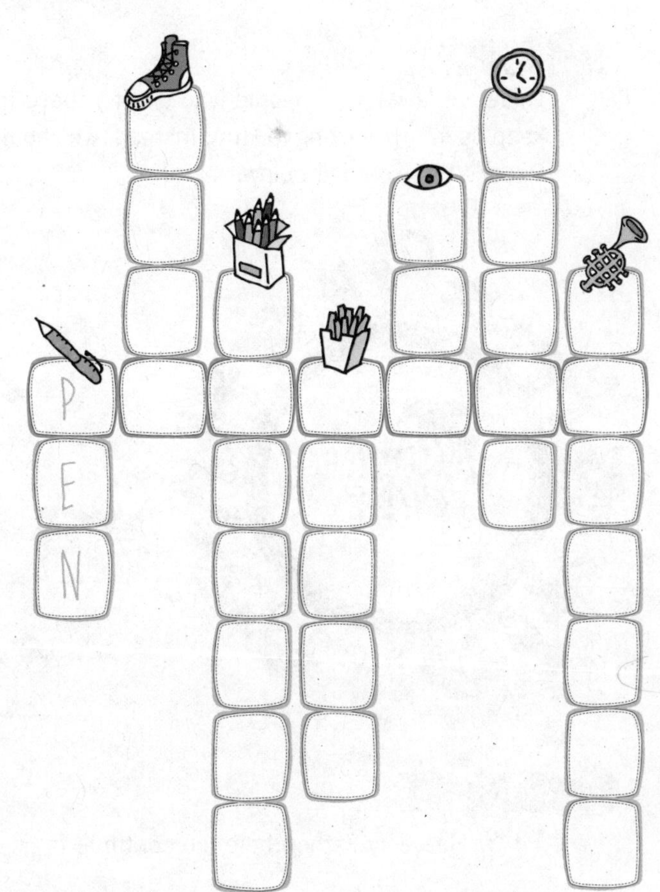

RESPOND

PRAY: Jesus, thank You for reminding me that I don't have to be perfect to follow You. Please help me follow You and trust You no matter what.

HIGHLIGHT

OLDER KIDS: Matthew 15:29-31
YOUNGER KIDS: Matthew 15:31
MEMORY VERSE: Proverbs 30:5

EXPLAIN

- Jesus continued to heal people and point them to worship God.
- The news of Jesus spread and crowds of people came to Him, bringing with them people to be healed.
- Through these healings, more people believed and gave glory to God.
- The religious leaders kept trying to find ways to get Jesus into trouble. Jesus didn't let them or their unbelief keep Him from showing others God's glory.

APPLY

There will always be people who don't believe in Jesus, but we must not let them keep us from believing in Him. Instead, we should continue to point others to Jesus. Decode the message below.

RESPOND

PRAY: Heavenly Father, help me continue to trust You and point others to You.

OLDER KIDS: Matthew 16:13-20
YOUNGER KIDS: Matthew 16:15-16
MEMORY VERSE: Proverbs 30:5

EXPLAIN

- Jesus asked the disciples who people said He was.
- Peter answered that Jesus is the Son of God.
- The disciples' belief in Jesus was important because He wouldn't always be with them. They needed to continue in their faith even when He was gone.
- Jesus had just finished explaining (through a parable) that He wanted the disciples to be cautious about listening to teaching from the Pharisees and Sadducees. Jesus explained that He is the Messiah, the Son of God. He warned the disciples not to tell others that He was the Messiah yet because the crowds misunderstood.

APPLY

We must have faith in Jesus, even if others do not believe in Him. Find the highlighted words above in the word search.

RESPOND

PRAY: Jesus, help me to have faith in You in every circumstance.

HIGHLIGHT

OLDER KIDS: Matthew 17:1-9
YOUNGER KIDS: Matthew 17:2,5-8
MEMORY VERSE: Proverbs 30:5

EXPLAIN

- Jesus took Peter, James, and John up on a mountain by themselves.
- Jesus was transformed (we call this the transfiguration), and they saw Moses and Elijah standing with Him.
- God spoke and told them to listen to Jesus. Jesus wanted the disciples to see His glory so their faith in Him would be stronger.
- Jesus wanted the disciples to be ready to continue His ministry after He was gone. They had to have strong faith, and Jesus was preparing them.

APPLY

Jesus wants to help our faith in Him grow. Write Proverbs 30:5 in the circle below to help you memorize it this week.

RESPOND

PRAY: Jesus, help my faith in You to grow.

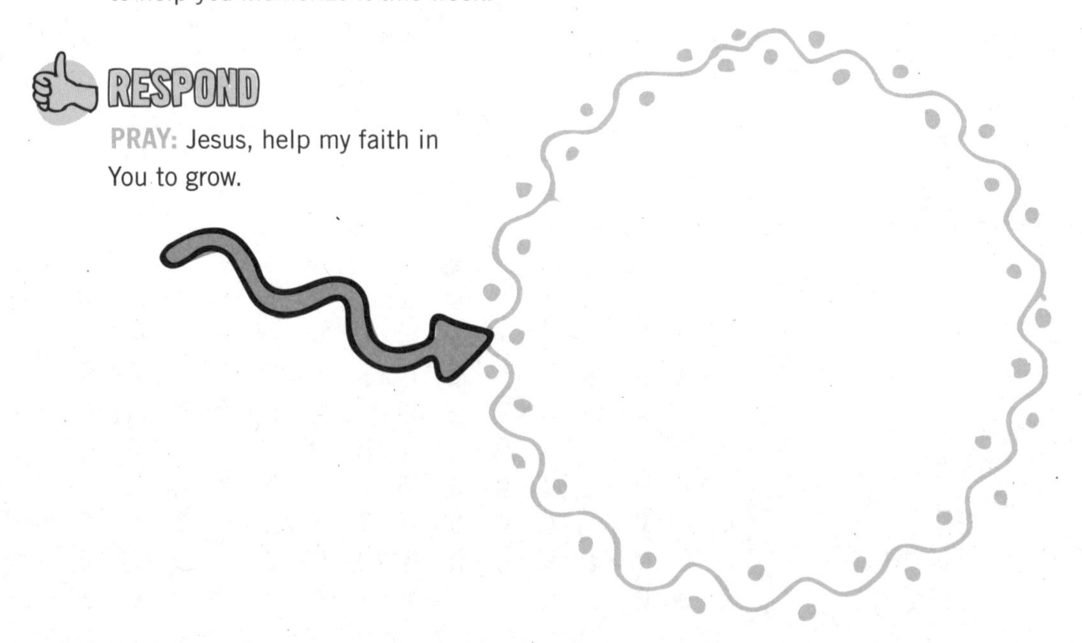

HIGHLIGHT

OLDER KIDS: Matthew 18:1-5
YOUNGER KIDS: Matthew 18:1-5
MEMORY VERSE: Proverbs 30:5

EXPLAIN

- The disciples were arguing about which one of them was the best.
- Jesus showed them a child and reminded them that humility, dependence on God, and childlike faith are the greatest things they can have.
- Jesus taught the disciples how they should live so they could teach others.
- Jesus taught the disciples about God's kingdom and about their personal lives. He knew it would be important for them to understand these things so they could teach others.

APPLY

We should focus on loving Jesus and following Him. Discuss: How can we focus on loving Jesus?

RESPOND

PRAY: Jesus, help me follow You with humility and faith.

HIGHLIGHT

OLDER KIDS: Matthew 19:23-26
YOUNGER KIDS: Matthew 19:25-26
MEMORY VERSE: Proverbs 31:8

EXPLAIN

- Jesus said it would be easier for a camel to go through the eye of a needle (a tiny hole) than for a rich man to get into heaven.
- Jesus taught that even something that seems impossible to people is possible with God.
- Jesus wanted people to know that the only way to heaven is through trusting Him. Salvation is only possible because of God's grace.
- Jesus used examples like a camel going through a tiny hole because they were easy for people to understand. People are to love God with all their hearts and cannot love money or anything else more than loving God.

APPLY

Nothing we do will get us eternal life with God. We can only have eternal life through Jesus. Discuss: What does forever mean? What do you think it will be like to spend forever with God?

RESPOND

PRAY: Heavenly Father, thank You for providing a way for me to spend forever with You.

HIGHLIGHT

OLDER KIDS: Matthew 20:9-16
YOUNGER KIDS: Matthew 20:9-16
MEMORY VERSE: Proverbs 31:8

EXPLAIN

- Jesus told a parable of a land owner who hired men at different times of the day to work for him.
- The land owner paid the men all the same, no matter how long the men worked.
- The men who began work in the morning were upset that the men who began work late in the day got paid the same amount they did. The land owner paid the men who started late the same because he was generous.
- Jesus used this parable to illustrate that God is generous with His grace—everyone receives the same grace from God.

APPLY

Our God is a generous God. He gives us grace and mercy when we don't deserve it. Cross out every other letter to reveal the hidden message.

God's grace is given to everyone ________.

RESPOND

PRAY: Heavenly Father, thank You for Your generous grace.

HIGHLIGHT

OLDER KIDS: Matthew 21:14-17
YOUNGER KIDS: Matthew 21:14-17
MEMORY VERSE: Proverbs 31:8

EXPLAIN

- Jesus was in the temple complex when children came in praising Him.
- The religious leaders were upset about the children praising Jesus.
- Jesus pointed out that the children were fulfilling Old Testament prophecy by praising Him.
- The religious leaders would not believe Jesus was truly the Messiah sent from God, and they did not want to accept anyone's praise of Him—even the praise of children.

APPLY

Kids can praise Jesus too! Place a check mark by all the ways you can praise Jesus. Is there anything on the list you would like to do more of?

RESPOND

PRAY: Jesus, I praise You for being the Son of God.

OLDER KIDS: Matthew 22:1-5
YOUNGER KIDS: Matthew 22:1-5
MEMORY VERSE: Proverbs 31:8

EXPLAIN

- Jesus used a parable to teach people about God's kingdom.
- In this parable, many people were invited to a wedding feast, but only a few chose to go.
- Just like the parable, God invites everyone to believe in Him, but only a few will.
- Jesus used this parable to explain that some people would refuse the invitation to trust God and enjoy Him forever in His kingdom. God wants everyone to trust Jesus as Savior, even though some will refuse.

Anyone who believes in Jesus will be saved. Jesus calls us, His disciples, to invite everyone to respond to the good news of Jesus. Discuss: Why is it important to tell others about Jesus, even though some will refuse to trust in Him for salvation?

RESPOND

PRAY: Jesus, thank You for making a way for me to enter God's kingdom. Help me to tell others about You.

WEEK 51 DAY 5

HIGHLIGHT

OLDER KIDS: Matthew 23:1-3
YOUNGER KIDS: Matthew 23:1-3
MEMORY VERSE: Proverbs 31:8

EXPLAIN

- Jesus spoke to the crowds and to His disciples about the religious leaders who refused to believe He was the Messiah.
- The religious leaders did not live like Jesus taught His followers.
- Jesus was unhappy with them because it was their job to teach people the Scriptures, but they were not teaching it properly.
- Jesus told the people to follow the Scriptures, but not to follow the example of the scribes and Pharisees. God is serious about His Word and what it teaches.

APPLY

God cares about how our words, attitudes, and actions influence others to follow Him. Find all the green letters to answer the question below.

S M D G O H S T Q C N A V O Z E Y
O W T U W X O M I S L A R E K B T
H J R F G E M P A L T I D Q A S I L
P X O Z I V C T D N R B E S M W G
T B G X J K O A Y M E W A O F K
N F Z E G M X S I B I A C N V H Q
C D U S U B K G W L S X O D M Y

We should always point people ☐☐☐☐☐☐

☐☐☐☐☐.

RESPOND

PRAY: Jesus, help me always point others toward You.

HIGHLIGHT

OLDER KIDS: Matthew 24:30-31
YOUNGER KIDS: Matthew 24:30-31
MEMORY VERSE: Psalm 150:6

EXPLAIN

- Jesus was teaching His disciples about the second time He will come to earth.
- Jesus will come back to earth on the clouds of heaven, in power and glory.
- Jesus will return with angels to gather His people.
- Jesus wanted His disciples to know that the world was not going to be kind to Christians. There will be wars. The sky will grow dark. The love in many people's hearts will grow cold. Jesus promised His return, though, and He will return with power and glory.

APPLY

Jesus will come to earth again with power and glory. Use the clue letters to fill in the crossword with the highlighted words above.

RESPOND

PRAY: Jesus, thank You for planning to come back to earth with power and glory.

HIGHLIGHT

OLDER KIDS: Matthew 25:31-34
YOUNGER KIDS: Matthew 25:31-34
MEMORY VERSE: Psalm 150:6

EXPLAIN

- Jesus told a parable about sheep and goats to explain judgment.
- He was talking about what will happen in the end times during God's final judgment.
- Jesus will separate His followers (sheep) from those who refused to follow Him (goats).
- Jesus taught His followers that not everyone will choose to follow Him, but it's important for believers to tell everyone the good news.

APPLY

We should tell others about Jesus because we want everyone to know about Him. Complete the sentence by unscrambling the words.

We should...

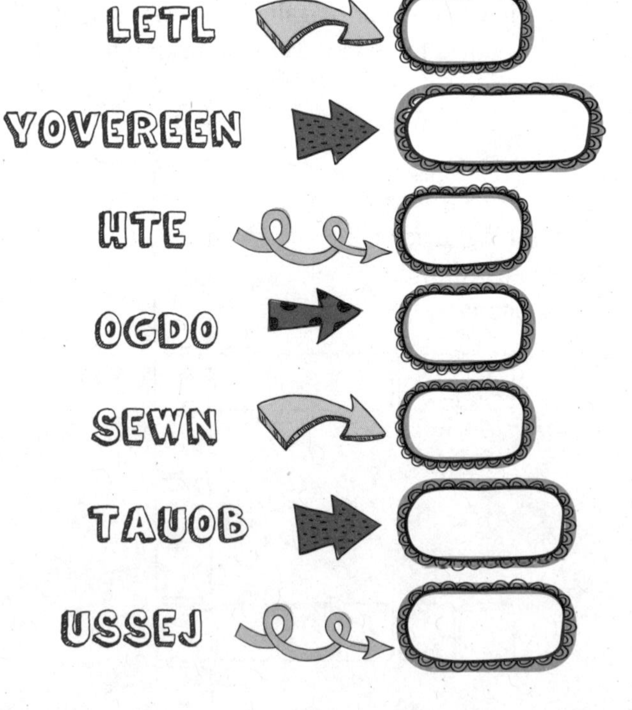

RESPOND

PRAY: Jesus, help me to tell others the good news about You.

HIGHLIGHT

OLDER KIDS: Matthew 26:1-2
YOUNGER KIDS: Matthew 26:1-2
MEMORY VERSE: Psalm 150:6

EXPLAIN

- Jesus told the disciples He would be arrested and crucified, but the disciples still didn't fully understand.
- Jesus knew all things because He is the Messiah. He knew the time had come for Him to be crucified.
- Jesus did not have to allow Himself to be crucified for sin, but He did it so people could be forgiven of their sins.
- Jesus is often called the Son of Man in the book of Matthew. The Jewish people recognized this name as the name of the Messiah they believed would come.

APPLY

Jesus was our perfect sacrifice. He gave His life and died on the cross so we can be forgiven of sin when we trust in Him. Use the maritime flags to decode the secret message to today's devotion.

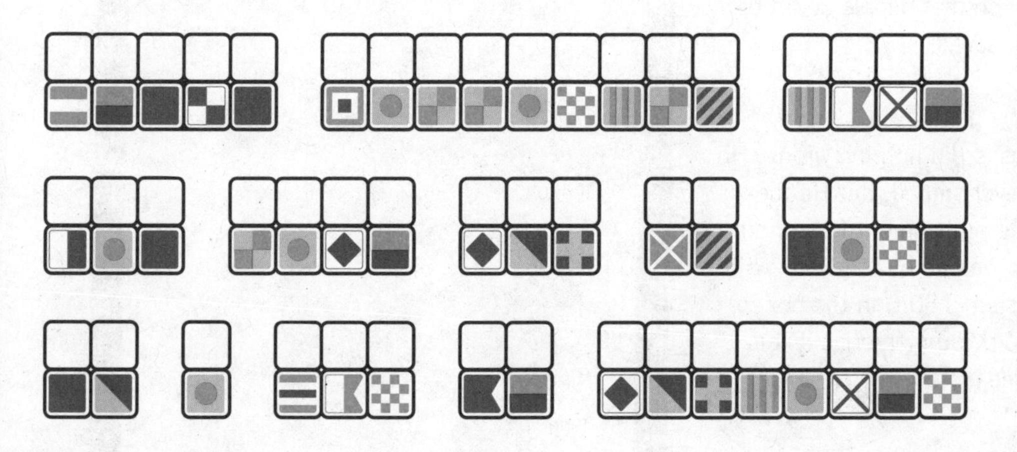

A B C D E F G H I J K L M N O P Q R S T U V W X Y Z

RESPOND

PRAY: Jesus, thank You for giving Your life so I can be forgiven.

HIGHLIGHT

OLDER KIDS: Matthew 27:27-31
YOUNGER KIDS: Matthew 27:27-31
MEMORY VERSE: Psalm 150:6

EXPLAIN

- Jesus was betrayed by Judas and arrested. The soldiers took Jesus to Pilate, the governor.
- The people wanted Jesus to be crucified even though He had done nothing wrong.
- Pilate's soldiers beat Jesus, made fun of Him, and placed a crown of thorns on His head.
- Jesus was betrayed by Judas, one of His own disciples. Pilate listened to the people and allowed Jesus to be crucified and killed by the Roman soldiers. Jesus endured horrible suffering, but He never complained, sinned, or stopped what was happening. Jesus obeyed God's plan and took the full punishment for sin so that people could be saved.

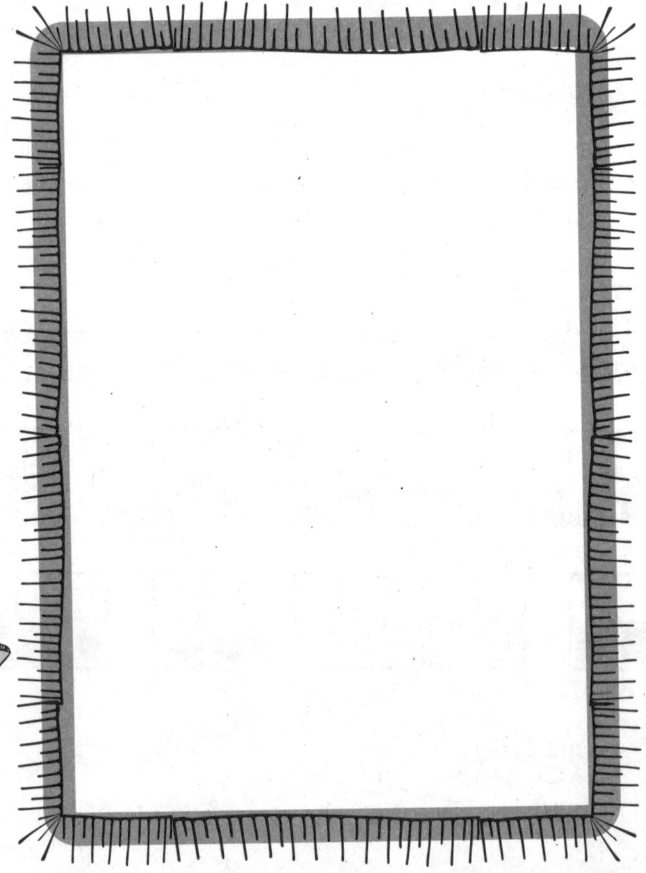

APPLY

Jesus did nothing wrong. He never sinned, but He took the punishment for our sin so we can be forgiven. Write Psalm 150:6 in the box to help you memorize it this week.

RESPOND

PRAY: Jesus, thank You for taking the punishment for my sin.

OLDER KIDS: Matthew 28:18-20
YOUNGER KIDS: Matthew 28:18-20
MEMORY VERSE: Psalm 150:6

EXPLAIN

- Jesus had risen from the dead and shown Himself to many people. Before He returned to heaven, He gave His disciples important instructions.
- Jesus' instructions were for them to make disciples wherever they went just like He did while on earth.
- Jesus promised to always be with them.
- The good news about Jesus is for everyone! It is the job of every Christian to tell people about Jesus as we go through life. Christians are called to pray for and tell other people about Jesus' forgiveness of sin all across the world.

Jesus wants you to tell others about Him. Who does Jesus want to know the good news? Solve the maze to find out.

PRAY: Jesus, help me to tell others about You.

CHURCH TEACHING PLAN

Use this teaching plan if your church wants a weekly kids' small group focused on *Foundations for Kids: New Testament*. You can group all of your kids together or divide into Younger Kids and Older Kids. *Foundations for Kids: New Testament* is written for 52 weeks of Bible study, 5 days per week. Your meeting could be set up to review what kids have read the week before or to preview what they will read on their own in the week ahead.

Foundations For Kids: New Testament uses the H.E.A.R. method. The acronym H.E.A.R. stands for Highlight, Explain, Apply, and Respond. Each of these four steps contributes to creating an atmosphere to hear God speak. Structure each meeting to go through the H.E.A.R. formula.

Each week, there will be 5 passages for Younger Kids to read and 5 passages for Older Kids to read, plus a memory verse for the week. The passages always overlap and are written to the same Bible truth. Each week your meeting should...

- **READ THE BIBLE PASSAGES.** God speaks through the Bible.
- **MEMORIZE THE WEEKLY VERSE.** Play a variety of Bible memory games where you write each word of the verse on a card, and the kids put the verse in order. You can hide cards throughout the room, run a relay race to put the cards together, make them into a puzzle, or turn over a card each time the kids say the verse.

EXPLAIN

Each day, Explain will have 4 bullets summarizing what happened in the verse and what the verse means. Explain each passage as you read it so kids can review what happened and make connections to their experience. Always make time for kids to ask questions.

APPLY

Every day, kids will have a learning activity to help them apply the Bible truth. This will make learning active and fun to complete these together as a group.

RESPOND

Give kids a few moments to respond in personal prayer, journal, or pray together as a group. Encourage kids to remember that prayer is part of a conversation with God.

GENERAL TIPS

1. Open every session by modeling how kids can pray before they have a quiet time with God. Pray and ask God to be with your time together and to speak to you.
2. Treat the Bible with respect and affirm its trustworthiness, authority, and reliability.
3. Ask kids what they think the passage means. Read together through Explain but be open to what each child is learning and how God speaks to the kids in your group.
4. Affirm that God loves and wants to have a relationship with each child.
5. Encourage kids any time they are able to complete their reading assignments outside of your time together.

WEEK 1

OLDER SCRIPTURE

Luke 1:26-33
Luke 2:4-7, 11-12
Luke 3:15-16; 21-22
Luke 4:1-13
Luke 5:4-11

YOUNGER SCRIPTURE

Luke 1:30-33
Luke 2:4-7, 11-12
Luke 3:21-22
Luke 4:1-4
Luke 5:9-11

MEMORY VERSE:

Proverbs 1:7

WEEK 2

OLDER SCRIPTURE

Luke 6:27-28, 31
Luke 7:12-16
Luke 8:43-48
Luke 9:46-48
Luke 10:25-28

YOUNGER SCRIPTURE

Luke 6:27-28, 31
Luke 7:12-16
Luke 8:47-48
Luke 9:46-48
Luke 10:27

MEMORY VERSE:

Proverbs 2:6

WEEK 3

OLDER SCRIPTURE

Luke 11:1-4
Luke 12:31-34
Luke 13:20-21
Luke 14:12-14
Luke 15:3-7

YOUNGER SCRIPTURE

Luke 11:1-4
Luke 12:31-34
Luke 13:20-21
Luke 14:12-14
Luke 15:3-7

MEMORY VERSE:

Psalm 1:6

WEEK 4

OLDER SCRIPTURE

Luke 16:10-12
Luke 17:11-19
Luke 18:35-43
Luke 19:39-40
Luke 20:20-26

YOUNGER SCRIPTURE

Luke 16:10
Luke 17:15-16
Luke 18:40-43
Luke 19:39-40
Luke 20:26

MEMORY VERSE:

Psalm 3:3

WEEK 5

OLDER SCRIPTURE

Luke 21:1-3
Luke 22:14-16
Luke 23:44-46
Luke 24:1-8
Acts 1:6-11

YOUNGER SCRIPTURE

Luke 21:1-3
Luke 22:14-16
Luke 23:44-46
Luke 24:1-3
Acts 1:8

MEMORY VERSE:

Proverbs 3:11

WEEK 6

OLDER SCRIPTURE

Acts 2:32-39
Acts 3:2-8
Acts 4:19-20
Acts 5:12-16
Acts 6:1-6

YOUNGER SCRIPTURE

Acts 2:36
Acts 3:6-8
Acts 4:19-20
Acts 5:12-16
Acts 6:1-6

MEMORY VERSE:

Psalm 9:9

WEEK 7

OLDER SCRIPTURE

Acts 7:54-60
Acts 8:34-38
Acts 9:1-9
Acts 10:34-36
Acts 11:27-30

YOUNGER SCRIPTURE

Acts 7:54-60
Acts 8:34-38
Acts 9:3-6
Acts 10:34-36
Acts 11:27-30

MEMORY VERSE:

Proverbs 4:23

WEEK 8

OLDER SCRIPTURE

Acts 12:6-11
Acts 13:1-3
Acts 14:21-22
James 1:2-3
James 2:14-17

YOUNGER SCRIPTURE

Acts 12:6-11
Acts 13:1-3
Acts 14:21-22
James 1:2-3
James 2:14-17

MEMORY VERSE:

Psalm 16:11

WEEK 9

OLDER SCRIPTURE

James 3:13-18
James 4:7-10
James 5:13-14
Acts 15:9-11
Acts 16:25-34

YOUNGER SCRIPTURE

James 3:13
James 4:7-8
James 5:13-14
Acts 15:11
Acts 16:29-31

MEMORY VERSE:

Psalm 18:2

WEEK 10

OLDER SCRIPTURE

Galatians 1:11-12
Galatians 2:19-21
Galatians 3:27-29
Galatians 4:6-7
Galatians 5:13-14

YOUNGER SCRIPTURE

Galatians 1:11-12
Galatians 2:19-21
Galatians 3:27-29
Galatians 4:6-7
Galatians 5:13-14

MEMORY VERSE:

Psalm 19:14

FOUNDATIONS: NT OUTLINE

WEEK 11

OLDER SCRIPTURE
Galatians 6:10
Acts 17:22-24
Acts 18:9-11
1 Thess. 1:2-6
1 Thess. 2:13

YOUNGER SCRIPTURE
Galatians 6:10
Acts 17:24
Acts 18:9-11
1 Thess. 1:2-4
1 Thess. 2:13

MEMORY VERSE:
Psalm 23:1

WEEK 12

OLDER SCRIPTURE
1 Thess. 3:12-13
1 Thess. 4:1-2, 7-8
1 Thess. 5:18
2 Thess. 1:5
2 Thess. 2:1-4

YOUNGER SCRIPTURE
1 Thess. 3:12-13
1 Thess. 4:1-2
1 Thess. 5:18
2 Thess. 1:5
2 Thess. 2:1-4

MEMORY VERSE:
Proverbs 10:27

WEEK 13

OLDER SCRIPTURE
2 Thess. 3:3-5, 13
Acts 19:1-5
1 Cor. 1:26-31
1 Cor. 2:10-13
1 Cor. 3:16

YOUNGER SCRIPTURE
2 Thess. 3:13
Acts 19:1-5
1 Cor. 1:30-31
1 Cor. 2:10
1 Cor. 3:16

MEMORY VERSE:
Proverbs 11:25

WEEK 14

OLDER SCRIPTURE
1 Cor. 4:1-5
1 Cor. 5:6
1 Cor. 6:19-20
1 Cor. 7:23-24
1 Cor. 8:13

YOUNGER SCRIPTURE
1 Cor. 4:1-2
1 Cor. 5:6
1 Cor. 6:19-20
1 Cor. 7:23-24
1 Cor. 8:13

MEMORY VERSE:
Proverbs 12:2

WEEK 15

OLDER SCRIPTURE
1 Cor. 9:24-27
1 Cor. 10:31
1 Cor. 11:3
1 Cor. 12:12-20
1 Cor.13:4-7

YOUNGER SCRIPTURE
1 Cor. 9:24-27
1 Cor. 10:31
1 Cor. 11:3
1 Cor. 12:12
1 Cor. 13:4-5

MEMORY VERSE:
Psalm 25:5

WEEK 16

OLDER SCRIPTURE
1 Cor. 14:40
1 Cor. 15:58
1 Cor. 16:13-14
2 Cor. 1:20-22
2 Cor. 2:9-10

YOUNGER SCRIPTURE
1 Cor. 14:40
1 Cor. 15:58
1 Cor. 16:13-14
2 Cor. 1:20
2 Cor. 2:10

MEMORY VERSE:
Proverbs 13:13

WEEK 17

OLDER SCRIPTURE
2 Cor. 3:4-6
2 Cor. 4:7-10
2 Cor. 5:17-20
2 Cor. 6:1-2
2 Cor. 7:10

YOUNGER SCRIPTURE
2 Cor. 3:4-6
2 Cor. 4:7-10
2 Cor. 5:17
2 Cor. 6:1-2
2 Cor. 7:10

MEMORY VERSE:
Psalm 27:10

WEEK 18

OLDER SCRIPTURE
2 Cor. 8:1-7
2 Cor. 9:6-8
2 Cor. 10:7
2 Cor. 11:30
2 Cor. 12:9-10

YOUNGER SCRIPTURE
2 Cor. 8:7
2 Cor. 9:7
2 Cor. 10:7
2 Cor. 11:30
2 Cor. 12:9-10

MEMORY VERSE:
Proverbs 14:12

WEEK 19

OLDER SCRIPTURE
2 Cor. 13:5-6
Mark 1:16-20
Mark 2:2-5
Mark 3:1-6
Mark 4:36-41

YOUNGER SCRIPTURE
2 Cor. 13:5-6
Mark 1:16-18
Mark 2:2-5
Mark 3:1-2, 5
Mark 4:37-39

MEMORY VERSE:
Proverbs 14:26

WEEK 20

OLDER SCRIPTURE
Mark 5:38-42
Mark 6:39-44
Mark 7:6-8
Mark 8:27-30
Mark 9:23-24

YOUNGER SCRIPTURE
Mark 5:40-42
Mark 6:39-44
Mark 7:6-8
Mark 8:27-30
Mark 9:23-24

MEMORY VERSE:
Psalm 33:4

WEEK 21

OLDER SCRIPTURE
Mark 10:13-16
Mark 11:4-10
Mark 12:13-17
Mark 13:32-37
Mark 14:17-20

YOUNGER SCRIPTURE
Mark 10:13-16
Mark 11:4-10
Mark 12:13-14
Mark 13:32-33
Mark 14:17-20

MEMORY VERSE:
Proverbs 15:1

WEEK 22

OLDER SCRIPTURE
Mark 15:37-39
Mark 16:1-8
Romans 1:16-17
Romans 2:11
Romans 3:21-24

YOUNGER SCRIPTURE
Mark 15:37-39
Mark 16:4-7
Romans 1:16-17
Romans 2:11
Romans 3:23

MEMORY VERSE:
Psalm 37:4

WEEK 23

OLDER SCRIPTURE
Romans 4:23-25
Romans 5:6-8
Romans 6:12-13
Romans 7:15
Romans 8:28

YOUNGER SCRIPTURE
Romans 4:23-25
Romans 5:6-8
Romans 6:12-13
Romans 7:15
Romans 8:28

MEMORY VERSE:
Psalm 37:23

WEEK 24

OLDER SCRIPTURE
Romans 9:30-32
Romans 10:9-13
Romans 11:33-36
Romans 12:1-2
Romans 13:4-7

YOUNGER SCRIPTURE
Romans 9:30-32
Romans 10:13
Romans 11:33-36
Romans 12:1-2
Romans 13:7

MEMORY VERSE:
Proverbs 16:9

WEEK 25

OLDER SCRIPTURE
Romans 14:10-12
Romans 15:5-6
Romans 16:19
Acts 20:7-12
Acts 21:30-36

YOUNGER SCRIPTURE
Romans 14:10-12
Romans 15:5-6
Romans 16:19
Acts 20:9-10, 12
Acts 21:30-31

MEMORY VERSE:
Proverbs 17:27

WEEK 26

OLDER SCRIPTURE

Acts 22:15-16
Acts 23:11
Acts 24:14-16
Acts 25:6-8
Acts 26:12-15

YOUNGER SCRIPTURE

Acts 22:15-16
Acts 23:11
Acts 24:14-16
Acts 25:7-8
Acts 26:13-15

MEMORY VERSE:

Proverbs 18:10

WEEK 27

OLDER SCRIPTURE

Acts 27:20-26
Acts 28:23-24
Colossians 1:9-10
Colossians 2:6-7
Colossians 3:12-17

YOUNGER SCRIPTURE

Acts 27:23-24
Acts 28:23-24
Colossians 1:9-10
Colossians 2:6-7
Colossians 3:12-17

MEMORY VERSE:

Psalm 51:10

WEEK 28

OLDER SCRIPTURE

Colossians 4:2-6
Ephesians 1:20-23
Ephesians 2:8-10
Ephesians 3:8-13
Ephesians 4:25-32

YOUNGER SCRIPTURE

Colossians 4:6
Ephesians 1:22-23
Ephesians 2:8-10
Ephesians 3:11-13
Ephesians 4:25-26

MEMORY VERSE:

Psalm 51:12

WEEK 29

OLDER SCRIPTURE

Ephesians 5:1-2
Ephesians 6:1-4
Philippians 1:20
Philippians 2:1-4
Philippians 3:13-14

YOUNGER SCRIPTURE

Ephesians 5:1-2
Ephesians 6:1-4
Philippians 1:20
Philippians 2:3-4
Philippians 3:13-14

MEMORY VERSE:

Psalm 51:17

WEEK 30

OLDER SCRIPTURE

Philippians 4:11-13
Philemon 1:8-10
Hebrews 1:1-4
Hebrews 2:18
Hebrews 3:1-6

YOUNGER SCRIPTURE

Philippians 4:13
Philemon 1:8-10
Hebrews 1:1-2
Hebrews 2:18
Hebrews 3:5-6

MEMORY VERSE:

Psalm 55:22

WEEK 31

OLDER SCRIPTURE

Hebrews 4:12-13
Hebrews 5:1-6
Hebrews 6:10-12
Hebrews 7:24-25
Hebrews 8:7,13

YOUNGER SCRIPTURE

Hebrews 4:12-13
Hebrews 5:5-6
Hebrews 6:10-12
Hebrews 7:24-25
Hebrews 8:7,13

MEMORY VERSE:

Proverbs 19:21

WEEK 32

OLDER SCRIPTURE

Hebrews 9:11-12
Hebrews 10:23-25
Hebrews 11:1-3
Hebrews 12:1-2
Hebrews 13:20-21

YOUNGER SCRIPTURE

Hebrews 9:11-12
Hebrews 10:23-25
Hebrews 11:1-3
Hebrews 12:1-2
Hebrews 13:20-21

MEMORY VERSE:

Psalm 67:1

WEEK 33

OLDER SCRIPTURE

1 Timothy 1:3-4
1 Timothy 2:1-4
1 Timothy 3:1-4
1 Timothy 4:11-12
1 Timothy 5:1-2

YOUNGER SCRIPTURE

1 Timothy 1:3-4
1 Timothy 2:1-4
1 Timothy 3:1-4
1 Timothy 4:12
1 Timothy 5:1-2

MEMORY VERSE:

Psalm 68:5

WEEK 34

OLDER SCRIPTURE

1 Timothy 6:17-19
2 Timothy 1:13-14
2 Timothy 2:15
2 Timothy 3:13-17
2 Timothy 4:1-5

YOUNGER SCRIPTURE

1 Timothy 6:18-19
2 Timothy 1:13-14
2 Timothy 2:15
2 Timothy 3:16-17
2 Timothy 4:2

MEMORY VERSE:

Proverbs 20:27

WEEK 35

OLDER SCRIPTURE

Titus 1:5-9
Titus 2:11-15
Titus 3:1-3
1 Peter 1:13-16
1 Peter 2:1-3

YOUNGER SCRIPTURE

Titus 1:5-6
Titus 2:11
Titus 3:1-3
1 Peter 1:13-16
1 Peter 2:1-3

MEMORY VERSE:

Proverbs 21:1

WEEK 36

OLDER SCRIPTURE

1 Peter 3:8-9
1 Peter 4:8-11
1 Peter 5:5-7
2 Peter 1:5-8
2 Peter 2:1-3

YOUNGER SCRIPTURE

1 Peter 3:8-9
1 Peter 4:8-11
1 Peter 5:5-7
2 Peter 1:5-7
2 Peter 2:1

MEMORY VERSE:

Psalm 84:10

WEEK 37

OLDER SCRIPTURE

2 Peter 3:17-18
John 1:1-5, 14
John 2:6-11
John 3:16-18
John 4:13-15

YOUNGER SCRIPTURE

2 Peter 3:17-18
John 1:1-2,14
John 2:7-8,11
John 3:16
John 4:13-15

MEMORY VERSE:

Proverbs 21:23

CHECK OUT

Foundations for Students: New Testament– A 260-Day Bible Reading Plan for Busy Teens (005810871)

FOUNDATIONS: NT OUTLINE

WEEK 38
OLDER SCRIPTURE
John 5:37-40
John 6:35
John 7:28-29
John 8:12
John 9:1-5

YOUNGER SCRIPTURE
John 5:37
John 6:35
John 7:28-29
John 8:12
John 9:3-5

MEMORY VERSE:
Psalm 86:5

WEEK 39
OLDER SCRIPTURE
John 10:14-18
John 11:17,39-44
John 12:44-50
John 13:34-35
John 14:5-6

YOUNGER SCRIPTURE
John 10:14-15
John 11:43-44
John 12:46
John 13:34-35
John 14:5-6

MEMORY VERSE:
Psalm 90:12

WEEK 40
OLDER SCRIPTURE
John 15:9-13
John 16:33
John 17:1-5
John 18:4-9
John 19:38-42

YOUNGER SCRIPTURE
John 15:12-13
John 16:33
John 17:1-5
John 18:4-6
John 19:41-42

MEMORY VERSE:
Psalm 96:2

WEEK 41
OLDER SCRIPTURE
John 20:24-29
John 21:15-17
1 John 1:5-9
1 John 2:3-6
1 John 3:1-3

YOUNGER SCRIPTURE
John 20:24-29
John 21:15
1 John 1:9
1 John 2:3
1 John 3:1

MEMORY VERSE:
Psalm 100:4

WEEK 42
OLDER SCRIPTURE
1 John 4:7-12
1 John 5:14-15
2 John 1:6
3 John 1:5-8
Jude 1:20-25

YOUNGER SCRIPTURE
1 John 4:11
1 John 5:14-15
2 John 1:6
3 John 1:5
Jude 1:20-21

MEMORY VERSE:
Psalm 103:1

WEEK 43
OLDER SCRIPTURE
Revelation 1:17-19
Revelation 2:7
Revelation 3:19-22
Revelation 4:11
Revelation 5:5

YOUNGER SCRIPTURE
Revelation 1:17-19
Revelation 2:7
Revelation 3:19-20
Revelation 4:11
Revelation 5:5

MEMORY VERSE:
Proverbs 26:20

WEEK 44
OLDER SCRIPTURE
Revelation 6:1-2
Revelation 7:9-10
Revelation 8:1-2
Revelation 9:20-21
Revelation 10:4

YOUNGER SCRIPTURE
Revelation 6:1-2
Revelation 7:9-10
Revelation 8:1-2
Revelation 9:20-21
Revelation 10:4

MEMORY VERSE:
Proverbs 27:17

WEEK 45
OLDER SCRIPTURE
Revelation 11:15
Revelation 12:10-12
Revelation 13:6-10
Revelation 14:6-7
Revelation 15:1

YOUNGER SCRIPTURE
Revelation 11:15
Revelation 12:10
Revelation 13:6-8
Revelation 14:6-7
Revelation 15:1

MEMORY VERSE:
Psalm 106:1

WEEK 46
OLDER SCRIPTURE
Revelation 16:17-18
Revelation 17:14
Revelation 18:1-2
Revelation 19:11-13
Revelation 20:1-3

YOUNGER SCRIPTURE
Revelation 16:17
Revelation 17:14
Revelation 18:1-2
Revelation 19:11-13
Revelation 20:1-3

MEMORY VERSE:
Psalm 119:10

WEEK 47
OLDER SCRIPTURE
Revelation 21:5-7
Revelation 22:1-5
Matthew 1:20-21,24
Matthew 2:1-2,9-12
Matthew 3:1-3

YOUNGER SCRIPTURE
Revelation 21:5-7
Revelation 22:1-5
Matthew 1:20-21
Matthew 2:1-2,9-12
Matthew 3:1-3

MEMORY VERSE:
Psalm 119:11

WEEK 48
OLDER SCRIPTURE
Matthew 4:1,10-11
Matthew 5:43-48
Matthew 6:9-15
Matthew 7:13-14
Matthew 8:14-17

YOUNGER SCRIPTURE
Matthew 4:1,10-11
Matthew 5:43-48
Matthew 6:9-15
Matthew 7:13-14
Matthew 8:14-17

MEMORY VERSE:
Psalm 119:105

WEEK 49
OLDER SCRIPTURE
Matthew 9:35-38
Matthew 10:5-8
Matthew 11:28-30
Matthew 12:33-35
Matthew 13:34-35

YOUNGER SCRIPTURE
Matthew 9:35-38
Matthew 10:5-7
Matthew 11:28
Matthew 12:33-35
Matthew 13:34-35

MEMORY VERSE:
Proverbs 29:22

WEEK 50
OLDER SCRIPTURE
Matthew 14:25-33
Matthew 15:29-31
Matthew 16:13-20
Matthew 17:1-9
Matthew 18:1-5

YOUNGER SCRIPTURE
Matthew 14:26-30
Matthew 15:31
Matthew 16:15-16
Matthew 17:2,5-8
Matthew 18:1-5

MEMORY VERSE:
Proverbs 30:5

WEEK 51
OLDER SCRIPTURE
Matthew 19:23-26
Matthew 20:9-16
Matthew 21:14-17
Matthew 22:1-5
Matthew 23:1-3

YOUNGER SCRIPTURE
Matthew 19:25-26
Matthew 20:9-16
Matthew 21:14-17
Matthew 22:1-5
Matthew 23:1-3

MEMORY VERSE:
Proverbs 31:8

WEEK 52
OLDER SCRIPTURE
Matthew 24:30-31
Matthew 25:31-34
Matthew 26:1-2
Matthew 27:27-31
Matthew 28:18-20

YOUNGER SCRIPTURE
Matthew 24:30-31
Matthew 25:31-34
Matthew 26:1-2
Matthew 27:27-31
Matthew 28:18-20

MEMORY VERSE:
Psalm 150:6

Disciple-Making Resources

Replicate.org

Our Replicate website is packed with tools to help create awareness for disciple-making. In addition to downloads and web-based content, the Replicate blog is a great source of insight and commentary on the current state of disciple-making.

The Growing Up Series

01 Growing Up. *Growing Up* is a practical, easy-to-implement system for growing in one's faith. It is a manual for making disciples, addressing the what, why, where, and how of discipleship. *Growing Up* provides you with transferrable principles for creating and working with discipleship groups, allowing you to gain positive information both for yourself and for others as you learn how to help others become better disciples for Christ.

02 Firmly Planted. Why is spiritual growth complicated? *Firmly Planted* is the second book in the Growing Up series. In biblical, practical, and simple terms, the book shares a roadmap for spiritual maturity. *Firmly Planted* addresses topics such as how you can be sure of your salvation, why your identity in Christ affects everything you do, how to overcome the three enemies that cripple a Christian's growth, a battle plan for gaining victory over temptation, and the indispensable spiritual discipline every believer must foster.

03 Bearing Fruit. *Bearing Fruit* is the third book in the Growing Up series. In this book, the reader will understand how God grows believers. Robby identifies seven places the word "fruit" is found in the bible: fruit of holiness, fruit of righteousness, fruit of soul-winning, fruit of the spirit, fruit of the praise, fruit of repentance, and fruit of giving. You will understand your role in the fruit bearing process of spiritual growth. *Bearing Fruit* is applicable for new and mature believers alike.